Party Attitudes Towards the EU in the Member States

IIII I I IIIIIIIIIIIIIIII IIIIIIIII IIII III
I0121427

In a moment when the EU is facing an important number of challenges, there is growing interest in understanding how parties influence the way Europe evolves as a political issue, notably how parties structure domestic competition over European issues and how they mobilise sentiments in referenda over European integration.

This book examines the views of national parties towards the European Union and the different facets of a supranational citizenship. It provides an in-depth investigation into the variations to the cross-national patterns in ten countries, including old and new member states and different EU regions. Using original and innovative concepts, data and research techniques the authors:

- explore whether parties formulate specific positions and preferences on the most particular aspects of the EU process;
- investigate whether the party's stance could be inserted into more pro-European, or more Eurosceptical attitudes;
- illustrate patterns of party contestation of EU issues in the member states and explain these patterns in the light of the main theoretical arguments.

Making an important contribution to party attitudes towards the EU and the Europeanisation of party politics, this book will be of interest to students and scholars of European politics, sociology, comparative politics, government and party politics.

Nicolò Conti is Assistant Professor at the Unitelma Sapienza University of Rome, Italy.

Routledge advances in European politics

Party Attitudes Towards the EU in the Member States

Parties for Europe, parties against Europe

Edited by Nicolò Conti

Routledge
Taylor & Francis Group

LONDON AND NEW YORK

First published 2014
by Routledge
2 Park Square, Milton Park, Abingdon, Oxfordshire OX14 4RN

and by Routledge
711 Third Avenue, New York, NY 10017

First issued in paperback 2015

Routledge is an imprint of the Taylor & Francis Group, an informa business

British Library Cataloguing in Publication Data
A catalogue record for this book is available from the British Library

Library of Congress Cataloging in Publication Data
Party attitudes towards the EU in the member states: parties for Europe, parties against Europe / edited by Nicolò Conti.
    pages cm. – (Routledge advances in European politics; 100)
    Includes bibliographical references and index.
    1. Political parties–European Union countries. 2. European Union countries–Politics and government–21st century. 3. Europe–Economic integration–Political aspects. I. Conti, Nicolò.
    JN50.P38 2013
    341.242'2–dc23
                                                                    2013021786

ISBN13: 978-1-138-93375-0 (pbk)
ISBN13: 978-0-415-62231-8 (hbk)

Typeset in Times New Roman
by Wearset Ltd, Boldon, Tyne and Wear

Contents

Figures

Tables

Contributors

Giacomo Benedetto is Lecturer in Politics at Royal Holloway, University of London.

Nicolò Conti is Assistant Professor at the Unitelma Sapienza University of Rome.

Santiago Delgado Fernández is Professor at the University of Granada.

Wojciech Gagatek is Assistant Professor in the Centre for Europe at the University of Warsaw.

Vít Hloušek is Associate Professor at the Masaryk University in Brno.

Nicolas Hubé is Associate Professor of Political Science at the University Paris 1 Panthéon-Sorbonne.

Petr Kaniok is Assistant Professor at the Masaryk University in Brno.

Vincenzo Memoli is Assistant Professor at the University of Catania.

Sofia Michalaki is a PhD student at the University of Athens.

Edalina Rodrigues Sanches is a PhD student at the Institute of Social Sciences, University of Lisbon.

José Santana Pereira is a post-doc Research Fellow at the Institute of Social Sciences, University of Lisbon.

Aleksandra Sojka is a PhD student at the University of Granada.

Diego Varela is Adjunct Professor at the Alexandru Ioan Cuza University of Iasi.

Réka Várnagy is Assistant Professor at Corvinus University of Budapest.

Rafael Vázquez-García is Lecturer at the University of Granada.

Susannah Verney is Assistant Professor at the University of Athens.

Claudius Wagemann is Professor at the Goethe University Frankfurt.

1 Introduction

Nicolò Conti

The context of the volume

In the last decade, there has been a growing interest in understanding how parties influence the way Europe evolves as a political issue or even as an emerging cleavage (Kriesi 2007; Down and Wilson 2010), notably how parties structure domestic competition over European issues and how they mobilise sentiments in referenda over European integration (Marks and Steenbergen 2004). This interest has become even more salient after the failure of the referenda on the EU held in countries such as France, the Netherlands, Sweden, Denmark and Ireland where not only the public, but also parties had often shown clear signs of disaffection for the EU. European issues have also become more salient after the outbreak of radical Eurosceptical parties in many member states. In the attempt to understand how parties structure patterns of contestation of the EU, the large-scale comparative literature has documented a cross-national tendency to structure party positions in a similar way (Marks and Steenbergen 2004). At the same time, however, other studies have shown some important differences across countries and geographic areas. Patterns of contestation of the EU are different in the old and in the new member states (Conti 2012). In the Nordic countries partisan Euroscepticism has always been persistent (Raunio 2008) and a mounting Euroscepticism has been documented in the new member states as well (Szczerbiak and Taggart 2002; Neumayer 2008). On the other hand, the South European member states have often been defined as a region where pro-European attitudes are exceptionally widespread and the symbiosis between integration, democratisation and modernisation was very effective in the eyes of domestic politicians and decision-makers (Conti *et al.* 2010), at least until the eruption of the economic crisis. It seems that the EU should produce a similar broad impact upon parties – consisting of a negative influence on parties' relevance 'in popular terms' (Mair 1995: 46–7) since their capacity to process key issues and be leading agents of interest aggregation and political representation was undermined consequent to the process of European integration (Gaffney 1996; Bartolini 1998, 2005; Hix and Goetz 2000) – in reality parties respond differently across the member states. In the attempt to advance in our knowledge of a phenomenon – i.e. party attitudes to the EU – that is relevant not only for democratic competition but also for the future of Europe, our research investigates in-depth the national parties in ten countries: a sample meant as representative of the wider EU since it covers old and new member states and different EU regions.[1]

At a moment when the EU is facing an important number of challenges, and given that its legitimacy and democratic capacities are increasingly questioned (Eriksen and Fossum 2004; Leconte 2010), it seems particularly important to address questions of *if, how* and *where* parties want the EU to grow. Moving from these broad research questions, this volume intends to make a contribution in comparative terms to the ever-growing literature on party attitudes towards the EU (Marks and Steenbergen 2004; Szczerbiak and Taggart 2008). Furthermore, it intends to contribute to the development of the recent literature on Europeanisation of party politics (Kuhlaci 2012; Ladrech 2002; Mair 2006; Poguntke *et al.* 2007). The interest of our study is, in fact, twofold. First, we describe the attitudes of parties towards the EU in-depth for a sizeable group of member states. Second, we relate the explanatory factors of party attitudes in the analysed countries to the main theoretical arguments available in the literature. We refine the theoretical framework that has originated from the comparative literature with some original speculations, in light of some new evidence that we were able to produce with our enquiry. Third, we analyse features of Europeanisation of the party system by considering to what extent the issue of Europe has been internalised by the system and absorbed into the main patterns of party competition. In particular, the empirical analyses will attempt to answer the following questions. *How is the EU depicted in the member states by parties? Can the EU rely on wide party consensus for its institutional performance and involvement in policy-making? Do projects of deeper integration find party support in the member states? Is there any identity issue that parties raise when they politicise the EU? Are these issues politically contested in the member states and, if so, what is the pattern of contestation they reflect?*

To achieve our research goals, we analyse an original set of data that was collected within the broader large-scale undertaking of the INTUNE project.[2] The main purpose of the project was to study the attitudes of several actors – elites, parties, masses, experts, media – towards the EU across several dimensions of the EU process. The theoretical foundations of this attempt originate from some recent reflections on the theme of citizenship and the EU. It is quite evident that over the last two decades the process of European integration has become more closely interwoven with the theme of citizenship. The fact that in the European treaties the concept of a European citizenship has received, starting with Maastricht, then with Amsterdam and Lisbon, an explicit mention and a precise legal definition is only the most visible and symbolic aspect of this trend. The fact that when citizens vote in EU referenda and in national and European elections they often express fears about the negative consequences of the EU process on their rights, duties, opportunities and constraints certainly is a more material aspect.

Citizenship developed within the national forms of political organisation with a multidimensional connotation, precisely under a *horizontal* and a *vertical* dimension (Cotta and Isernia 2009). Traditionally, the horizontal dimension has to do with the creation of a polity, thus with the definition of its membership. The second is instead related to the allocation of powers and responsibilities within the aforementioned polity. The horizontal meaning of citizenship rests, therefore, on a series of (ascribed and achieved) criteria through which one is, or becomes, a citizen – i.e. a full member of a polity – while the others, even if residents in the same territory, are considered part of the out-group of non-citizens. The vertical dimension concerns the citizens' entitlement to the rights of control and influence over the political authorities, and the right to receive services, care and protection from the same authorities. This dimension is thus linked both to the authoritative structure of the polity and to its policy scope. Benhabib (2002a, 2002b) and Bartolini (2005: 211) maintain that these dimensions are rooted in the normative principles of democratic government, as they nurture the legitimacy and democratic quality of government at any level. The two authors also maintain that these dimensions, and therefore citizenship at large, are being substantially impacted by the EU process. With respect to the impact of the EU, the vertical and horizontal dimensions of citizenship also represent the focus of the analyses carried out by the INTUNE project. In this volume we present the results of the analyses on national parties, while other works document the findings on national elites (Best *et al.* 2012), citizens (Sanders *et al.* 2012a, 2012b) and media (Bayley and Williams 2012). The book builds on and further expands the special issue edited by Conti (2010), 'Which Europe do Parties Want? A View from France, Italy, Portugal and Spain'. More countries are included in this new analysis and a larger time frame allows us to explore the most recent developments of contemporary times, and to refine the theoretical arguments that explain party attitudes to the EU. The research was funded by the INTUNE project; compared to the original group of scholars involved in the research more authors have joined the cooperative effort that made this book possible.

The method

Inspired by the above theoretical reflections, our main attempt was to move beyond the study of broad, or uni-dimensional, attitudes to the EU, in order to assess party attitudes across distinct (functional and symbolic) dimensions of citizenship. Particularly, research under the INTUNE project considers the horizontal dimension of citizenship as it is directly connected to the conceptual dimension of *identity* and the vertical dimension through the two dimensions of *representation* and *policy scope*. The national experts involved in the project carried a manifesto analysis – a methodology that is widely used to study party policy positions and issue preferences (Bara and Weale 2006; Budge *et al.* 2001; Klingemann *et al.* 1994; Gabel and Hix 2004; Laver 2001) – in order to describe party attitudes to the EU. Manifestos represent an extensive source of information with which to map the positions of parties across a large number of issues. Making use of a common coding scheme (see Appendix to the book), the national experts coded in particular the Euromanifestos that were issued by domestic parties to contest elections for the European Parliament (EP) extracting from the text the content analytic variables that can well describe their positions on a set of different EU issues across the above three dimensions. These documents do not have a focus as narrow or as specialised as other party documents (i.e. position papers on EU treaties, or parliamentary debates on ratification of EU legislation); on the contrary they are broad enough to represent an appropriate documentary source for the analysis of party preferences on the many faces of the EU process as studied by the INTUNE project.

We analysed a long period of time up to the most recent European elections of 2009, so we were also able to document change in party positions that was consequent to developments in treaty-making, enlargement, monetary unification and so on. Unfortunately, since our investigation ends in 2009, we were not able to fully document party attitudes after the economic crisis reached a peak in Europe. In the future, our method could be applied for the analysis of the Euromanifestos of the 2014 EP elections, in order to update the picture and to document change with even greater deepness. Furthermore, some time asymmetries have been introduced in the chapters in order to better represent the country-specific situations. To start with, since our analyses are based on Euromanifestos, in the new member states a systematic study of these documents could be carried only after their accession in the EU and participation to European elections (i.e. 2004 and 2009). In Italy the change in the party system was so ample over time that we opted for an accurate depiction of the main differences between the pre- and post-1994 systems and then we focussed on the most recent reality after the transitional years of the so-called Second Republic. For countries like Britain, although in the presence of a remarkable degree of continuity of the party system, a crucial swap in the attitudes towards Europe occurred between left and right in the long term, so it was important to document this path by extending the analysis to include a longer time frame. In spite of these time asymmetries, the chapters on the old member states all cover the period 1994–2009 and additionally they make reference to the period before when deemed relevant; chapters on the new member states refer to 2004–2009 but the analyses are complemented with narratives on the accession period as well.

The manifesto analysis allowed us to examine party positions beyond their salience in the public discourse. As a matter of fact, only some of the contents in the manifestos are actually salient in the discourse channelled through the media. This is the result of a process of selection of contents by the media that often inflates contentious issues over consensual ones, and uncomplicated issues over complex ones. Therefore, when mapping the positions of parties on complex multidimensional issues, the manifesto analysis allows remarkable levels of precision and depth that otherwise would not be allowed with the analysis of media discourse. For this reason, we do not make any assumption about the interest for such issues of any actor beyond parties, for example citizens certainly have more limited information about the specific aspects of EU integration. Our goal is instead to document party attitudes towards the EU based on original party sources such as manifestos, hence the results of our analyses cannot be extended to any other actor beyond parties here considered as unitary actors. Actually, we recognise that the party official stance is often different from the one of voters, and even of individual party members. To make some examples, we show that in the British case, in the 1980s the attitudes of the Conservative party towards Europe were milder than those of their leader Margaret Thatcher. Eventually, this disagreement contributed to the ejection of Thatcher by her own party, something that could well be anticipated by a careful reading of the conservative manifestos of the time. Furthermore, the manifestos of the Czech Civic Democrats reflect the stance of a less Eurosceptical party than is commonly perceived – overall they show a more balanced stance than the individual attitudes of some of their party leaders (often more prominent in the media). On the contrary, in the case of Berlusconi's party in Italy, People of freedom, we could clearly trace the roots of a mounting Euroscepticism that for a long time has not been very evident in the media and that only recently has become more recognised.

The research on Euromanifestos that we present in this volume allows us, first, to assess whether parties formulate *specific positions* and preferences on the most particular aspects of the EU process. Second, it investigates whether their *stance* could be inserted into more pro-European, or more Eurosceptical attitudes. Third, it illustrates *patterns* of party contestation of the EU issues in the member states. These are the main descriptive goals of our work. Furthermore, it attempts to explain these patterns, in the light of the main theoretical arguments available in the literature and of some original proposals that we formulate in order to refine our *understanding* of the problem. Finally, our work contributes to enhancing knowledge about the mechanisms of the interaction between the EU and domestic politics in the member states, particularly from the point of view of the level of *penetration* and of the *mechanics* that EU issues play in party competition and programmatic supply.

Describing party attitudes

This volume has been structured as a set of country studies that all apply the same framework for analysis. I have already framed party attitudes towards the EU as the main problem that we investigate. Accordingly, we defined the dependent variables of our study as the party positions on a set of EU issues, along the three dimensions of identity, representation and policy scope. Finally, as I illustrate in the following section, from the most recognised explanatory arguments available in the literature and from the original conjectures advanced by the authors of the volume, I derive the independent variables whose impact we test in the chapters.

As it is typical of any empirical study based on content analysis, as this one is, a fundamental methodological problem concerns what should be observed. Many studies observe the salience of themes – usually measured through word, sentence or quasi-sentence counting – but then scholars face the problem of the low salience of themes that are too specific although important. Our purpose, instead, is precisely to document positions that are very specific and that refer to multiple dimensions of the EU process so, inevitably, they occupy only some limited sections of the Euromanifestos. At the same time, however, our analysed issues find an empirical equivalent in other studies. The overlapping will allow us to compare our results with those that have emerged from studies that have made use of different research techniques to analyse the attitudes of other actors towards specific aspects of the EU process, through use of elite (Best *et al.* 2012) and mass surveys (Sanders *et al.* 2012a, 2012b). Indeed, any analysis of the salience of our selected themes based on the more traditional techniques of salience measuring would result in small values and in very limited variations across cases. A solution would be to aggregate specific themes into broader macro-themes, a strategy adopted for example by Gabel and Hix (2004). It is one, however, that works against our efforts to analyse some of the most specific components of party attitudes to the EU. For this reason, the authors of this volume propose some alternative methodological approaches to analyse very specific textual information, regardless of the dedicated number of words. Making use of a combination of qualitative and quantitative methods we show that it is possible to make use of documents, such as party manifestos, to analyse even very specific party positions, an attempt otherwise addressed in the past by use of other techniques, such as a survey of politicians or an expert survey, that surely have points of strength but also some of weakness (Hooghe *et al.* 2004; Ray 1999).[3]

In their descriptive analyses, authors consider the level of *relevance* of EU issues in the different countries, whether parties *contest* and how parties *divide* upon such issues in their programmatic stance. Additionally, they document the *consistency* of party attitudes across different dimensions of the EU process. In order to assess the level of congruence of party attitudes across the different faces of the EU process and of its impact on citizenship, in their chapters, the authors make cross-reference to attitudes towards different themes *within* the same dimension, as well as towards themes in *different* dimensions. The European menu is indeed rich and different parties choose different mixes in line with their different agendas and policy priorities, but also with their short-term strategies in the domestic scene. At the same time, European integration is a multidimensional phenomenon impacting on multiple values and beliefs. Sometimes parties develop attitudes towards the EU across these different dimensions that are consistent, but some other times they develop attitudes that are much less coherent and even implausible. Only the extreme positions (hard Euroscepticism and Euro-federalism) are simple but, as we show in the book, they are shared only by a minority of parties. We document that the large mainstream contains, on the contrary, a variety of positions that are often much less geometrically coherent and not so similar across countries.

Ultimately, the study that we present in this volume is primarily a contribution to research on party attitudes to the EU that is original and innovative from the conceptual, as well as from the methodological point of view, but it also presents a bulk of descriptive empirical evidence that could certainly become a point of reference for future research.

Explaining party attitudes

To explain variations in the attitudes of parties certainly is a major goal of this work, one that allows our research to be inserted within the broader theoretical debate of the comparative literature. In this respect, it is important to note that some of the main empirically grounded arguments that are available pertain to ideology and to party competition, either in terms of a left/right competition, or of a mainstream/radical party divide. In particular, many scholars consider the pattern of opposing mainstream to radical parties as a main pattern of contestation of the EU (Szczerbiak and Taggart 2008; Conti 2012), with the former parties supposedly expressing an underlying support for the EU, as opposed to the latter who express rejection. At the same time, evidence of an ideological divide on the EU, although of lower intensity, has also been found along the division between left and right (Hix *et al.* 2007; Marks and Steenbergen 2004; Ray 1999; Tsebelis and Garrett 2000), with left parties described as more pro-European than right parties, particularly since the 1990s. Another explanatory argument that we can find in the literature concerns the impact of the government/opposition status of a party on its stance on the EU (Sitter 2001), but the empirical evidence to support this argument is quite limited, especially in large-scale analyses, and incumbency in government has been found to play, at best, only a secondary influence. In particular, Conti (2012) shows that the discourse of the party central office through party manifestos, being addressed to the party rank and file and more broadly to the citizens, tends to be more ideological, more linear and less influenced by the competition between government and opposition at the domestic level. It is instead the stance of the party in public office that is more strategic, as MPs (and also MEPs) are more sensitive to the influence played by the costs and benefits offered by the position they occupy with respect to the national government (Best *et al.* 2012; Hix *et al.* 2007).

It has also been argued that party responses to the EU may not be structured, in particular not along the aforementioned lines of party competition. The EU may actually represent a *sleeping giant* (Van der Eijk and Franklin 2004), and even a *combustible issue* (Evans 1999) that could gradually introduce *political disorder* in the party system (Conti 2007). The idea behind this argument concerns the supposedly transversal nature of the European issue in some countries, like some other issues that give birth to coalitions cutting across the political spectrum. When they do not fit the patterns of party competition and they produce instead some maverick coalitions, these issues could also give rise to forms of *depoliticisation*. For example, this is the case when parties prefer not to take responsibility for decisions over some given issues, instead they leave their members (and supporters) free to take their own positions. From the party perspective, this can be seen as a rational response to the internal conflict these issues would produce if the party tried to come up with a univocal position. Therefore, it is a way to minimise the costs of conflict upon the party itself. For example, Aylott (2002) shows that in the Scandinavian countries, the party leaderships have attempted to compartmentalise the different arenas in which they operate, with the specific purpose of isolating the potentially damaging impact of the EU. Consequently, parties have often made use of referenda in order to decide on contentious matters related to the EU, where norms of party discipline have been suspended in order to avoid intra-party struggles. For example, parties in France have experienced internal splits consequent to their contrasting positions on the EU that have caused serious disorder and centrifugal tendencies in the party system, especially at the time of European elections and of referenda on the EU (Marthaler 2005, 2009). Mair (2006) argues that, in the presence of such phenomena, the EU may bring instead a depoliticisation of certain political questions, in other words the abstention of parties from the direct political management of given critical issues. The problem of the disconnection of parties from the direct control of a growing number of political issues is certainly well known (Blondel and Cotta 2000; Cerny 1990, 1996), though it is one that has never been systematically investigated. Mair suggests that party scholars should take this phenomenon seriously and, in particular, they should start to consider this kind of indirect impact as one face of Europeanisation.

In the country chapters of the volume, we test the validity of the above explanatory arguments pertaining to ideology and to the government/opposition strategy of parties. As well, the alternative scenario of transversalism of the EU issue is also considered. Where appropriate, the impact of other country-specific determinants on party attitudes is documented and discussed at length by the authors. We show that there are cross-national factors that can well explain party choices on the EU. But many times there are country-specific factors behind such choices, such as the national interests and culture, the varieties of capitalism, the attitudes towards the domestic government and even the perceived external threats to the state. Member states still present national specificities that are difficult to accommodate in a unique Europe-wide party system and a genuine supranational space for contestation of the EU has not emerged yet. On the contrary, we show in the book that contestation of the EU has become even more national specific, particularly after accession of the new members. Ultimately, the volume documents how, in the member states, national and cross-national driving factors interact to shape party contestation of the EU, in a context that we can well describe as one of *growing domestication* of the issue of European integration. Indeed, national contexts filter party responses to the EU. And beyond the well-known pattern opposing mainstream to radical parties of both extremes, it would be hard to find other configurations of party contestation of the EU that are really valid across all countries. On the contrary, we show that despite broad convergence within party families and EP groups (Hix *et al.* 2007), the attitudes of parties towards the EU really are scattered, especially with respect to the most specific aspects of European integration.

In the end, from an explanatory point of view, our analysis allows us to specify under what patterns (if any) party attitudes towards the EU can be modelled in a large group of member states. Additionally, we explain why such patterns have emerged, focussing our attention on both cross-national and national specific factors. Finally, we discuss the fit between the EU issue and the domestic party system, particularly how well the former has been internalised by the latter in its cleavage structure or, eventually, how seriously the EU constitutes a combustible issue whose effects on the party system could be disordered and even maverick.

Key findings of the book

National differences

Our survey of party attitudes towards the EU shows very clearly that *attitudes do not follow a linear cross-national pattern*. Substantial differences are visible among member states and regions of the EU. Within the group of surveyed countries, the South European members are the most Europhile; particularly in the dimension of policy scope, parties are ready to delegate competence to the EU in a large number of policies. In these countries, the EU is not necessarily seen as fully democratic or accountable to citizens, nor it is the object of greater affection or identification, yet it is considered a more efficient power than the national government. Indeed, even in these countries attitudes towards the EU are more cautious on issues of European identity and political representation. Moreover, Euroscepticism is on the rise in these countries too and the economic crisis and related austerity measures are not the only explanation of such a phenomenon. In fact, increased reservations on the EU developed even before the crisis, particularly in Italy and Portugal. But not in Spain or in Greece where until 2009 Euroscepticism was really a fringe phenomenon confined to radical minority parties. Thus, any recent surge of Euroscepticism in these countries marks a shift from long-rooted widespread support (Conti *et al.* 2010) to a completely new situation. It is to be seen whether in the long term these countries will move to a more pessimistic camp enduringly.

Our study shows that parties in the new member states (Czech Republic, Hungary, while Poland is more divided) are reluctant towards most solutions in favour of deeper integration. Although the deepening of European integration usually determines an increased salience of Europe in domestic political debates (Van der Eijk and Franklin 1996), we also found that the salience of EU-related themes in these countries is overall limited, especially in the policy dimension (although citizens are enthusiastic about extensions to EU policy scope, primarily because of institutional failings at home; see on this Sanders *et al.* 2012a). Otherwise, in the new member states parties are overtly reluctant about the supranational mode of decision-making, while they are concerned about the defence of national identity and interests. On these issues, they clearly voice their views and demarcate themselves from parties in the new member states. Although during the accession period, in these countries the EU was framed as an optimistic normative theme by governments (Neumayer 2008), we found that the party discourse after accession is one of nationally introverted fashion, where preferences about future developments present inner elements of resistance to deeper integration. Party attitudes in these countries might be a reflection of their recent entry in the EU and their asymmetric experience with EU affairs compared to parties in the old member states. Thus, over the long term, parties in the new member states may fill in the gaps and clarify their preferences on the EU beyond the current broad reluctance. However, in the context that we were able to depict, Euroscepticism proves particularly loud in these countries as rejection of the EU on the side of radical parties goes together with limited support for the EU by mainstream parties.

In the remaining group of countries that we analysed (France, Germany, Great Britain) party attitudes are very diverse and each country is rather unique. In France, attitudes towards European integration are fluid. Beyond the firm opposition of radical and sovereignist parties, the stance of the other parties varies a great deal across the analysed dimensions following ideological beliefs, as well as short-term calculations. In the EP elections (as well as in referenda on Europe), parties can be more expressive about their views than in French presidential or parliamentary elections where centripetal pressures prevail and divisions on the EU are boiled down to favour intra-party unity and coalition-building. So, when the goal at stake is not the formation of national government, but EU issues or EP elections, French parties divide and really make Europe an issue of party competition. They do so following a new cleavage that has emerged in the French political scene creating new enmities and alliances; but also depending on their domestic institutional position and their short-term strategies specifically designed to challenge their adversaries at home.

On the contrary, in Germany, there is wide consensus on the EU among the main parties. Attitudes are overwhelmingly positive and criticisms are rare – the only exception is represented by radical parties that are clearly more Eurosceptic, but also quite irrelevant in the German system. For most German parties, Europe is an optimistic and rather serene issue, not one of contrasting views, and the programmatic supply on the EU is quite plain and definitely convergent.

In Britain, the main feature of EU politicisation is determined by the presence of fierce Euroscepticism among mainstream parties, specifically the Labour party until the 1990s then the Conservative party. Due to inter-party dissent, EU issues have been of high salience in the programmatic supply and in different moments even the two main parties have alternatively emphasised with radical tones the danger of European integration to British sovereignty. Opposite to Germany, Britain represents within the group of analysed countries a principal example of recurrent pessimistic normative representations of the EU. However, the positive stance of those parties in the pro-European camp is more conventional than some would expect and can well be compared to that in other countries of similar international status, such as France.

In the end, the comparative landscape that we were able to describe raises many questions as to the supposed cross-national tendency to structure party positions in a similar way (Marks and Steenbergen 2004). In actual fact, when we investigate the specific aspects of European integration, we find that patterns of contestation of EU issues are rather different, politicisation of the EU is multifaceted across countries and, as it is shown by many examples in the book, very often it mirrors the political discussion 'at home'. Our findings in the book converge with those of the survey of national political elites of the INTUNE project. These elites have also been described as diverse and their contradictory preferences on European integration are deeply rooted and conditional on the social and political settings in national contexts (Best *et al.* 2012).

Salience

Overall, *representation and scope of governance are the most salient dimensions* in the Euromanifestos. We found that, although relevant for citizenship, identity is not a very salient theme in the European discourse of domestic parties. In some moments, there was greater emphasis on a European shared identity especially in those countries with a problematic nationalistic past, particularly those losing the Second World War (Italy and Germany), but this phenomenon declined over time. Sometimes the national and the European layers of identity are mentioned with concurrent emphasis, other times references to national identity outweigh references to European identity. Actually, where identity is salient, we found that it is often characterised by the attempt to defend national identity, or to mark the distance from the out-group of non-Europeans, more than to build European citizenship rooted in a set of EU-led values. This is particularly true for radical parties and for parties in the new member states who often insert reference to identity in stories of moral panic and defence from outside enemies, such as immigrants or big powers like the United States or Russia (on this see also Matonyte and Morkevičius 2012). Hence, within a context of comparatively low salience, identity issues are addressed by parties predominantly with a rather introverted approach and to demarcate a distance between in-group and out-group, not to support the building of a true European meta-culture. This is a specification of Hooghe and Marks' (2009) argument on the increased importance of identity in the public discourse on Europe.

Thus, the dimensions with greater salience are the two functional ones of representation and scope of governance. Still, the analyses in the different chapters show that salience varies a great deal depending on the cases; even in these two dimensions parties sometimes keep silent on many considered issues. On the one hand, in some countries parties address issues that exceed the scope of our analyses, and this is strongly linked to national specificities (e.g. in the Czech Republic an extraordinary emphasis was given to energy issues after the Czech presidency of the EU pushed the subject in the agenda). On the other hand, we found that many parties that support Europe and its integration are sometimes little communicative on the specific aspects of the process. It is the same for many parties that criticise Europe as well. So, how do we interpret such *lack of salience of important EU issues* like those of representation, policy or identity? The analyses that are presented in the book show that the national context makes a difference. Saliency theory postulates that, in order to distinguish themselves, parties compete through selective emphasis on those issues that they consider most favourable for electoral success, particularly those position issues on which opinion is divided (Budge and Farlie 1983). On the contrary, parties are less interested in contesting valence issues – those that are uniformly liked (or disliked) – as these do not allow parties to demarcate from each other. Hence, lack of salience could be taken as a sign of the fact that in some countries Europe has become a valence issue and parties do not find it electorally profitable to politicise their support or criticisms so uniform attitudes are within the national context. At the same time, lack of purposefulness on the different aspects of integration could be taken as the sign of preference for the status quo, hence as broad appreciation for the EU. Indeed, in some countries approval is so widespread that the EU has been ruled out of party competition. In some other countries, however, we found that the EU is widely perceived more pessimistically but here as well it is not a very salient issue. Ultimately, the EU can be a matter of divergence among parties, or one of consensus on either optimistic or pessimistic viewpoints. In case of divergence, the overall salience of the EU tends to be greater and differences in specific party preferences on the EU more tangible. On the contrary, when the EU constitutes a valence issue of either optimistic or pessimistic fashion, we observed it is less salient in the party system and positions become way less distinct. It has emerged from our analyses that parties tend to diverge on EU issues in Britain, France, Greece, Portugal and Italy; to converge on optimistic views in Germany and Spain; to converge on pessimistic viewpoints in the Czech Republic, Hungary and (less) Poland (where some features of divergence are also present).

If it is easier to understand why those parties who converge optimistically make Europe a non-issue or one of limited salience, it is more difficult to understand why those parties who would like to change things do not fight for this goal. It could well be that the limited impact of parties on the EU process makes them unable to overturn EU decisions once in office. So, these parties tend to surrender to the EU system and not to propose real alternatives to the current trajectory of the EU given that they would not be able to put them into effect anyway. Parties politicise issues and make them salient if they see electoral advantage in doing so (Hooghe and Marks 2009), but beyond broad criticism it is very difficult for parties to fulfil pledges that imply a change of the EU. The EU makes the scope of manoeuvring of parties more limited and restricts their capacity to shape the political system in which they operate (Ladrech 2009), hence their silence on the issue. In future research, it would be interesting to compare the stance of parties on the EU with that on other issues of pessimistic consensus, in order to assess whether they are all affected by a similar lack of salience. At this moment, it is relevant to note that this is the closest scenario to what Mair (2006) defined as depoliticisation of the EU, meaning a situation where parties abstain from management of certain critical issues, even though they are not happy with the status quo and they would like reality to be very different from what it actually is.

Euroscepticism

The general trend in Europe is one of *mounting Euroscepticism*. Over time, criticisms to the EU have become more steadily expressed than support for the EU. The new member states represent in this sense a real challenge, as they constitute a bloc of countries where resistance to deeper integration is rather widespread (see also Conti and Memoli 2012). But the EU is increasingly a divisive issue in the old member states as well. It should be noted that opposition to the EU is rarely absolute, on the contrary it has become a firm idea (even of radical parties) to consider the EU as a necessity and European integration an inevitable process. For example, we found some overtly Eurosceptical parties – as *Libertas* in France, the *Republikaner* in Germany, the Northern League in Italy, *Samoobrona* in Poland and most radical left parties particularly in Southern Europe – to progressively support some areas of (present and future) integration. Thus, in the member states it has become very difficult to find parties that reject the very idea of the EU process. At the same time, however, it has become equally difficult to find Euro-federalists who advocate the deepening of integration in all fields. Even where support for the EU is voiced, only rarely is it an enthusiastic and unconditional one; instead many pro-European parties moved from Euro-enthusiasm to more conditional support over time, even in countries like Germany and the South European member states. Certainly, parties that have a principled support for the EU tend to show a linear stance across the different dimensions, so their attitudes are rather consistent and predictable. This, however, includes only a minority group of Euro-federalists such as the Spanish Socialist party, the Italian Democratic party, the Greens and other minor centre-left parties in France. However, the large majority is made of parties who express a continuum of stances and who support (or oppose) the EU with varying intensity in the different dimensions. Their approach is more pragmatic when compared with the group of Euro-federalists; they accept the EU as a system but their analysis of the costs and benefits allocated within this system becomes more and more severe over time. This could be due to the costs of integration that have gradually become tangible for member states and national governments.

Certainly, the decisions of any government cannot always be of a positive-sum kind, and those of the EU government are no exception to that. Hence, in times of great empowerment of this supranational level of government, the costs – not only the benefits – of EU policies and constraints on the member states have become significant and the feelings that the EU inspires have become mixed, as it would be towards any government. It is certain, however, that although the integration process is more established and unquestioned in its very essence than it was in the past, it has become the object of a mounting mistrust by the national parties who less and less represent an engine for creation of a broad (permissive) consensus on the EU, hence a shift towards dissensus (Hooghe and Marks 2009). In this book we document that European integration stopped being a propulsive idea even of traditionally pro-European party families – earlier the Christian-democrats, then the socialists – while at the same time Euroscepticism has become a more determined attitude – even if one of a broad kind that may actually include a constellation of irreducible positions.

Indeed, evidence in the book of a wide range of preferences on the side of Eurosceptical parties (particularly radical parties, but also some mainstream ones) could raise the question of whether or not they can all be classified as Eurosceptic. The answer would be positive if we define Euroscepticism as opposition to the current trajectory of the EU. But beyond this broad posture, Euroscepticism (as well as pro-Europeanism) can be better characterised as a continuum of stances that could not be locked into static definitions of either categorical or typological nature. Opposition to the EU varies a great deal among parties, throughout countries and across dimensions of the EU process. It is to be seen whether at the European, as well as at the national level, these diverse stances can manage to unite in anti-EU coalitions capable of stipulating some credible alternative path for the EU. In the meanwhile, it is certain that these parties can contribute to create a pervasive sense of discontent with the EU that can really play a detrimental impact on its popular legitimacy (see Eichenberg and Dalton 2007; De Vries and Edwards 2009).

Explaining party attitudes and assessing Europeanisation of the party system

The analyses in the different chapters show that the factor that can best explain party attitudes towards the EU is the mainstream–radical party divide. This factor is a good predictor of attitudes in the Czech Republic, France, Germany, Hungary and also in the Europhile southern member states where attitudes tend to be more benevolent and Euroscepticism is overall more limited. In Great Britain and Poland Euroscepticism can definitely be associated with radical parties, however radical opposition to the EU has also concerned some major parties and, therefore, it is not a phenomenon that can be confined to political radicalism and minor parties exclusively.

On the contrary, the left–right divide has an influence of lower intensity in the analysed countries. Actually, where a left–right divide really is at work, it does not follow a linear tendency: in some countries we found that the left is slightly more pro-European than the right and in other countries we found the opposite. Any expectation of a left–right differentiation on the EU proved false particularly in Central and Eastern Europe, but the influence of this factor is dubious in the old member states as well. The left comes out as more pro-European than the right in Great Britain, Italy and Spain especially since the mid-1990s, but not in the Czech Republic, France, Germany, Greece, Hungary, Poland where the attitudes of left and right tend to be balanced, or we found even a more Europhile right. Finally, the evidence that we were able to produce suggests that all sorts of patterns are possible within member states with respect to this variable.

As to the relationship between attitudes to the EU and the government–opposition status of parties, we found a combined effect of this factor with the mainstream–radical party divide. Those parties who are more radical also tend to be confined to opposition and it is true that they also tend to hold Eurosceptical attitudes. However, as to mainstream parties, incumbency plays less of a role. It is true that in some countries (France, Hungary) the incumbent parties often tend to externalise the focus of their discourse talking more about Europe. For an incumbent party shifting the focus of discourse to the European level can be a natural effect of greater exposure to the EU arena while in government, but it can also represent a strategy to draw the attention away from the performance of the government at home, whose popularity is often under test in second-order elections of this kind. It is also true that in some other countries (Portugal), parties tend to be more supportive of the EU when in government. However, these are not general rules and in most other countries incumbency does not play a significant role in shaping party attitudes to the EU. Most parties do not change their attitudes once in government (although they might change their institutional behaviour), also Euroscepticism can spread even among the incumbent parties (see Britain, Czech Republic, France, Italy, Poland).

Beyond these factors that are prominent in the literature, party attitudes are often influenced by country-specific factors that, given their specificity, are less well known and more difficult to classify. These include calculations for purposes of domestic party competition (such as coalition-making, inter-party distancing or convergence, citizens' attitudes and voter-targeting), as well as national economic interests (net recipient countries are motivated to boil-down opposition to the EU). Whereas in the past twenty years most of the comparative literature has attempted to demonstrate the existence of cross-national patterns of EU politicisation, the evidence that we were able to produce demonstrates that the EU is instead politicised to a large extent under the impact of national specific factors: hence it becomes another face of domestic politics.

As I have illustrated above, in some countries this process takes the form of (either optimistic or pessimistic) consensus, then the EU becomes depoliticised, while Europeanisation as a process that leads to change in the domestic system looks asleep. In other countries, the EU is the object of specific party competition that is, however, subsumed by the main patterns at work domestically (particularly mainstream–radical competition). These are cases where politicisation of the EU is encapsulated in the pre-existing patterns of party competition and Europeanisation does not produce real change but absorption. Only in rare cases (France in our sample) the EU plays a maverick impact on the party system, cross-cutting the existing patterns with a potential disruptive impact (that in the French case only the centripetal pressures of the semi-presidential system prevent from becoming really explosive and unfitting the system). In the end, the book shows that although the format of national party systems has not changed consequent to the impact of the EU (parties whose main reason for existence is Europe are very rare), the mechanics of issue-making together with the repertoire of parties have been impacted more effectively. In most cases, the impact was smooth and parties managed to accommodate EU issues in the party system by either absorption or depoliticisation. It is to be seen, however, whether in the future unfitting politicisation of the EU will become more recurrent or, instead, depoliticisation and well-fitting politicisation will continue to work as the two main alternatives, as it has been in the long period that we have documented in the book.

Notes

1 With the only exception of the Nordic countries that were unfortunately not included in the research.
2 The INTUNE project (Integrated and United: A Quest for Citizenship in an Ever Closer Europe) was financed by the Sixth Framework Programme of the European Union, Priority 7, Citizens and Governance in a Knowledge Based Society (CIT3-CT-2005-513421).
3 A clear advantage of the manifesto analysis is its reliance on primary sources (party official platforms), instead of reliance on previous knowledge and the second guessing of the experts who judge party positions.

References

Aylott, N. (2002) 'Let's discuss this later: Party responses to Euro-division in Scandinavia', *Party Politics*, 8(4): 441–61.
Bara, J. and A. Weale (eds) (2006) *Democratic Politics and Party Competition*, Abingdon: Routledge.
Bartolini, S. (1998) 'Exit options, boundary building, political structuring: Sketches of a theory of large-scale territorial and membership retrenchment/differentiation versus expansion/integration (with reference to the European Union)', EUI Working Papers, SPS 98/1, Florence: European University Institute.
Bartolini, S. (2005) *Restructuring Europe: Centre Formation, System Building and Political Structuring between the Nation-state and the European Union*, Oxford: Oxford University Press.
Bayley, P. and G. Williams (2012) *European Identity: What the Media Say*, Oxford: Oxford University Press.
Benhabib, S. (2002a) *The Claims of Culture: Equality and Diversity in the Global Era*, Princeton, NJ: Princeton University Press.
Benhabib, S. (2002b) 'Citizens, residents and aliens in a changing world: Political membership in the global era', in U. Hedetoft and M. Hjort (eds) *The Postnational Self: Belonging and Identity*, Minneapolis, MN: University of Minnesota Press.
Best, H., G. Lengyel and L. Verzichelli (eds) (2012) *The Europe of Elites: A Study into the Europeanness of Europe's Economic and Political Elites*, Oxford: Oxford University Press.
Blondel, J. and M. Cotta (2000) *The Nature of Party Government*, New York: Palgrave.
Budge, I. and D. Farlie (1983) Party competition: Selective emphasis or direct confrontation? An alternative view with data. In H. Daalder and P. Mair (eds) *Western European Party Systems: Continuity and Change.* London: Sage Publications.
Budge, I., H.D. Klingemann and A. Volkens (eds) (2001) *Mapping Policy Preferences*, Oxford: Oxford University Press.
Cerny, P. (1990) *The Changing Architecture of Politics: Structure, Agency, and the Future of the State*, London: Sage.
Cerny, P. (1996) 'International finance and the erosion of state policy capacity', in P. Gummett (ed.), *Globalisation and Public Policy*, Cheltenham: Edward Elgar.
Conti, N. (2007) 'Domestic parties and European integration: The problem of party attitudes to the EU, and the Europeanisation of parties', *European Political Science*, 6(2): 192–207.
Conti, N. (2010) 'Which Europe do parties want? A view from France, Italy, Portugal and Spain', *Perspectives on European Politics and Society*, 11(2), special issue.

Conti, N. (2012) 'The EU in the programmatic statements of domestic parties', in H. Best, G. Lengyel and L. Verzichelli (eds) *The Europe of Elites: A Study into the Europeanness of Europe's Economic and Political Elites*, Oxford: Oxford University Press.

Conti, N. and V. Memoli (2012) 'The multi-faceted nature of party-based Euroscepticism', *Acta Politica*, 47: 91–112.

Conti, N., M. Cotta and P. Tavares de Almeida (eds) (2010) 'European citizenship in the eyes of national elites: A southern European view', *South European Politics and Society*, 15(1), special issue.

Cotta, M. and P. Isernia (2009) 'Citizenship in the European polity: Questions and explorations', in C. Moury and L. de Sousa (eds) *Institutional Challenges in Post-Constitutional Europe: Governing Change*, London: Routledge.

De Vries, C.E. and E.E. Edwards (2009) 'Taking Europe to its extremes: Extremist parties and public Euroscepticism', *Party Politics*, 15(1): 5–28.

Down, I. and C.J. Wilson (2010) 'Opinion polarization and inter-party competition on Europe', *European Union Politics*, 11(1): 61–87.

Eichenberg, R. and R.J. Dalton (2007) 'Post-Maastricht blues: The welfare state and the transformation of citizen support for European integration, 1973–2002', *Acta Politica*, 42(2): 128–52.

Eriksen, E.O. and J.E. Fossum (2004) 'Europe in search of legitimacy: Strategies of legitimation assessed', *International Political Science Review*, 25(4): 435–59.

Evans, G. (1999) 'Europe: A new electoral cleavage?' in G. Evans and P. Norris (eds) *Critical Elections: British Parties and Voters in Long-Term Perspective*, London: Sage.

Gabel, M.J. and S. Hix (2004) 'Defining the EU political space: An empirical study of the European election manifestos, 1979–1999', in G. Marks and M. Steenbergen (eds) *European Integration and Political Conflict*, Cambridge: Cambridge University Press.

Gaffney, J. (ed.) (1996) *Political Parties and the European Union*, London: Routledge.

Hix, S. and K. Goetz (2000) 'Introduction: European integration and national political systems', *West European Politics*, 23(4): 1–26.

Hix, S., A. Noury and G. Roland (2007) *Democratic Politics in the European Parliament*, New York: Cambridge University Press.

Hooghe, L. and G. Marks (2009), 'A postfunctionalist theory of European integration: From permissive consensus to constraining dissensus', *British Journal of Political Science*, 39: 1–23.

Hooghe, L., G. Marks and C. Wilson (2004) 'Does left/right structure party positions on European integration?' in G. Marks and M. Steenbergen (eds) *European Integration and Political Conflict*, Cambridge: Cambridge University Press.

Klingemann, H.D., R.I. Hofferbert and I. Budge (eds) (1994) *Parties, Policies and Democracy*, Boulder, CO: Westview Press.

Kriesi, H. (2007) 'The role of European elections in national election campaigns', *European Union Politics*, 8(1): 83–108.

Kulahci, E. (ed.) (2012) *Europeanisation and Party Politics*, Colchester: ECPR Press.

Ladrech, R. (2002) 'Europeanization and political parties', *Party Politics*, 8(4): 389–403.

Ladrech, R. (2009) 'Europeanization and political parties', *Living Reviews in European Governance*, 4(1), available at www.livingreviews.org/lreg-2009-1.

Laver, M. (ed.) (2001) *Estimating the Policy Positions of Collective Actors*, London: Routledge.

Leconte, C. (2010) *Understanding Euroscepticism*, Basingstoke: Palgrave Macmillan.

Mair, P. (1995) 'Political parties, popular legitimacy and public privilege', in J. Hayward (ed.) *The Crisis of Representation in Europe*, London: Frank Cass.

Mair, P. (2006) 'Political parties and party systems', in P. Graziano and M. Vink (eds) *Europeanization: New Research Agendas*, Basingstoke: Palgrave Macmillan.

Marks, G. and M. Steenbergen (eds) (2004) *European Integration and Political Conflict*, Cambridge: Cambridge University Press.

Marthaler, S. (2005) 'The French referendum on ratification of the constitutional treaty, 29 May 2005', EPERN Referendum Briefing No. 12, Brighton: Sussex European Institute.

Marthaler, S. (2009) 'European Parliament election in France, June 7 2009', European Parliament Election Briefing No. 31, Brighton: Sussex European Institute.

Matonyte, I. and V. Morkevičius (2012) 'The other side of European identity: Elite perceptions of threats to a cohesive Europe', in H. Best, G. Lengyel and L. Verzichelli (eds) *The Europe of Elites: A Study into the Europeanness of Europe's Economic and Political Elites*, Oxford: Oxford University Press.

Neumayer, L. (2008) 'Euroscepticism as a political label: The use of European Union issues in political competition in the new member states', *European Journal of Political Research*, 47(2): 135–60.

Poguntke, T., N. Aylott, E. Carter, R. Ladrech, and K.R. Luther (eds) (2007) *The Europeanization of National Political Parties*, Oxford/New York: Routledge.

Raunio, T. (2008) 'Softening but persistent: Euroscepticism in the Nordic EU countries', *Acta Politica*, 42(2): 191–217.

Ray, L. (1999) 'Measuring party orientations towards European integration: Results from an expert survey', *European Journal of Political Research*, 36(2): 283–306.

Sanders, D., P. Bellucci, G. Tóka and M. Torcal (2012a) *The Europeanization of National Politics? Citizenship and Support in a Post-Enlargement Union*, Oxford: Oxford University Press.

Sanders, D., P. Magalhaes and G. Tóka (2012b) *Citizens and the European Polity: Mass Attitudes towards the European and National Polities*, Oxford: Oxford University Press.

Sitter, N. (2001) 'The politics of opposition and European integration in Scandinavia: Is Euro-scepticism a government-opposition dynamic?' *West European Politics*, 24(4): 22–39.

Szczerbiak, A. and P. Taggart (2002) 'Europeanisation, Euroscepticism and party systems: Party-based Euroscepticism in the candidate states of central and eastern Europe', *Perspectives on European Politics and Society*, 3(1): 23–41.

Szczerbiak, A. and P. Taggart (eds) (2008) *Opposing Europe: The Comparative Party Politics of Euroscepticism*, I–II vols, Oxford: Oxford University Press.

Tsebelis, G. and G. Garrett (2000) 'Legislative politics in the European Union', *European Union Politics*, 1(1): 5–32.

Van der Eijk, C. and M. Franklin (1996) *Choosing Europe? The European Electorate and National Politics in the Face of Union*, Ann Arbor, MI: University of Michigan Press.

Van der Eijk, C. and M.N. Franklin (2004) 'Potential for contestation on European matters and national elections', in G. Marks and M. Steenbergen (eds) *European Integration and Political Conflict*, Cambridge: Cambridge University Press.

2   France

Nicolas Hubé

Introduction

The main purpose of this chapter is to link the general attitude of French political parties towards EU integration (since 1989) with their positions in political arenas and with historical junctures, and to show that in the French case the interdependency between these factors is particularly strong. Party positions on European integration (whether supportive or critical) is '*related to voter alignments, ideology, interests and identity*' and then translated into party competition in the context of the party system (Sitter 2001, 37, emphasis added).[1] The attitudes towards the EU that have emerged in France have always been somehow critical (Bossuat 2007; Schmidt 2006; Crespy 2010). Certainly, this is due to a large number of factors including the country status of leading power within the EU, a greater international influence in the international scene than other member states and a strong national sentiment that is historically rooted (Schmidt 2007; Gaxie *et al.* 2011). In France, attitudes towards the EU have always been more critical and complex than in most of the other countries considered for this book. Following many other EU member states, French civil society has now largely overstepped the 'permissive consensus' once pointed out by Lindberg and Scheingold which relied on a global factitious adhesion to European prospects, moving to a 'constraining dissensus' (Down and Wilson 2008). As Percheron (1991) showed and confirmed 20 years later by Gaxie *et al.* (2011), there are different logics behind attitudes towards the EU. The present situation is now closer to what we could describe as a process of politicization through involvement, as Weber (1976) explained for the changing French society of the nineteenth century. Indeed, dynamics of European integration are really politicizing the debate and even modifying the French partisan field and the way French diplomacy defends its strategic interests in the European co-decision process (Crespy 2010; Milner 2006). This phenomenon is not new but has structured the French field since the beginning of European integration and the rejection of the European Defence Community in 1954 (Bitsch *et al.* 2007). This has a 'dis-inhibiting effect' on French debate: voices against one specific European project or the whole European integration have no ineffable and delegitimizing effect on those who express them.

Euroscepticism is one position in the political field among others (Neumayer 2008; De Vries and Edwards 2009). More generally, it 'has become an integral part of politics in Europe' (Brack and Costa 2012, 106), having a growing impact on national and European political structures, without being a homogeneous phenomenon (Conti and Memoli 2012). Institutional as well as political conditions are indeed of the utmost importance to scrutinize parties' varying attitudes on European matters, as Sitter (2001) pointed out. More generally, going back to Bourdieu's field theory (1991), we will consider the way parties are positioning themselves in the *national* competition[2] in a relational approach: parties are collections of individuals, groups and coalitions with different and divergent views and interests. Political competition is a symbolic struggle around a set of issues, so that ideology and strategy are closely related, and cannot be considered as totally independent factors. Consequently, Euroscepticism (but also pro-Europeanism) is a 'classification tool' (Neumayer 2008, 141; also De Vries and Edwards 2009). However, the existing literature tends to describe these attitudes by using a static approach. The scientific literature refers to ideology and party attitudes to the EU, either in terms of a left/right competition (Hix and Noury 2009; Marks and Steenbergen 2004; Ray 1999; Tsebelis and Garrett 2000) and/or of a mainstream/radical party divide (Conti 2007, 2012; Schmitt and Thomassen 1999; Taggart and Szczerbiak 2008). Beyond the role of ideology, Deloye (2008) and Conti (2012) explained resistance to European integration by a specific institutional configuration (to be in office or not). This chapter analyses the INTUNE data (52 Euromanifestos and also position papers of French governments between 1989 and 2009) in order to understand the variation in political attitudes across parties.[3] It proposes a complementary insight into the ideological explanations of party attitudes towards the EU by focusing on two main factors of variation: the institutional position of parties and time effects. I will consider the dimensions of citizenships (Cotta and Isernia 2009) as one index[4] and I will attempt to scatter a map of the positions of French political parties between 1989 and 2009 along such index.

Institutional position and variation in party attitudes

One source of variation in party attitudes to the EU that I am going to explore concerns the institutional position of a party in the domestic political scene. To get a more accurate view of attitudes towards Europe, it is necessary to explore the parties' electoral strategies, as well as the alliances they forge in the electoral competition. We can address the question by taking a first example. During the European elections in 1989, the *Union pour la démocratie française* (UDF – Union for the French Democracy/Christian Democrat) was associated with the *Rassemblement pour la République* (RPR – Rally for the Republic/Conservative). Both right-wing parties were at this time in parliamentary opposition. They defended the idea that 'to build a European Union means to give to the European level some needed competences and to keep away some others which defend the

freedom of citizens, companies, local authorities and States' (UDF-RPR 1989).
These parties were back in government in 1993 and remained united for the 1994
European elections, even though internal divisions appeared in the meantime.
Some members of the UDF created a dissident right-sovereignist party called the
Movement for France or MPF (Gautier 2007). At the same time, the Gaullist
Minister of the Interior (RPR) Charles Pasqua created his own sovereignist
party, the Rally for France (RPF). This new party – along with the MPF – was
still a member of the governmental coalition, but it developed a very strong
Eurosceptical point of view:

> Give back its voice to each people, through their respective parliaments/Roll
> back the technocrats of the Commission … Share roles between the nations
> and Brussels. The European Union produced by the Maastricht Treaty tries
> to merge the states in a supranational entity. We refuse this monstrosity.
>
> (RPF 1994)[5]

In 1999, the RPF and MPF made an alliance. In the 1990s, the RPF was what we
can call an 'outsider' party, with severe critical positions against the right-wing
parties from which it originated. At the same time, it maintained the alliance
with these parties in the national government and at the regional level. Its manifesto entitled 'Our project for the other Europe' consisted of a rough attack
against the consensual attitudes of all the other French parties accused of scrap-
ing the debate on Europe: 'The union gets stronger, at both sides of the political
spectrum, on the European project whose purpose seems to be reduced to this
threefold stance: *Yes to Maastricht, Yes to Schengen, Yes to the GATT, as soon
as possible*'. The RPF proposed an alternative path to European integration:

> That is the reason why, against the corroding consensus, in opposition to the
> Maastrichtian proposals of the other parties committed to carry on with the
> present policy, we propose a radical change, to allow France, within Europe,
> to keep its place in the modern world.
>
> (RPF 1994)

In 2009, again, the MPF and the little regionalist 'Hunting, Fishing and Traditions Party' (CPNT) presented a common autonomous list named *Libertas* in the
EP elections. At the same time they were about to join the UMP (in August) and
had had alliance with it for regional and local assemblies. *Libertas*' position is
somehow critical:

> Europe is a necessary dimension of our future. For years, it has been too
> technocratic and undemocratic, far away from the initial draft of the found-
> ing fathers of Europe. The Brussels Commission drifts towards more cen-
> tralism, dirigism and dogmatism. *Libertas* wants to drive a new boost to
> Europe. [...] For a European Europe, this means without Turkey.
>
> (*Libertas* 2009)

This means that party-based Euroscepticism is not only an opposition or protest strategy of parties (Sitter 2001, 27), but in France for some small and non-pivotal parties it can be a firm position even when they are in government. Euromanifesto contents should be interpreted in the light of what we know about the context in which these opinions are expressed. Positions are both strategic and ideological: they are taken in order to distinguish one party from its competitor and at the same time they are 'allowed' by the partners in order to cover each fringe of one political wing. They are also structured by the logic of the national political field (Bourdieu 1991).

For instance, the main characteristic of the French institutional system is indeed to be a semi-presidential regime and the legislative voting system is a two-round system, in which majority parties are over-represented and minority parties do not really endanger the balance between parliamentary forces. This is the reason why I propose to use the category of 'outsider' party, in addition to 'mainstream' and 'radical'. In horse races, outsiders are challengers who run in the shade of those who dominate the competition. Their chances of victory at first order elections may be small but they have to be taken into account as they can disturb well-established predictions of victory. Applied to the French political context, this expression keeps the same meaning. Outsider parties can be seen as auxiliary political formations for majority parties, but not as pivot parties that can coalesce with parties on both sides of the political spectrum. These are parties small in size but with some coalition potential. They can be either moderate or radical, and for this reason the use of the concept of outsider that we propose here is different from the one made by Schedler (1996) when he refers to anti-establishment parties. Depending on the point in time, they can be in government, in the opposition or in the parliamentary majority without holding any governmental office. They can be 'important' at regional level and have therefore to be cherished. When in the majority, in general their members have occupied ministerial office, either with key posts (e.g. State Minister and Minister of the Interior with Pasqua – RPF – between 1993 and 1995 or Defence Minister with Hervé Morin, Nouveau Centre, between 2007 and 2010) or not (e.g. Minister of Sports with Marie-Georges Buffet – *Parti Communiste Français* [PCF – French Communist Party]) and Minister of Regional Planning and Environment with Dominique Voynet (*Les Verts* – Greens – between 1997 and 2002) depending on the role that the majority party intends to give to its coalition partners. In the time period under consideration (1989–2009), this has been the case for the Communist Party in 1984 and 1999, the Greens in 1999, for the UDF and the RPF in 1994, for the Nouveau Centre in 2009. Being auxiliary forces they often seek to attract residual votes that are not captured by the major parties. European elections as second-order elections are a good opportunity to voice an original point of view – also on Europe – to distance themselves from major parties, but also to win some seats, i.e. some positions to offer to party members. In fact, European elections are one of the few elections based on a proportional voting system on a national (from 1979 until 1999) or quasi national (eight large constituencies) level since 2004.[6] Furthermore, given the fact that they never have control of the government, and therefore they never take full responsibility for the performance of the government, they may be less interested in the government–opposition dynamics than major parties.

It is more useful instead to consider the impact of being in government or in the opposition for major parties. When conducting an exploratory analysis I noticed that when in government, major parties tend to concentrate their arguments in the Euromanifestos on European matters, referring less to domestic issues. For example, when the *Parti Socialiste* (PS – Socialist Party) was in office in 1989, its Euromanifesto mainly focused on social and institutional European issues:

> The constructive work that we wish to do together to develop a harmonious global programme includes ... Social Europe, based on high levels of social protection and dialogue between the social partners, an effective health and social security system and also redistribution of benefits to society as a whole, with particular attention to those in need.... For Socialists, Social Europe is a basic element for the construction of a citizens' Europe.
>
> (PS 1989)

Furthermore, in 1994, the right-wing governmental coalition of the RPR and the UDF specified the identity bases of the European integration process: 'The European Union will not be built on the mutilation of our respective identities but by sharing a cultural diversity which makes our true wealth.' Again 10 years later, the presidential UMP party made its pronouncements 'resolutely in favour of the "Federation of Nation-States" defined by Jacques Chirac, Valéry Giscard d'Estaing, Helmut Kohl or Jacques Delors' (UMP 2004). However, when in opposition – conservative RPR/*Démocratie Libérale* (DL – Right liberal) at the time of European elections in 1999 and the socialist PS in 2004 – these parties were much more inclined to import national competition in their Euromanifestos and to challenge the government's performance in Europe: 'The real issue of these European Elections is the choice between the Europe of Freedom and the Socialist Europe.... That's why, in this poll, national as well as European issues are strongly intertwined' (RPR/DL 1999).

> The attitude of the President of the Republic and of the French government is actually in this context methodologically counterproductive and analytically wrong. Misplaced arrogance towards new members states, brutal and casual breakdown of the Stability Pact without proposing a serious strategy to boost growth and employment ... It is also dangerous: demagogic attacks against the European institutions feed nationalism and all kinds of populism.
>
> (PS 2004)

In 2009, the two major parties (PS and UMP) and also the outsider *Front de Gauche* (FG, former communist party) were particularly inclined to import

Table 2.1 Parties, party family, governmental positions and European positioning

	1989	1994	1999	2004	2009	
			LUTTE OUVRIERE/LIGUE COMMUNISTE REVOLUTIONNAIRE		*LUTTE OUVRIERE*	FAR LEFT
			Trotskyist/Extra-Parliamentary *Weak support*	Trotskyist/Extra-Parliamentary *Strong support*	Trotskyist/Extra-Parliamentary *Weak support*	
					NOUVEAU PARTI ANTICAPITALISTE Trotskyist/Extra-Parliamentary *Weak Support*	
	PCF Communist/Non-governmental *Weak support*	*PCF* Communist/Non-governmental *Negative*	*PCF* Communist/Non-governmental *Weak support*	*PCF* Communist/Non-governmental *Weak support*	*FRONT DE GAUCHE* Communist/Non-governmental *Weak support*	
		L'AUTRE POLITIQUE Lefts-sovereignist/Non-governmental *Negative*				
	PARTI SOCIALISTE Social-Democrats/Governmental *Weak support*	*PARTI SOCIALISTE* Social-Democrats/Non-governmental *Strong support*	*PARTI SOCIALISTE* Social-Democrats/Governmental *Strong support*	*PARTI SOCIALISTE* Social-Democrats/Non-governmental *Weak support*	*PARTI SOCIALISTE* Social-Democrats/Non-governmental *Weak support*	
		LES VERTS Greens/Non-governmental *Strong support*	*LES VERTS* Greens/Governmental *Weak support*	*LES VERTS* Greens/Non-governmental *Neutral*	*EUROPE ECOLOGIE LES VERTS* Greens/Non-governmental *Strong support*	
	PARTI RADICAL Centre-left/Non-governmental *Strong support*	Centre-left/Non-governmental *Strong support*	Centre-left/Governmental *Strong support*	*PARTI RADICAL DE GAUCHE* Centre-left/Non-governmental *Strong support*		

RPR and UDF	RPR and UDF	UDF	MOUVEMENT DEMOCRATE
Conservative, Liberal and Christian-Democrat/Non-governmental *Weak support*	Conservative, Liberal and Christian-Democrat/Democrat/Governmental *Strong support*	Liberal and Christian-Democrat/Governmental *Strong support*	Liberal and Christian-Democrat/Non-governmental *Strong support*
	RPR and DEMOCRATIE LIBERALE Conservative and Liberal/Non-governmental *Strong support*	*UMP* Conservative and Liberal/Governmental *Weak support*	*UMP and NOUVEAU CENTRE* Conservative and Liberal/Governmental *Weak support*
Others/Extra-parliamentary *Weak support*	*CPNT* Others/Extra-parliamentary *Negative*	Others/Extra-parliamentary *Weak support*	*LIBERTAS* Nationalists/Extra-parliamentary *Weak support*
MAJORITE POUR L'AUTRE EUROPE Nationalists/Governmental *Negative*	*RPF/MPF* Nationalists/Extra-parliamentary *Neutral*	*MOUVEMENT POUR LA FRANCE (MPF)* Nationalists/Extra-parliamentary *Weak support*	*DEBOUT LA REPUBLIQUE* Nationalists/Non-governmental *Negative*
		RASSEMBLEMENT POUR LA FRANCE (RPF) Nationalists/Extra-parliamentary *Neutral*	
FN Extreme-right/Extra-parliamentary *Negative*	*FN* Extreme-right/Extra-parliamentary *Negative*	*FN* Extreme-right/Extra-parliamentary *Neutral*	*FN* Extreme-right/Extra-parliamentary *Negative*
Others/Extra-parliamentary *Negative*	Others/Extra-parliamentary *Negative*		

FAR RIGHT

national issues into their Euromanifestos. Opposition parties denounced the poor performance of the government one year after its defeat at regional and local elections: 'What we want is first of all to transform the elections into an arm wrestling between our People and Nicolas Sarkozy' (FG 2009) or 'The French turnaround on this [social] issue, following the victory of Nicolas Sarkozy, gave a majority to the most antisocial liners' (PS 2009). Back to its Gaullist tradition, the governing UMP proposed a plebiscite for the President and its action in Europe:

> France in Europe, not just 6 months of Presidency, it is a will and a sustained action that Nicolas Sarkozy wants to print. He continues to take his responsibility. Return of the willingness, of the desire to act, to give a real meaning to the European integration is our vision of Europe. It is the vision that bears the Presidential Majority, with Nicolas Sarkozy. At every level of European institutions, it is this desire that must govern the European action.
>
> (UMP 2009)

Finally, some words on the 'extra-parliamentary' parties. In France, this category concerns the fringes of the political spectrum (the National Front on the far right, the Trotskyist parties *Lutte ouvrière* [LO – Workers' Struggle] and *Ligue Communiste Révolutionnaire* [LCR – Revolutionary Communist League][7] on the far left) as well as the regionalist Hunting, Fishing and Tradition Party (CPNT). Given that their institutional position does not change, their stance is a firm ideologically constructed one. Conscious of limited institutional opportunities, the CPNT wrote in 1999 in the Euromanifesto: 'Our vocation was never to take some definitive places in the institutions of power. We only want to sit in the European Parliament to defend the voices of those who want to protect their origins and identity' (CPNT 1999).

The most stable party on the European issue is probably the National Front (FN) whose critical positions are always focused on immigration, globalization, technocrats and anti-establishment arguments. It occurred in 1994, when it clearly explained its vision:

> A France whose laws should not be subordinated to the directives of Brussels. A France mastering its borders which must be retained under French control. A France where major decisions are made at home, not in Washington, Brussels, New York, Frankfurt and Luxembourg.
>
> (FN 1994)

The same arguments appeared in the same wording in 1999, 2004 and 2009. The FN is the only constantly negative party (in our index). The FN is the only radical party with a great audience, although rarely represented (only between 1986 and 1988 and since June 2012 with two MPs) in the National Assembly and only in some regional or European assemblies. This firm extreme-right positioning is at the same time ideological and strategic, as could be noticed during the last Presidential campaign when Marine Le Pen slightly 'softened' its position on immigration but not on the European issue.

In the end, it seems that the impact of institutional positions on the way French parties tackle European issues takes several forms. In the major mainstream parties, we should be able to find greater sensitivity to the institutional elasticity which derives from holding or not holding public office. Other parties like the National Front or the Trotskyist parties should not be sensitive at all as they are out of any elective positions. Outsider parties should be less sensitive to government responsibility than major parties and more interested in producing an original stance that could distinguish them from larger parties. The index results (Figures 2.1 and 2.2) partially confirm this hypothesis. Mainstream and governmental parties are the most Euro-supportive parties but with a majority of weak supporters. The UMP in 2004 and 2009 as the PS in 1989 are only weak Euro-supporters. There is the same proportion (about 40 per cent) of strong supporters within the outsider and non-governmental group – something that clearly distinguishes them from radical and extra-parliamentary parties. There is however a significant difference of outsider as well as non-governmental parties: they are more negative and neutral than mainstream parties (about 20 per cent). But we can also note that about 10 per cent of governmental parties express negative views of European integration.

At the same time, there is a significant difference with radical and extra-parliamentary parties: about 40 per cent of the former and 30 per cent of the latter are negative towards European integration and about 20 per cent are neutral. Almost no one is a strong Euro-supporter but, surprisingly, about 40 per

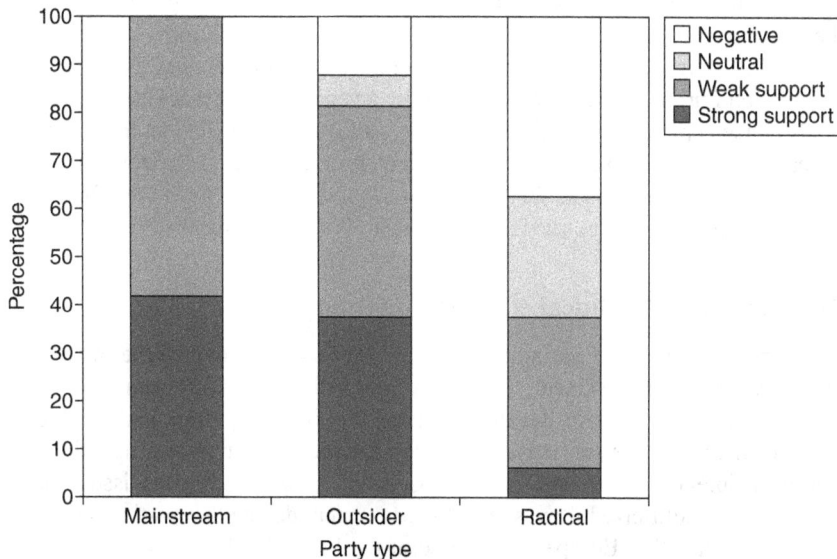

Figure 2.1 General attitude and party type.

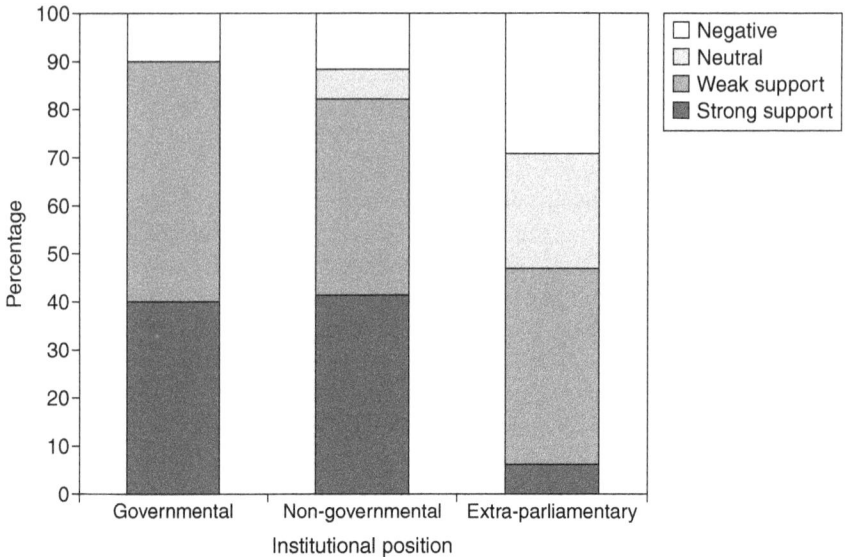

Figure 2.2 General attitude and institutional position.

cent are weak Euro-supporters. The Trotskyist parties are a good example of this contra-intuitive result: they are against the 'liberal European integration' but at the same time supporters of a 'European socialist integration' (LO/LCR 2004 and LO 2009), calling for a 'real' supranational European democracy. In 2004, they appear to be 'strong supporters' but of their (socialist) Europe.

In other words, a political party does not only aim at reiterating fixed political attitudes on Europe, but also seeks to propose a general set of what Gaetano Mosca (1939) once depicted as 'political formulas'. But we have to add that these formulas narrowly depend on the institutional, ideological and political context in which they are stated (Mastropaolo 2004), as well as on the time factor. In the following section, we present an empirical representation of this phenomenon.

Time effects and political elasticity

A second main factor of variation concerns what could be named the 'historical elasticity' of political stances. Over time, the salience of European issues has changed in French public debate. Both on the side of parties and of public opinion there is a greater sense of the impact (both positive and negative) of European integration on daily life. Consequently, some European issues have become more politicized. It was after the Maastricht debate that parties started to speak about 'another Europe', 'a Europe of the People and no more the techno-cratic Europe of Maastricht' (RPF 1994). In the discourse of extra-parliamentary parties, the democratic deficit becomes an argument that is strongly voiced:

And when we criticize the anti-democratic character of the European integration process, it is because we would prefer a development based on a democratic political Europe, new institutions, control exerted by the people on all decisions at all possible levels. To sum up, we support the creation of a new democratic Europe.

(LO–LCR 1999)

Other specific issues make their appearance in the discourse on the EU. For the CPNT Europe should defend the regions, agriculture and local traditions (Mischi 2007).[8] For the socialists, communists and Trotskyists Europe should defend the worker's rights against the market and international finance. The argument of a 'Social Europe' is also used in the domestic competition (Crespy 2010). In 1989, for the socialists (in government at the time) 'a social Europe is the founding element of a citizens' Europe. The European Social Charter is its touchstone and should be acknowledged by all Member States' (PS 1989). But the communist party, which was an outsider party at the time, maintained:

1. It is necessary to stop the social regression and the attacks to social rights … 2. We have to fight against the hegemony of financial powers and multinational companies … The candidates of the Socialist party declare they want what they call 'a Social Europe', while in France they implement an austerity policy … Facts prove it: on European integration socialists have adopted the same principles as the right-wing parties.

(PCF 1989)

Ten years later, the European social agenda was still mobilized against the socialist government by the extra-parliamentary alliance of LO–LCR, which proposed 'to oppose the policy of the [present socialist] government which does not fight enough against unemployment and poverty' (LO–LCR 1999).

Not surprisingly, in the 2009 elections all parties mentioned the financial crisis. For the mainstream Socialist Party, the outsider Greens and the Christian-Democrats (*Mouvement démocrate* – MODEM), 'Europe is our only chance to fight against the crisis and overcome the immense challenges we face' (MODEM 2009). The only strong Euro-supporters are the Greens and the MODEM. For the governing UMP and also for the nationalist outsider parties (*Libertas, Debout la République*), if the crisis is European, the solution is only national, i.e. intergovernmental. The best argument supporting this position was Nicolas Sarkozy's Presidency: 'And in the financial and economic crisis, initiative and proposals came from Europeans. Presiding the European Union, Nicolas Sarkozy has shown that this is possible. That Europe knows how to act and protect when it is directed' (UMP 2009). On both ends of the political axes, this crisis is an argument to criticize the system and the establishment. The far-left depicts the 2009 crisis as it did in 1999: a crisis of capitalism, of a bourgeois Europe cut off from the people's reality: 'crisis now unites the destiny of workers in Europe' (LO 2009). For the extreme-right, immigration, elites, mainstream parties and bankers are the main culprits.

The Europe of Brussels, one that supports Sarkozy, the UMP and the PS, is a Europe governed by technocrats cut off from reality, [Europe] of industries relocated to China, of services to India, of American agriculture, of jobs destroyed and of people increasingly poor. It is also a Europe colonized by immigration [...], a Europe in a process of Islamisation that is about to make Turkey a member. These are the results of the betrayal of politicians and financial elites, their boundless loyalty to free trade and unbridled globalism.

(FN 2009)

When studying attitudes towards Europe, one should take into consideration the fact that EU issues evolve according to a temporal and contextual framework. Electoral cycles and party institutional positions certainly have an influence on party competition over the EU. But party strategies are particularly visible for the topics that have become hard issues (such as a social Europe) in the national public debate. Looking at the historical variations (Figures 2.3 and 2.4), there is a global trend of decreasing strong enthusiasm, but also of *negativeness*. There are fewer and fewer strong supporters, while negativity almost disappeared in 2004 (characterizing the FN and the nationalist *Debout la République*). Each party type is affected by this general trend: radical parties are going from negativity to neutralism or weak supports, whereas mainstream are going from Euro-enthusiasm to weak support.

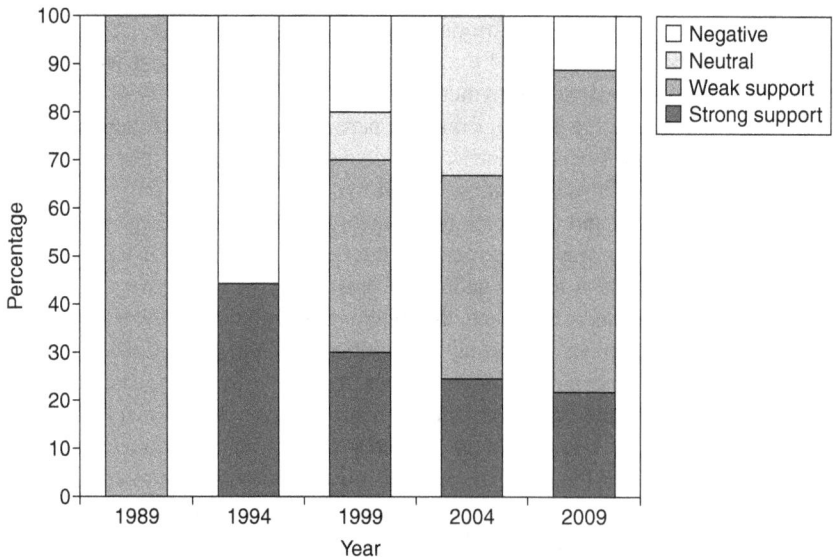

Figure 2.3 General position in time.

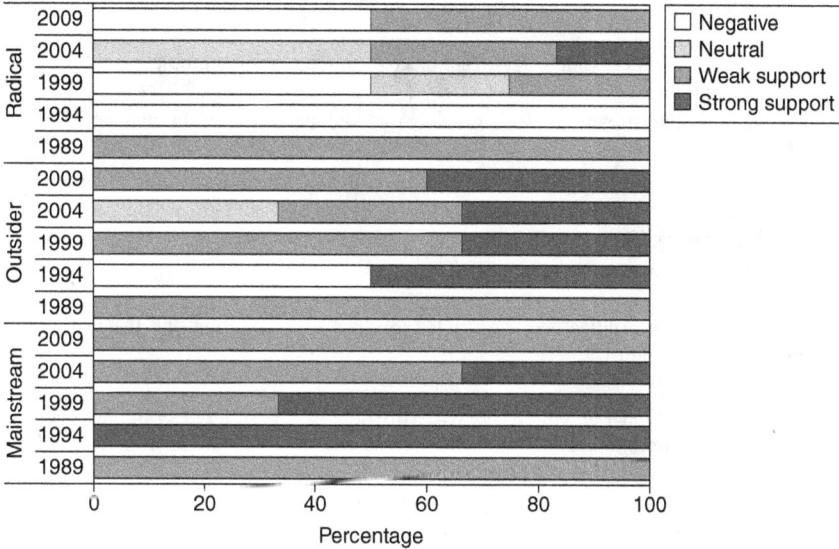

Figure 2.4 General attitude and party type in time.

A French political map of party attitudes[9]

As Conti pointed out (2007, 2012), cleavage lines are evolving and may spread disorder and unprecedented contestation inside the national political spectrum. Considering a longitudinal dimension in the study of party attitudes towards the EU will be an appropriate means to show for different historical junctures the evolution of attitudes consequent to the electoral cycle and to developments in European integration.

Box 2.1 Methodological notes

A multiple correspondence analysis (MCA) provides a simplified representation of the space built by the dependent variables used, in our case it is a map of the party positions on European integration. To work out our analysis, we have carried out several MCAs. We have used the software program R 2.8.1. With 11 variables used, the first axis summarizes 15.68 per cent, the second 8.87 per cent and the third 8.36 per cent of the variance, a good result using this method (Benzécri 1992). MCA provides a representation of the main structure of a dataset in a scatter of points, i.e. social spaces. Results (see Table 2.a.1 in the Appendix to this chapter) are presented in synthetic indexes of weights of the modalities of each variable, from the most influential to the least. Each axis shows us a structure of correlations among variables. Axes are not constructed a priori, but are the results of the statistical correlations among variables (Durand 1998).

Five of the selected variables concern the nature of the analysed party/document:

1 type of document (party manifesto or governmental programme);
2 party family;
3 nature (mainstream, radical, outsider) of the party in the French political context;
4 institutional position of the party in the domestic arena at the time the document was issued (in government, only in parliament or outside the parliament);
5 date of the document.

Five questions are indicators of attitudes towards representation and the institutional setting of the EU:

6 European impact on country matters (favourable opportunities bringing benefits and improvements to the country, or negative constraints limiting and constraining countries' freedom);
7 national action in Europe (preference for a leadership position for their country in the EU, or for cooperation, adaptation or opting-out);
8 EU decision-making (preference for a supranational, intergovernmental mode, a mixed position or national preference);
9 subsidiarity in the EU (positive or negative reference to);
10 democratic deficit of the EU (reference or lack of reference to).

One variable informs on the position on European identity:

11 reference to supranational, national or sub-national identity, or to mixed layers of identity.

After calculation of correlations within axes, we have carried out several multiple linear regressions on the first three axes considered as continuous dependent variables (for another example, see Chiche and Haegel 2002).

A first dimension evidenced by the analysis consists of two opposite poles. In Figure 2.1 the first axis summarizes the division between radical Euro-critics and mainstream Euro-supporters. This division is quite common in the European context and it is well documented by comparative works (Taggart and Szczerbiak 2008). The dimensions of citizenship pointed out by Cotta and Isernia (2009) are intertwined. On one side of the spectrum, we can find the extreme right,[10] nationalists, extra-parliamentary and radical parties, and non-defined parties in a left–right scale such as the CPNT. They express preferences in favour of opting out of the building blocks of the EU, endorse strong protection of national interests, severely criticize European institutions and call for a shift-back of powers to the member states. They allow different identities to co-exist, but with an explicit ranking in favour of the national/sub-national layer. Finally, they develop a negative vision of federalism and deepening of European integration and think that decision-making in the EU should depend on unanimity voting, i.e. it should be kept intergovernmental. On this side of the axis (but less polarized) are also left-sovereignists,[11] Trotskyists and, closer to the centre, communists.

Mainstream parties (social democrats, conservatives, liberals and Christian-Democrats) can be found on the opposite pole of the axis. They maintain that Europe broadly functions in a democratic way but that it suffers, at the same time, from a democratic deficit. This is a more critical attitude than the one found for many counterpart parties in the other countries considered in this book (see also Conti 2010). Moreover, in their view, European and French identities can co-exist and are complementary. They are in favour of mixed supranational and intergovernmental decision-making, depending on the issue area, and support greater subsidiarity in EU policy-making. They want France to take an active part in European decision-making, but at the same time they underline the importance of working together with the other member states to define common aims (Gaxie and Hubé 2012a, 2012b). They also make reference to a common European identity and consider France to have mainly benefited from the EU. These parties create a Euro-supporter, but not necessarily a federalist pole. As a matter of fact, their stance in favour of supranational decision-making and subsidiarity in the EU – key elements of European federalism – characterizes this pole less than the other factors mentioned above. A division can also be observed between periods of more widespread support for the EU (1989–1991 and 1999–2001) and periods of more widespread criticism, around the time of EU referenda (1994 and 2004–2005, see Table 2.a.1 in the Appendix to this chapter).

It is important to note that on this side of the axis we find both governmental and non-governmental parties, as well as major and outsider parties. On this axis, parties in governing positions are overall more inclined to positive attitudes than non-governmental parties (although the range of variation within each of these two clusters is quite large). Furthermore, parties are ordered in this horizontal axis along a continuum from Euro-critics (radical and extra-parliamentary parties) to Euro-supporters (mainstream and governmental parties), with positions in between occupied by other parties (outsider and non-governmental parties), so that parties are ordered from radical to mainstream (outsiders have in-between positions) and from extra-parliamentary to government parties (parties in non-governmental position are in-between).

The left–right division has no impact on the structure of the positions on the EU of the French parties. This evidence goes against the theoretical argument on the impact of left/right on party attitudes to the EU that is maintained by several authors with respect to other countries (Conti 2010; Hix and Noury 2009; Marks and Steenbergen 2004; Ray 1999; Tsebelis and Garrett 2000). On the contrary, our findings confirm the argument on the dyadic mainstream–radical pattern of party positions on the EU (Taggart and Szczerbiak 2008), to which a tryadic mainstream–outsider–radical pattern could be added specifically for the French case.

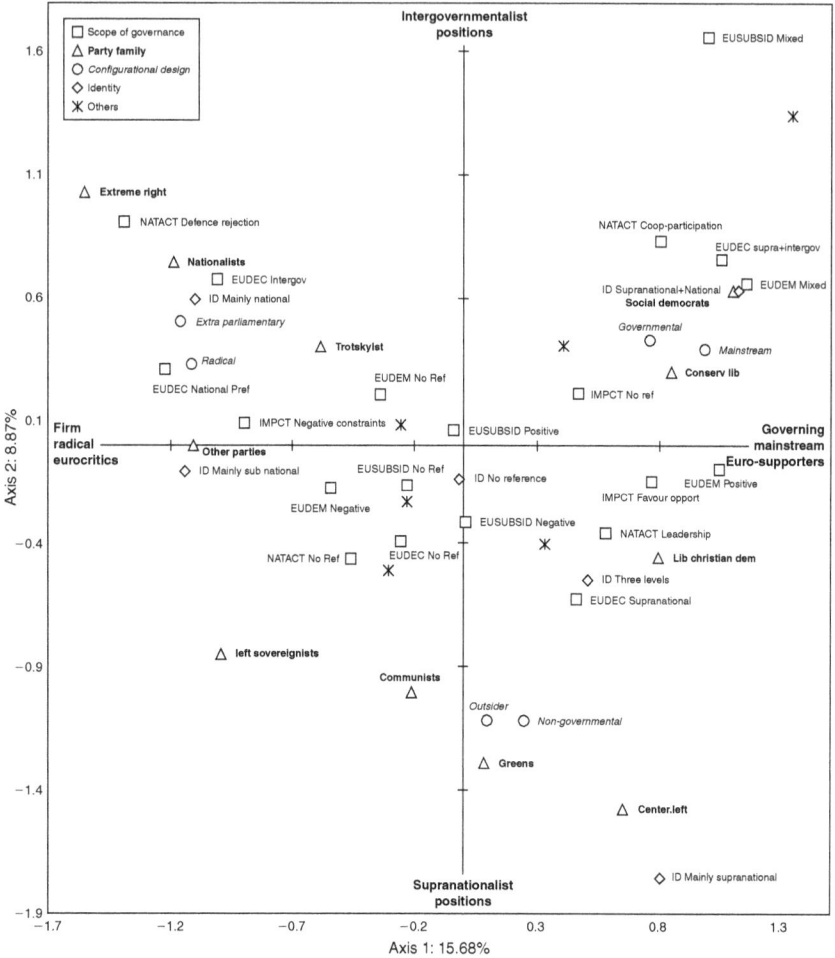

Figure 2.5 Parties and parties' positions on axes 1 and 2.

The second axis mainly opposes outsider parties with supranationalist positions to the other (mainstream or radical) parties (see Figure 2.5). At one end of this second axis, we find programmes mainly characterized by explicitly positive references to European identity. They also express preferences in favour of EU decisions made by majority voting. Those involved are the centre-left, green, non-governmental, outsider, communist and left-sovereignist parties. The liberal and Christian-Democratic party (UDF) is also found on this side of the axis. Such positions were asserted more strongly in 1994 (when the French left was in opposition) and (slightly less visibly) in 1989–1991. At the opposite side of the axis are government parties as well as nationalists and the extreme right, who express mixed feelings on EU subsidiarity, a pledge for protection of national sovereignty, either support for mixed supranational/intergovernmental decision-making in the EU or open defence of strict intergovernmental decisions, and mixed feelings on European identity or open defence of national identity. This second axis makes it possible for us to understand the specific contribution of outsider parties (especially of the left) to the political discourse on the EU in France and also in Europe (Brack and Costa 2012). These parties present themselves as an alternative to both major and radical parties, introducing a form of support for the supranational mode of decision-making otherwise rare in the French party system where, as we have seen, reluctance towards delegation of national sovereignty is quite widespread. Finally, a third axis gives us little additional information about the spatial positioning of parties (therefore, it is not shown here).[12] This axis mainly shows a division between the different radical parties. The well-known resistance of these parties to European integration shows no ideological convergence between right- and left-wing oppositions (Deloye 2008, 681; Neumayer 2008; De Vries and Edwards 2009; Conti and Memoli, 2012). Consequently, in France, party-based Euroscepticism does not use the same arguments on both sides of the political spectrum.

The above three axes define political maps that give a clear representation of parties' positions on issues related to the development of European governance and identity. They show that governing parties are in an institutional position that drives them to be broadly more positive towards the EU than the other parties. However, on issues concerning delegation of powers to the EU, they are more intergovernmentalist and less federalist than the outsider parties. In Figure 2.5 intergovernmentalist Euro-supporters are located in the top-right area of the map, whereas Euro-rejects are in the top-left area. Overall, the most Europhile are outsider parties (centre-left, greens, UDF) which are located in the bottom-right area. In the end, our analysis shows the validity of the argument of the mainstream vs radical nature of party attitudes towards the EU: the former show various degrees of support for the EU, while hard Euroscepticism can only be found among the latter. However, some specifications are necessary in the French case as communists are not necessarily as Eurosceptic in all dimensions of the EU process as one may expect when we accept the mainstream vs radical argument. Furthermore, the argument on the left vs right nature of party attitudes towards the EU is definitely not valid in the French case, where competition on the EU does not overlap with this line of conflict (left and right parties share similar positions in the different quadrants of the map). As was noticed before, French mainstream parties and/or governing parties are more inclined to be intergovernmentalist than federalist. This is probably due to France's status of a 'big' founding member state, reluctant to lose its sovereignty (Gaxie and Hubé 2012b).

The analysis shows that only few of the variables under consideration are correlated (also Conti 2010). Pro-Europeanism in one field does not necessarily overlap with Europhilia in other aspects. Regressions of various variables in the factorial axes show correlations mainly among variables within the representation dimension.[13] However, these relationships are strong in the first axis but very weak in the other two, so even these variables do not correlate systematically in the represented space. As we discussed above, parties on the right side of the first map (Figure 2.5) share positive or (near to the centre) mixed views on the legitimacy of European institutions, on their responsiveness and on the decision-making mechanisms in the EU. Parties on the left side share negative views on these issues. References to national identity and national symbols are located on the left side of the axis (although with weak correlations). Conversely, reference to European identity is located on the right side of the map. We then tested if the first two axes (considered as indexes that aggregate the variables shown in Table 2.a.1 in the Appendix to this chapter) correlate with policy (for a list of analysed policies, see the Appendix to this book). We found that support for the EU in one dimension does not produce support in the other dimensions. Furthermore, we found that support for the Europeanization of one policy field does not associate with the same support in other policy fields. The only partial exception (although with weak correlations) is the policies of what used to be the second and third pillars of the EU that mildly correlate with the first and second axes. Parties at the bottom-right quadrant of the map tend to be in favour of an exclusive supranational or a mixed national/supranational competence in foreign and security policies, as well as in justice affairs. Parties in the top-left quadrant tend to share a preference for the exclusive national competence in these fields as well as in the fields of immigration and social policy.

Finally, it would be interesting to enquire if party positions, in particular those expressed in the Euromanifestos, could be thought of as strategic electoral positions in the pursuit of electoral gains. We found no relation between the positions expressed by parties and their results in the polls. Even where the stance of a party is the result of a strategy for party competition, this stance seems far away from voters' choices (Bourdieu 1991).

Final remarks

This chapter shows that the relevance of European issues in the French political debate has grown since 1989. French parties divide over such issues, along the lines opposing (1) major parties to radical and outsider parties, and (2) governmental (i.e. in office) parties to non-governmental (i.e. not in office) and extra-parliamentary parties. Left or right positioning, on the other hand, does not impact the pattern of contestation of the EU issue in the French case. The consistency of party-based positions is overall limited: attitudes vary a great deal from one field to another (but also within the same field), so that support for the EU in one field (representation) does not necessarily translate into support in another field (policy).

Parties divide upon a set of EU issues, so their touchstone of dissent (Taggart 1998; Crespy and Verschueren 2009) varies across the analysed dimensions, producing in the end a peculiar pattern that differs from the more traditional patterns of party competition in France. Additionally, variation emerges over time. In the French case, some junctures are particularly critical for the establishment of party-based Euroscepticism (the years around 1994 and 2004). This work aimed to emphasize that in order to understand party competition on the EU, strategy and ideology have to be analysed. Ultimately, in France, European elections really are both about national competition and positioning on European integration (Neumayer 2008).

Acknowledgements

The author would like to thank M.-H. Bruère and Y. Deloye for their participation in the coding of the Euromanifestos (1989–2004), Muriel Rambour for her help in the previous version (Hubé and Rambour 2010) and Laure Neumayer for her constructive reading of this text.

Appendix

Table 2.a.1 Weights of each variable's modality in the definition of the three first factorial axes

Axis 1		Axis 2		Axis 3	
PART_FAM: Extreme.right	-1.54608021	IDMULTIP: Mainly.supranational.identity	-1.749557096	IDMULTIP: Mainly.supranational.identity	-1.53082182
NATACT: Defence.rejection	-1.38698462	EUSUBSID: Mixed	1.656456440	IDMULTIP: Mainly.sub.national	1.52411388
DOCTYP: Government.Programm	1.34513762	PART_FAM: Centre.left	-1.475352578	EUDEC: No.reference	1.39888142
EUDEC: National.preference	-1.22445049	DOCTYP: Government.Programm	1.336735142	PART_FAM: Other	1.32765732
PART_FAM: Nationalists	-1.18861785	PART_FAM: Greens	-1.286972170	DATE2: 1989.91	1.28421092
Extra.parliamentary	-1.15956826	Non.governmental	-1.115793311	IMPCT: No.reference	1.20079975
EUDEM.Mixed	1.15768936	TYP_PART: Outsider	-1.115660338	PART_FAM: Nationalists	-1.17019971
IDMULTIP.Mainly.sub.national	-1.14118816	PART_FAM: Extreme.right	1.030938010	PART_FAM: left.sovereignists	1.01448767
IDMULTIP: Supranational … National	1.12295208	PART_FAM: Communists	-1.001539568	NATACT: Defence.rejection	-1.01361384
TYP_PART: Radical	-1.11313330	NATACT: Defence.rejection	0.906480699	EUDEC: Intergovernmental	-0.99415011
PART_FAM: Other	-1.10772931	PART_FAM: left.sovereignists	-0.844965614	EUSUBSID: No.reference	0.98578180
PART_FAM: Social.democrats	1.10242198	NATACT: Cooperation.participation	0.828685434	NATACT: No.reference	0.95359839
IDMULTIP: Mainly.national	-1.09896049	EUDEC: Mixed.supranational.and. intergovernmental	0.754452187	PART_FAM: Extreme.right	-0.87791055
EUDEC: Mixed.supranational.and. intergovernmental	1.05671568	PART_FAM: Nationalists	0.744932990	EUDEM: No.reference	0.86625665
EUDEM: Positive	1.05337110	EUDEC: Intergovernmental	0.671282919	PART_FAM: Centre.left	-0.80813655
EUDEC: Intergovernmental	-1.00596608	EUDEM: Mixed	0.653733638	EUSUBSID: Negative	-0.79019955
EUSUBSID: Mixed	1.00077131	IDMULTIP: Supranational … National	0.630000371	EUDEM: Positive	-0.60723045
PART_FAM: left.sovereignists	-0.98946891	PART_FAM: Social.democrats	0.627937506	IDMULTIP: Supranational … National Sub.national	0.51495399
TYP_PART: Mainstream	0.98345610	EUDEC: Supranational	-0.624061217	EUDEC: National.preference	-0.45938960
IMPCT: Negative.constraints	-0.89436291	IDMULTIP: Mainly.national	0.594909248	NATACT: Leadership	-0.44361081
PART_FAM: Conservatives_liberals	0.84476411	IDMULTIP: Supranational … National Sub.national	-0.543948675	PART_FAM: Greens	0.42824235
NATACT: Cooperation.participation	0.80466848	DATE2: 1994	-0.507174717	IDMULTIP: Mainly.national	-0.37811114
IDMULTIP: Mainly.supranational.identity	0.79937427	Extra.parliamentary	0.504944746	DATE2: 1994	-0.35961468

PART_FAM: Liberals_christian_democrats	0.79483961	NATACT: No.reference	-0.457010031	EUDEC: Supranational	-0.35565093
IMPCT: Favourable.opportunities	0.76428918	PART_FAM: Liberals_christian_democrats	-0.451039778	PART_FAM: Social.democrats	0.32958827
Governmental	0.75925413	Governmental	0.426577377	PART_FAM: Liberals_christian_democrats	-0.28427860
PART_FAM.Centre.left	0.64820574	DATE2: 1999.2001	0.406338976	PART_FAM: Conservatives_liberals	-0.27858285
PART_FAM: Troskist	-0.58118626	DATE2: 1989.91	-0.402243004	DOCTYP: Government.Programm	0.26835746
NATACT: Leadership	0.57909240	PART_FAM: Trotskyist	0.401953992	Non.governmental	-0.23938614
EUDEM: Negative	-0.53795417	TYP_PART: Mainstream	0.3901.1449	TYP_PART: Outsider	-0.22735012
IDMULTIP: Supranational ... National ... Sub.national	0.50614415	EUDEC: No.reference	-0.387020430	IDMULTIP: No.reference	-0.22532681
IMPCT: No.reference	0.46826543	NATACT: Leadership	-0.353236789	PART_FAM: Trotskyist	0.19887210
EUDEC: Supranational	0.46259674	TYP_PART: Radical	0.327654680	EUSUBSID: Mixed	0.19632954
NATACT: No.reference	-0.46131982	EUSUBSID: Negative	-0.311967289	IMPCT: Negative.constraints	-0.19208524
DATE2: 1999.2001	0.40494823	EUDEC: National.preference	0.306552937	PART_FAM: Communists	-0.15028208
EUDEM: No.reference	-0.33935568	PART_FAM: Conservatives_liberals	0.298485037	IMPCT: Favourable.opportunities	-0.14147025
DATE2: 1989.91	0.33155497	DOCTYP: Euromanifesto	-0.229154596	Governmental	0.12213004
DATE2: 1994	-0.30387043	IMPCT: No.reference	0.206301553	TYP_PART: Radical	0.08457855
EUDEC: No.reference	-0.25660380	EUDEM: No.reference	0.205850367	EUSUBSID: Positive	-0.08285673
DATE2: 2004.05	-0.25548964	EUDEM: Negative	-0.173519256	EUDEM: Mixed	-0.08028627
Non.governmental	0.24386011	EUSUBSID: No.reference	-0.162361228	Extra.parliamentary	0.07065793
EUSUBSID: No.reference	-0.23113308	IMPCT: Favourable.opportunities	-0.145756674	IDMULTIP: Supranational ... National	0.06808458
DOCTYP: Euromanifesto	-0.23005902	IDMULTIP: No.reference	-0.133976700	TYP_PART: Mainstream	0.06280143
PART_FAM: Outsider	-0.21005976	IDMULTIP: Mainly.sub.national	-0.101920612	NATACT: Cooperation.participation	0.04843801
TYP_PART: Outsider	0.09617018	EUDEM: Positive	-0.094479979	DOCTYP: Euromanifesto	-0.04600414
PART_FAM: Greens	0.08117475	IMPCT: Negative.constraints	0.088450959	EUDEC: Mixed.supranational.and. intergovernmental	0.03692225
EUSUBSID: Positive	-0.04129738	DATE2: 2004.05	0.084414249	DATE2: 1999.2001	0.03459477
IDMULTIP: No.reference	-0.01619645	EUSUBSID: Positive	0.062298495	EUDEM: Negative	0.03241882
EUSUBSID: Negative	0.00910102	PART_FAM: Other	0.003972195	DATE2: 2004.05	-0.02932293

Notes

1 A previous analysis from 1989 to 2004 was published in Hubé and Rambour (2010). The author would like to thank Muriel Rambour for her help on this former paper.
2 Even if there is a strong Europeanization of the political competition and also a strong impact of Euroscepticism (Brack and Costa 2012), the strategic interest of these second order elections remains mainly national.
3 We start the analysis from 1989 as for the first two elections only four manifestos are available. Manifestos will be quoted with the party's acronym and the year of the election. For example (PS 1989) for the Socialist Party manifesto during the 1989 election.
4 As explained below, we used a multiple component analysis. But I first built an index of general attitude towards European Integration, adding three questions (MEMBERSHIP, NATACT and EUDEC). For MEMBERSHIP, negative constraints, Defence/rejection and National preference were always coded –1. No reference coded 0. Favourable opportunities were coded 1. For NATACT, leadership was coded 1 and cooperation 2. For EUDEC, mixed answers were coded 1, intergovernmental 2 and supranational 3. In the end, the index goes from –3 to 6. I considered negative scores as 'negative attitude'; those with answers from 1 to 3 as 'weak support', and those from 4 to 6 as 'strong support', the 0 score as 'neutral'.
5 All quotations are the author's own translations.
6 Regional elections are also based on a proportional voting in 22 constituencies since 1986.
7 In 2009: Nouveau Parti Anticapitaliste, NPA – New Anticapitalist Party.
8 The party received 4 per cent of votes in the EP elections in 1989 and 1994; 6.77 per cent and six MEPs in 1999; 2 per cent in 2004. In 2009, it joined the right-sovereignists party MPF under a common banner: *Libertas*: 4.80 per cent of votes and no MEP elected.
9 Some minor changes in the coding system between the first and the second wave prevented me from conducting the MCA for the whole period. However, this analysis can be considered as illustrative of a considerable period of time (1989–2004) and the clear patterns that have emerged would not be put substantially under question by inclusion of 2009. For more details on the research technique see Hubé and Rambour (2010).
10 Modalities defining this first pole of the first axis are mentioned hereafter in decreasing order of positive contribution to the first factorial axis. It means that 'Party family: extreme right' and 'National action in Europe: Defence/rejection' display the highest weight on the first axis on the 'euro-critic' side. See Table 2.a.1 in the Appendix.
11 Left-sovereignists are defending a 'Europe of Nations' against federalism but are close to the other left parties on other issues.
12 For details see Hubé and Rambour (2010, 155).
13 Due to space constraints, we do not present the tables here, but they are available on demand.

References

Benzécri, Jean-Paul (1992) *Correspondence Analysis Handbook*, New York: Dekker.
Bitsch, Marie-Thérèse, Loth Wilfried and Charles Barthel (eds) (2007) *Cultures Politiques, Opinions Publiques et Intégration Européenne*, Bruxelles: Emile Bruylant.
Bossuat, Gérard (2007) 'La culture politique des dirigeants français face au défi de la construction européenne (1943–2005)', in Marie-Thérèse Bitsch, Loth Wilfried and Charles Barthel (eds) *Cultures Politiques, Opinions Publiques et Intégration Européenne*, Bruxelles: Emile Bruylant, pp. 7–26.

Bourdieu, P. (1991) 'Political representation: elements for a theory of the political field', in P. Bourdieu (ed.) *Language and Symbolic Power*, Cambridge, MA: Harvard University Press, pp. 171–202.

Brack, Nathalie and Olivier Costa (2012) 'Beyond the pro/anti-Europe divide: diverging views of Europe within EU institutions', *Journal of European Integration*, 34, 2: 101–111.

Chiche, Jean and Florence Haegel (2002) 'Les connaissances politiques', in Gérard Grunberg, Nonna Mayer and Paul M. Sniderman (eds) *La Démocratie à l'épreuve*, Paris: Presses de Sciences po, pp. 273–292.

Conti, Nicolò (2012) 'The EU in the programmatic statements of domestic parties', in Heinrich Best, György Lengyel and Luca Verzichelli (eds) *The Europe of Elites: A Study into the Europeanness of Europe's Economic and Political Elites*, Oxford: Oxford University Press, pp. 192–207.

Conti, Nicolò (2007) 'Domestic parties and European integration: the problem of party attitudes to the EU, and the Europeanisation of parties', *European Political Science*, 6: 192–207.

Conti, Nicolò (ed.) (2010) 'Which Europe do parties want? A view from France, Italy, Portugal and Spain', a special issue of *Perspectives on European Politics and Society*, 11, 2.

Conti, Nicolò and V. Memoli (2012) 'The multi-faceted nature of party-based Euroscepticism', *Acta Politica*, 47, 2: 91–112.

Cotta, Maurizio and Pierangelo Isernia (2009) 'Citizenship in the European polity: questions and explorations', in Catherine Moury and Luis De Sousa (eds) *Institutional Challenges in Post-Constitutional Europe: Governing Change*, London: Routledge, pp. 71–94.

Crespy, Amandine (2010) 'When "Bolkestein" is trapped by the French anti-liberal discourse: a discursive-institutionalist account of preference formation in the realm of EU multi-level politics', *Journal of European Public Policy*, 17, 8: 1253–1270.

Crespy, Amandine and Nicolas Verschueren (2009) 'From Euroscepticism to resistance to European integration: an interdisciplinary perspective', *Perspectives on European Politics and Society*, 10, 3: 377–393

Deloye, Yves (2008) 'Ce que résister veut dire ou les paradoxes d'une construction européenne face aux contingences historiques et aux logiques politiques nationales', *Revue Internationale de Politique Comparée*, 15, 4: 679–685.

De Vries, Catherine and Erica Edwards (2009) 'Taking Europe to its extremes: extremist parties and public Euroskepticism', *Party Politics*, 15, 1: 5–28.

Down, Ian and Carole Wilson (2008) 'From "permissive consensus" to "constraining dissensus": a polarizing union?' *Acta Politica*, 43: 26–49.

Durand, Jean-Luc (1998) 'Taux de dispersion des valeurs propres en ACP, AC et ACM', *Mathématiques et sciences humaines*, 144: 15–28.

Gautier, Olivier (2007) 'L'Autre Europe du Mouvement pour la France (MPF) et l'européanisation du souverainisme', in Olivier Baisnée and Romain Pasquier (eds) *L'Europe telle qu'elle se fait. Européanisation et sociétés politiques nationales*, Paris, CNRS Editions, pp. 123–143.

Gaxie, Daniel and Nicolas Hubé (2012a) 'Elite views on European institutions', in Heinrich Best, György Lengyel and Luca Verzichelli (eds) *The Europe of Elites: A Study into the Europeanness of Europe's Economic and Political Elites*, Oxford: Oxford University Press, pp. 122–146.

Gaxie, Daniel and Nicolas Hubé (2012b) 'On national and ideological background of elites' attitudes toward European 'nstitutions', in Kauppi Niilo (ed.) *A Political Sociology of Transnational Europe*, Colchester, UK ECPR Press, pp. 165–190.

Gaxie, Daniel, Nicolas Hubé and Jay Rowell (eds) (2011) *Perceptions of Europe: A Comparative Sociology of European Attitudes*, Colchester, UK: ECPR Press.

Hix, Simon and Abdul Noury (2009) 'After enlargement: voting patterns in the sixth European parliament', *Legislative Studies Quaterly*, 34, 2: 159–174.

Hubé, N. and M. Rambour (2010) 'French Political parties in campaign (1989–2004): for a configurational analysis of political discourses on Europe', *Perspectives on European Politics and Society*, 11, 2: 146–166.

Marks, Gary and M. Steenbergen (2004) *European Integration and Political Conflict*, Cambridge: Cambridge University Press.

Mastropaolo, Alfio (2004) 'La double théorie de la classe politique de Gaetano Mosca', *Revue Internationale de Politique Comparée*, 11, 4: 611–630.

Milner, H. (2006) 'YES to the Europe I want, NO to this one: Some reflections on France's rejection of the EU constitution', *PS: Political Science and Politics*, 39, 2: 257–260.

Mischi, Julian (2007) 'L'impact communautaire sur la politisation des classes populaires en milieu rural: Le cas des chasseurs de gibier d'eau', in Olivier Baisnée and Romain Pasquier (eds) *L'Europe telle qu'elle se fait: Européanisation et sociétés politiques nationales*, Paris: CNRS Editions, pp. 145–165.

Mosca, Gaetano (1939) *The Ruling Class*, New York: McGraw-Hill.

Neumayer, Laure (2008) 'Euroscepticism as a political label: the use of European Union issues in political competitions in the new member states', *European Journal of Political Research*, 47, 2: 135–160.

Percheron, A. (1991) 'Les Français et l'Europe: acquiescement de façade ou adhésion véritable?' *Revue Française de Science Politique*, 41, 3: 382–406.

Ray, L. (1999) 'Measuring party orientations towards European integration: results from an expert survey', *European Journal of Political Research*, 36, 2: 283–306.

Schedler, A. (1996) 'Anti-political-establishment parties', in *Party Politics*, 2, 3: 291–312.

Schmidt, Vivien A. (2006) *Democracy in Europe*, Oxford: Oxford University Press.

Schmidt, Vivien A. (2007) 'Trapped by their ideas: French élites' discourses of European integration and globalization', *Journal of European Public Policy*, 14, 7: 992–1009.

Schmitt, Hermann and Jacques Thomassen (1999) 'Distinctiveness and cohesion parties', in Hermann Schmitt and Jacques Thomassen (eds) *Political Representation and Legitimacy in the European Union*, Oxford: Oxford University Press, pp. 111–128.

Sitter, N. (2001) 'The politics of opposition and European integration in Scandinavia: is Euro-scepticism a government–opposition dynamic?' *West European Politics*, 24, 4: 22–39.

Taggart, P. (1998) 'A touchstone of dissent: Euroscepticism in contemporary Western European party systems', *European Journal of Political Research*, 33, 3: 363–388

Taggart, P. and A. Szczerbiak (eds) (2008) *Opposing Europe: The Comparative Party Politics of Euroscepticism*, Oxford: Oxford University Press.

Tsebelis, G. and G. Garrett (2000) 'Legislative politics in the European Union', *European Union Politics*, 1, 1: 5–32.

Weber, Eugen (1976) *Peasants into Frenchmen: The Modernization of Rural France, 1880–1914*, Stanford, CA: Stanford University Press.

3 Germany

Claudius Wagemann

Introduction

It is a central (and too often overlooked) problem in comparative research and comparative methodology how to define the time frame of the investigation (see Bartolini 1993; Pierson 2003). Indeed, when conducting macro-comparative research in the sense of comparing nation states, the researcher has to be aware of the fact that one and the same year can have different meanings in different countries. 'Time' in this sense is not an only quantitative category, but also a qualitative category. This is also the case when we look at the four European elections which are at stake here. If we take the first election in the 1990s, namely the European election of 1994, this was the last election during the Mitterand era in France, the first after the breakdown of the old party system in Italy, and the first in Germany after re-unification, with the initial enthusiasm already being over. One does not need to refer to the concept of a 'second order election' (Reif and Schmitt 1980) in order to understand that this means that the 1994 European elections in France, Italy, and Germany happened in different national contexts. These contexts also had their effect on the various manifestos.

This makes it necessary to first briefly describe the national context of the various European elections in Germany. Our analysis starts with the year 1994. This is the first European election after the fall of the GDR and German re-unification. The year 1994 was also called a 'Superwahljahr' (super election year), because it was characterized by an unprecedented number of local, regional, and national elections. Among others, the German *Bundestag* was elected in general elections later that year. Although there was, after more than ten years in office, no enthusiasm about Federal Chancellor Helmut Kohl's incumbent government composed of the Christian Democrats (CDU and CSU) and the Liberals (FDP), times were not yet mature for a change, not least due to the not very inspiring political performance by the Social Democratic (SPD) leader of the time, Rudolf Scharping (Gibowski 1995). Thus, the year 1994 marks a situation in German politics where 'Politikverdrossenheit' (tiredness about politics) was a frequently discussed phenomenon and in which no major political actor seemed to be attractive for the electorate.

In late 1998, half a year before the subsequent European elections of 1999, the situation changed: Gerhard Schröder managed to overthrow the Kohl government. The general perception was that an era had come to an end (Feist and Hoffmann 1999). The coalition of SPD and Greens also understood its government as a general reform of the German society: a redefinition of the German role in international politics and an ecologically oriented tax system were part of this tendency as well as the introduction of same-sex marriages. However, when the European elections of 1999 were held, the Schröder government was living through its first deep crisis: the unexpected resignation of the minister of finances, Oskar Lafontaine, in early 1999 made clear that the new harmony between left-wing and more centrist Social Democrats was nothing than a nice illusion. The European elections were consequently held in a phase in which the incumbent SPD–Green government lost many regional elections.

The situation of 2004 was not so different: again, the Schröder government was in difficulties, after having won the previous national elections (Pappi and Shikano 2003). These difficulties finally resulted in anticipated national elections in 2005 in which the Schröder government lost and which led to Angela Merkel's Chancellorship (Hilmer and Müller-Hilmer 2006).

The Merkel Chancellorship also characterized the 2009 European elections. These elections were held in the outgoing phase of the 'Grand Coalition' of CDU, CSU, and SPD (Helms 2006) – although this arrangement had not been wanted by the partners before the 2005 elections, public satisfaction with it was surprisingly very high. Merkel herself counted as one of the main reasons of the success of the government. Consequently, the 2009 electoral campaigns for the general and the European elections were rather soft, without too much polarization. The year 2009 was also the year after the outbreak of the banking and economic crisis which since then has not left the European continent. However, Merkel's and her finance minister's guarantee for German savings in late 2008 avoided a general panic and also stabilized Merkel's and her government's good reputation.

Germany is also particular in that its party system did not undergo very deep disruptures in that era. Certainly, this does not mean that there were only marginal changes, but, compared to other countries, the German party system remained largely stable. The two big political parties, CDU and SPD, were shrinking over time, but no third party came close to the status as a *Volkspartei*. In a similar way, the CSU, the Bavarian equivalent to the CDU, lost its absolute majority of seats in 2008, but is still the dominant political actor in Bavaria. The FDP did not undergo any meaningful changes in that period, and the Greens became a stable political actor as part of the Federal Government for seven years. The most notable changes can be observed to the very left and the very right of the political spectrum: the right-wing *Republikaner* which are part of the sample here lost their importance over the period of analysis and were replaced by the much more radical and thus also much more worrysome National Democratic Party (NPD) subsequently. The left-wing PDS, later *Linkspartei* and today

Die Linke, did not only change its name every once in a while, but also developed from an East German nostalgic party to a left-wing rival of the SPD. The effects of this development of the PDS can, above all, be seen in the 2009 European election.

Thus, although the party system has certainly undergone some modifications during the period of analysis, these were comparatively minor: no political party entered the system, no one dropped out, and no one fell or rose disproportionately. This means that over-time changes in the electoral manifestos are not due to a recomposition of the party system, but to changing substantial preferences of the single actors.

1994 – creating the new Europe

For our analysis, the year 1994 marks the point of departure. This is especially meaningful in the German case, since the 1994 European elections were the first ones after German re-unification. This event also added a further political actor to the otherwise rather stable German party system, namely the PDS, the official successor of the ruling party in the autocratic GDR system, which would develop into the voice of the German left later on, under changing names.

General attitude towards Europe

In 1994, however, the then PDS was still a strange mixture of a post-communist, nostalgic, and East German regionalist party. This was also expressed by a general discontent (variable MEMBERSHIP) about European integration which was only similar to the extreme right-wingers' (i.e. the *Republikaner*'s) attitude (for this, see also De Vries and Edwards 2009). Certainly, the PDS acknowledged that European integration also provided advantages for citizens, but stated that it mainly served the interests of big companies and banks, while mass unemployment and poverty were on the rise. It also criticized that war had returned to Europe (obviously referring to the war in ex-Yugoslavia) and that the continent was still divided between East and West – the PDS has also frequently used the latter argument in the German national context.

The *Republikaner* instead frame their critique mostly in terms of the Maastricht Treaty and express their fears that German financial contributions to European integration would be too high. With the PDS, they share the general aversion against the liberalization of the markets, but they also refer to a potential moral decline of Europe.

The other political parties have a mixed (CDU, SPD, and Greens) or positive (CSU and FDP) evaluation of the impact of European integration. This is especially surprising in the case of the CSU whose attitude to European integration has often been described as not too positive. The Greens add one more aspect to the picture, describing parts of the European integration process as an undemocratization of the European polity; the manifesto explicitly refers to the Treaty of Maastricht.

When it comes to the role of the own country in the European Union (NATACT), a strange alliance of CSU, Greens, FDP, and *Republikaner* affirms a leadership role for Germany – certainly the *Republikaner* rather for reasons of national identity, something which is very probably not the case for the Greens; the other parties do not express explicit opinions on this.

The data is even less telling when the question is addressed as to how the EU decision-making processes should be organized (variable EUDEC). Only the SPD makes a clear statement in favour of supranational modes. More precisely, the SPD proposes a right of initiative for the European Parliament, a co-decision procedure between the Parliament and the Council, and a general majority voting for the Council.

Identity

Nearly all political parties (apart from the SPD and the PDS) make references to some kind of Europeanness (variable IDEU). The picture is even clearer when it comes to references to shared cultural elements (EUCULTUR) which are made by all political parties, apart from the PDS. As far as the national level is concerned, the picture is more varied. A general reference to national identity (IDNAT) is made by the two political parties furthest to the right (*Republikaner* and CSU) and, more paradoxically, by the Greens. Cultural elements (NACULTUR) are mentioned by the Greens, the PDS, and the *Republikaner*. And it is absolutely no surprise that the two mostly regionally acting political parties, namely the Bavarian CSU and the PDS with its strongholds in the post-communist East, are the only political parties which have some reference to the sub-national level: the CSU with regard to identity (IDSUB) and the PDS with regard to culture (SBCULTUR).

If we look at these variables from a more case-oriented perspective, then we can observe that it is the traditional parties of the 'old' Germany, namely the CDU, the SPD, and the FDP which exclusively focus on a European identity and/or a European culture, respectively. On the other hand, no single party exclusively focuses at the national or the sub-national level. It is interesting to see that precisely those parties which can be interpreted as the cornerstones of the early post-war German Republic are the strongest advocates of Europeanness in 1994.

Policies and scope of governance

As for the level of governance for single policies, there is a clear tendency towards supra-national solutions. The options 'supranational only' (33 per cent) or 'supranational + national' (36 per cent) clearly dominate, followed by 'national only' (12 per cent), 'supranational + national + subnational' (5 per cent) and 'national + sub-national' (2 per cent). However, there are differences between both single policy issues and single parties. 'Supranational only' slightly dominates defence policy, immigration policy, and environmental policy, while the mixed solution of 'supranational + national' is preferred for foreign policy and justice and crime policy. 'Only national' policy is indicated only in a very selective manner: following the *Republikaner*, defence policy and social policy should be exclusively national policies, while the CDU proposes this for justice and crime policy and for immigration policy; the CSU also wants an only national immigration policy. Social policy presents itself as a deviant case, because it is here where the sub-national level (among others levels) is also proposed, by the CDU, the CSU, and the Greens.

Very clear supranational preferences are presented by the SPD which proposes a 'supranational only' approach for nearly all policy issues; only for social policy (a core topic of the SPD), a mixed approach is preferred. Similar tendencies with at least half the number of policy issues to be regulated at the 'supranational only' level are visible within the Greens and the PDS; the PDS claims, above all, for more collaboration in social policy (this confirms similar findings in Conti and Memoli 2012). A very mixed approach is observable for the FDP, while CDU and CSU combine the mixed preferences with some 'national only' statements, and the *Republikaner* show a clear tendency towards 'national only'. It is surprising, though, that the *Republikaner* concede at least a mixed level to justice and crime policy which could be considered a core subject of the *Republikaner*. The CSU (and in part also the SPD) justifies most of its preferences for a stronger European component with the subsidiarity principle: fighting terrorism and coping with organized crimes requires a more European and joint reaction. The *Republikaner* also use the examples of crime and terrorism, but render the EU and its open borders responsible for these problems.

Representation and democracy

Regarding the democratic deficit, only the *Republikaner* surprisingly mention the way in which democracy is applied in the EU in a favourable manner. This is counter-intuitive, since it would rather be the typical mode of a right-wing populist political party to criticize the application of democracy in the EU. Other political parties are either negative (Greens, PDS) or mixed (CDU, SPD, FDP). Such different actors as CDU, CSU, FDP, the Greens, and the PDS explicitly refer to the subsidiarity principle, the SPD more implicitly. The topic of 'democracy' is addressed, sometimes very boldly, such as in the case of the FDP which simply claims that the EU has to become 'more democratic'. The *Republikaner* make the concrete proposal of introducing referenda into the EU political system.

1999 – after the Kohl era

The late 1990s marked the end of Helmut Kohl's Chancellorship. This 16-year-long era saw German re-unification and a further intensification of European integration through the introduction of the single market and the creation of the European Union at Maastricht. With regard to all these events, Helmut Kohl was claimed to be notably involved. However, in 1998, the German voters decided for a profound change and voted in favour of Gerhard Schröder's red–green alliance of the SPD and the Greens. This was the first (and up to the time of writing, last) time in German post-war history that no member of a previous government continued to be part of the new executive. This particular institutional disrupture was accompanied by a deep and notable policy change. Ecologically oriented tax measures, the end of nuclear energy, and societal reforms, such as the introduction of same-sex marriages, were among the first decisions of the new government.

General attitude towards Europe

In this particular moment of German history, it is indeed only the *Republikaner* who see a negative impact of European integration on German matters (variable MEMBERSHIP). Compared to five years before, the PDS has given up its unfavourable position and has moved to a mixed attitude. It is joined in this by the Greens. However, the PDS presents a very differentiated view: while European integration as such is supported, its then institutional form is harshly criticized. The positive evaluation of CSU and FDP with regard to the impact of Europe on the domestic situation is confirmed in 1999, and this group is additionally joined by the CDU so that the old Kohl coalition presents itself as a clearly pro-European alliance in this sense.

The plea for a leadership role for Germany in the European Union (variable NATACT) is still confirmed by the Greens, the FDP, and the *Republikaner*; different from five years before, however, there are now also two political parties which are more in favour of cooperation and participation, namely, the CDU and the SPD. The CDU explicitly considers the variety which can be found within Europe as an important asset. Similarly, the SPD manifesto mentions the parallel need of respecting national identities and driving forward European integration.

While five years before hardly any political party had an explicit standpoint on how to organize EU decision-making processes (variable EUDEC; only the SPD was clear about preferring supranational modes), this picture is now more differentiated: the SPD is joined in this opinion by the CDU and the FDP, while the Greens and the PDS opt for a more intergovernmental approach.

At this point, we can dare the claim that there is a kind of 'grand coalition' of CDU and SPD in wanting more European integration through more supranational competences and more shared responsibilities (on the validity of the left–right axis for European integration, see also Hooghe *et al.* 2004). On the other hand, the Greens take on a rather Germany-centred approach. It is also notable that, while the out-voted party alliance of CDU, CSU, and FDP has rather similar standpoints, more differences occur between the two partners of the new national government, that is, the SPD and the Greens.

Identity

There is a unanimous confirmation of the existence of European identity (variable IDEU). Different from 1994, this is less clear for shared European cultural elements (EUCULTUR) which are only made by the CDU, the SPD, and the

PDS. With regard to national identity (IDNAT) and national culture (NACUL-TUR) the grand coalition of CDU and SPD reappears (in case of identity joined by the CSU) – this is a small contradiction to our findings from above where CDU and SPD were portrayed as political parties which are in favour of more supranational elements of integration. It is also astonishing that, with regard to the two nation-state-oriented items, nearly all values regarding the 1999 elections are different from their counterparts in 1994. This can either mean a complete change in attitude (for which, however, no reasons could be imagined) or simply a kind of indifference towards these topics.[1] As for the sub-national level (IDSUB and SBCULTUR), it is only the CSU which mentions this while it is disregarded by the East German regionalist party PDS. This is – similar to the not only negative evaluation of European integration – a further instance of the maturation of the PDS as a political party, but also of the PDS turning towards a less regionalist and a more left-wing (and thus not only regionally oriented) agenda.

Policies and scope of governance

The general picture on policies and the level of governance has not changed very notably between 1994 and 1999. Again, there is a clear tendency towards supranational solutions, and again the option 'supranational + national' is in the lead (45 per cent, compared to 36 per cent five years before) compared with 'supranational only' (33 per cent, as in 1994). 'National only' is clearly less important (5 per cent compared to 12 per cent), becoming equal to 'supranational + national + subnational' (5 per cent, as in 1994). Different from 1994, 'national + sub-national' is not given any more (in 1994, 2 per cent), while the combination 'supranational + sub-national' now exists (2 per cent).

While this looks like a confirmation of the situation in 1994, some changes have occurred within the single policy issues: while the 'supranational only' option is confirmed for defence policy and the supranational–national mixture for justice and crime policy, in foreign policy those preferences prevail which only consider the supranational level (while it was mixed before), while environmental policy moves from the exclusively supranational level to a mixed level of supranational and national governance. However, the differences are very subtle. Again, social policy stands out, because it is again here where a combination of all levels (supranational, national, and sub-national) is advocated, namely by the CDU and the SPD.

If we look at the single political parties, the most astonishing comparison has to be made for the SPD which, in 1994, favoured exclusively supranational approaches for nearly all policies and now advocates more mixed supranational–national governance. It seems that being the leading party of the national government also makes them re-detect the national level of governance. As for the rest, there are no clear tendencies within single political parties; only the PDS is predominantly marked by a 'supranational only' preference and the *Republikaner* by a 'supranational + national' idea. This is meaningful insofar as the *Republikaner* do not seem to promote a very nation-alistic idea of policy-making, but propose to keep the national component, combining it with supranational elements. The CSU is particular as it brings the sub-national component back in and wants (as the only political party) a 'national only' strategy for immigration. As becomes evident from the mani-festo, the CSU refers above all to the question of political asylum where a 'fairer distribution' of asylum seekers is proposed. Also, international crime remains an issue for the CSU; this might have contributed to the CSU's idea of renationalizing immigration policy. However, since this was an intensively discussed topic at the time, it is no surprise that the manifestos of the SPD, the Greens, and the FDP also refer extensively to the asylum question, but opposite to the CSU they define it as a joint European challenge.

Representation and democracy

When looking at the problem of democratic deficit, there is – different from five years before – a very critical attitude. Despite the CDU (which does not make a reference), all political parties evaluate EU democracy negatively. The CSU (and to a more limited extent and with different emphases also the SPD and the Greens) sees, above all, a problem of transparency and too much bureaucracy and refers back to the subsidiarity principle. The FDP and the PDS also mention subsidiarity as a central principle, with the FDP additionally making the explicit claim for a European Constitution with guaranteed Fundamental Rights.

2004 – towards the end of the Schröder Chancellorship

The 2004 electoral campaign was already characterized by the crisis which eventually led to the resignation of the Schröder government in 2005. Schröder's previous 2002 electoral victory was a consequence of several factors: the PDS was very weak at that time; the candidate of CDU and CSU, Edmund Stoiber, did not enjoy notable sympathies outside Southern Germany; and Gerhard Schröder had won many sympathies and could present himself as a successful crisis manager during floods which, after a long period of rain, had hit Eastern Germany (Roberts 2003). However, this victory did not stop the crisis of the Schröder government. Some labour market reforms ('Hartz' reforms) led to mass protests in the summer 2004, a re-emergence of the PDS as the new political party 'Die Linke' (supported by many prominent ex-members of Schröder's SPD), a failure at the elections in North Rhine-Westphalia in 2005, the subsequent resignation of the Schröder government, and Angela Merkel's election as head of a new government in the autumn of 2005. While most of these consequences were visible only after the European elections, it goes without saying that already the European elections were char-acterized by the upcoming problems of the Schröder government and by the labour market reforms as a general topic.

General attitude towards Europe

With the country and its economy being in crisis, it is no surprise that after a certain period of a positive evaluation of Europe's impact on Germany (variable MEMBERSHIP), the attitude has turned astonishingly negative: the *Republikaner* continue to be sceptical, wanting a Europe of nation states, and also the PDS, after a more positive attitude five years before, has turned negative. The PDS already anticipates the topic with which it will be successful in the future: it underlines that European policies are wrong in dismantling social security systems and leading to mass unemployment; a broad policy change would be needed. However, these somewhat extreme parties of the German political spectrum are joined in their negative attitude by the CSU and the SPD. The CSU links the problems at the European level with the national level: Chancellor Schröder's SPD is warned not to exploit the problems at the European level in order to cover its own failure at the national level. The FDP, for which foreign and European integration policy has always been important, shows mixed feelings with regard to the impact of the EU on country matters. It sees itself as an advocate who takes care of the citizens' justified critique. The only two parties which consider the opportunities more favourable are thus the CDU and the Greens.

This also has an effect on the question of national action in Europe (variable NATACT). While the year 1999 has shown a somewhat more open positioning towards cooperation and participation, now the CSU, the SPD, the Greens, and the FDP see a leadership position for Germany; only the CDU and the PDS (two admittedly very different parties) opt for cooperation and participation.

As in 1994, there are hardly any statements in 2004 on how to organize the EU decision-making processes (variable EUDEC). Only the FDP shows an intergovernmental tendency. European institutions do not seem to be fashionable at this point in German history.

Identity

With regard to identity questions, 2004 is less marked by differences, compared to general questions of European integration. The existence both of a European identity (variable IDEU) and of shared European cultural elements (EUCULTUR) is largely confirmed, with minor deviances (the Greens on both variables, the SPD on the cultural one). It is again surprising that even the *Republikaner* see the existence of a European identity positively. However, this happens through a differentiation from globalization as an even more dangerous trend: globalization is understood as a dominance of the strongest that, in this case, would be the United States. References to patterns of national identity (IDNAT) and a shared national culture (NACULTUR) are further reduced: only the centre-right and right-wing parties CDU, CSU (only cultural elements), and *Republikaner* (only identity) underline this level; the CDU sees the nation state as a guarantee for the preservation of identity and cultural variety. Also, the sub-national level (IDSUB and SBCULTUR) is again only mentioned by the CSU; following the manifesto of the CSU, the regional is an important element of identity formation.

Policies and scope of governance

If we now assume that the crisis in Germany around 2004–2005 would have led to a plea for more national approaches in policy making, we are proven wrong. While there had hardly been any notable changes between 1994 and 1999, we now see a dominance of the 'supranational only' preference (48 per cent, compared to 33 per cent in 1999) over the mixed category of 'supranational + national' (33 per cent, compared to 45 per cent). The 'national only' category has completely disappeared (5 per cent in 1999), while other combinations are mentioned only occasionally ('supranational + sub-national'; 'supranational + national + sub-national'; national + sub-national; all 2 per cent).

However, looking at the single policies, we can observe an important trend: while in past campaigns, there had been very different opinions on single policy issues, there is now close to unanimity *within* most of the single policy issues. Foreign policy and defence policy are preferred as 'supranational only' policies by all political parties, to a lesser extent also justice and crime policy (where only the CDU and the CSU would like to reserve some competences for the national level). The picture changes when it comes to more contested policy issues of that time, namely immigration policy and social policy where a mixture of supranational and national processes are predominantly preferred; only the FDP and the PDS are in favour of a 'supranational only' approach towards immigration, while, for social policy, the two regionally based parties, PDS and CSU, prefer some importance for the sub-national level. When it comes to environmental policy, the picture is more mixed with, however, a certain dominance for the mixed approach. We can thus see that, environmental policy being a small exception, more importance is claimed for more highly contested policy issues, while those issues which did not characterize German national politics at that time (foreign, defence, and justice policies) are 'left' to the supranational level.

With regard to the single political parties, no huge differences are observable. The most supranationally oriented party is again the PDS. Also, the Greens, the FDP, and the SPD (in this order) predominantly prefer a 'supranational only' approach. This is a bit different for the CDU and the CSU where mixed preferences slightly prevail, in the case of the CSU enriched by a sub-national component (which is also shared by the PDS). Above all, with regard to unemployment, the CSU sees the responsibility with the national system. This was probably also inspired by the job crisis in Germany at that time. In terms of foreign policy, both CDU and CSU underline the strategic importance of combining a European way with a close cooperation with the US. This is probably an answer of the more trans-Atlanticist political parties of the then opposition against the preferences of the Schröder government for a more European way which mainly found its expression a year before the European elections, namely during the Iraq War. This means that – different from previous years – interpretation is straightforward: both the regionalist component as well as the left–right axis (interpreted in the sense of a libertarian attitude) come to the fore. The *Republikaner* hardly make any statements on the governance levels, but is not as anti-European as one might think: rather, it claims a closer cooperation of Europe in order to be a strong unit against outside influences; one can suspect that this is also a plea against too much immigration.

Representation and democracy

After a nearly exclusive negative evaluation of European democracy in 1999, this picture is more varied in 2004: while the CSU continues to have a negative opinion, the then government partners SPD and Greens evaluate the state of European democracy positively. All other political parties are undecided and see both negative and positive aspects. Subsidiarity continues to be the most important principle (put forward by all political parties, apart from the SPD). The Greens also claim for more participatory processes and more equality between different societal groups. The PDS is in favour of a referendum on the European Constitution and asks for a strengthening of non-parliamentary groups. The FDP asks for concrete reforms of the European institutions. Both the CDU and CSU want less bureaucracy at the European level. The SPD is vaguer in its affirmations, by just claiming a 'Europe of the citizens'.

2009 – markets in crisis

In 2009, the Euro crisis as we understand it today was still about to come. No European rescue packages had to be negotiated; this crisis was more national and more global at the same time, but the specifically European variant of the crisis, including the question whether or not certain countries should be excluded from the common currency, was still vague. Also, further steps of European integration were yet not part of national policy discourses.

With regard to German domestic politics, however, the year 2009 is interesting: as with 1994, 2009 was a year in which the European elections preceded the general national elections by only some months. The elections occurred in a moment of great consensus between the citizens and national policy making. Although being created out of a difficult electoral result, the grand coalition of CDU, CSU, and SPD, which had governed Germany during the previous four years, had led to significant policy results and had been proven to be a relatively calm period of German politics. Above all, the close cooperation between CDU Chancellor Angela Merkel and her SPD finance minister Peer Steinbrück implied much confidence of the citizens in their political leaders during the banking crisis. Consequently, Merkel won the subsequent general elections and could then govern the country with her own majority (together with the FDP), without having to rely on the SPD as a partner.

General attitude towards Europe

A clear finding can be seen for the evaluation of Europe's impact on Germany (variable MEMBERSHIP): the political parties which were already seen as the most probable winners of the subsequent national elections, namely the CDU, the CSU, and the FDP, see that European integration has provided above all favourable opportunities. The *Republikaner* have a negative evaluation, while all other political parties do not make explicit statements on this. With regard to national action in Europe (variable NATACT), hardly any statements can be found; only the *Republikaner* propose defence/rejection. When it comes to EU decision making (variable EUDEC), the general attitude has become rather sceptical (while the year 2004 was largely characterized by indifference): a supranational approach is preferred by the Greens, an intergovernmental approach by the *Republikaner*, and the CDU (claiming respect for the identity of single member states) and FDP prefer a mixed strategy. However, there is a novelty with regard to previous years: CSU and SPD are very harsh and want competences back to the national level. The CSU explicitly wants a reduction of decision-making competences at the European level and a reorganization of the federal, regional, or even local decision-making level; also the SPD underlines the principle of affectedness: if citizens are directly concerned by a decision, then the closest decision-making level has to be preferred: local, regional, and national politics thus prevail over European politics.

Identity

Also in terms of identity, the European dimension loses importance, while national patterns come to the fore. Belongingness to Europe is less framed in terms of a general identity of civic type (variable IDEU), but more with regard to shared European cultural elements (EUCULTUR). Only the CDU and the Greens affirm the existence of a European identity, while shared cultural elements are affirmed by all political parties, apart from the CSU. The CSU underlines the cultural specificities of the single member states. We also see a notable difference when we look at the national level. While this has been largely disregarded in past years, the shared national culture (NATCULTUR) is mentioned by all political parties (apart from the CDU). However, the confirmation of national identity (IDNAT) remains underdeveloped (only the CDU, the Greens, and the *Republikaner* mention it). The sub-national level is mentioned in the CDU manifesto (IDSUB) and the CSU and *Republikaner* manifestos (SBCULTUR); the *Linke* (ex-PDS), now transformed in a left-wing political party with regional strongholds, but with a clearly reduced regionalist component, does not refer to sub-national elements any more. The *Republikaner* continue to be ambiguous in its evaluation of shared cultural elements: while, on the one hand, the importance of the European nation state is emphasized, further European integration is seen as a possibility for a strong standing in the world.

Policies and scope of governance

When it comes to the scope of governance for the single policy issues, we first have to affirm that the 2009 manifestos were more difficult to code in this respect than those of previous elections. No less than 29 per cent of the combinations of parties and policy issues could not be assessed. (The following percentages are, however, calculated with *all* possible party-issue combinations as a common basis, in order to assure comparability with previous years). Despite all crises and despite all renationalization of the political discourse which is evident from the findings demonstrated above, the 'supranational only' preference remains in the clear lead (43 per cent compared to 48 per cent five years before). The mixed variant of 'supranational + national' clearly falls behind (14 per cent compared to 33 per cent in 2004); this is a further reduction of this value. However, the preference for the 'national only' category, which had disappeared in 2004, rises again to 10 per cent. Other combinations are mentioned very marginally ('sub-national only'; 'supranational + national + sub-national'; both 2 per cent).

Looking at the single policies, we can confirm the finding for 2004, namely that foreign and defence policy are largely attributed to the supranational level only; this is now predominantly also the case for immigration and social policy. Only with regard to justice and crime policy, the mixed approach is preferred; a 'national only' preference can also be confirmed for justice and crime policy (*Linke* and *Republikaner*) and social policy (FDP and *Republikaner*). Environmental policy is an odd case in this respect, since hardly any statements on this can be found from the manifestos; it does not seem to be an important policy issue in 2009.

If we look at the single political parties, no huge differences are observable, similar to 2004. However, some changes have occurred: the CDU has moved from a more mixed to an 'only supranational' approach (while the CSU has stayed to the mixed preferences, presenting Bavaria and Germany as policy models for the European Union as a whole), while the FDP has moved in the opposite direction towards more mixed levels of governance. It is also interesting that the *Linke* – more strongly advocating its left-wing agenda than its predecessor PDS had done – is not so convinced about supranational policy making any more, although it sees Europe as a continent promoting the idea of the welfare state and being an example of successful peace policy. With regard to the supranational variant, we can observe that the Greens are the strongest supporters of supranational policy making, closely followed by the SPD. In general, the year 2009 presents the Greens as a very profiled and strong pro-European political party. The EU is portrayed as a political actor which, through its decisions, would have often inspired single nation states and influenced their policy preferences. In this sense, the EU serves as a model of policy substance. The SPD sees the strength of the EU precisely in a common strategy for a social pact on economic stability; for the fight of international terrorism; and for ensuring the security in the world, including the question of poverty and human development.

Representation and democracy

While we could not confirm Euroscepticism for the single policy issues, we fall back to 1999 when it comes to the democratic deficit: negative statements dominate (CSU, SPD, Greens, and *Republikaner*), positive statements cannot be identified, only the CDU and the FDP present a mixed evaluation. It is interesting to see that the justifications of the attitudes become more and more concrete: the CDU, the SPD, the Greens, and the *Linke* propose yet another attempt for a European Constitution, with the SPD emphasizing above all the role of single citizens and the political parties; the *Linke* additionally renews its earlier claim for a referendum on a European Constitution; the CSU makes clear proposals for including the German institutions (the *Bundestag*, the *Bundesrat*, and the various *Landtage* are explicitly named); the Greens draw attention to the question of the freedom of opinion; and the *Republikaner* are the most critical actor, by claiming a fundamental reform of the European institutions which would put an end to the disadvantages which Germany would undergo as a consequence from the majority decisions taken in the EU. The subsidiarity principle is also again mentioned (as in all the years before), above all by the CSU and the *Linke*.

Final remarks: European elections in Germany

While there are certainly some party preferences which are focused on the process of European integration, many affirmations mirror the political discussion 'at home'. The various points in time for which the analysis is performed indicate a clear relation between the general political situation in Germany and parties' strategies for the European elections. That notwithstanding, there are, of course, some more specific attitudes with regard to tipping points: the 1994 manifestos include some references to the Treaty of Maastricht; and, after 1999, the European Constitution (or the possibility of such a constitution) is mentioned. However, most party preferences on the European integration process understood as the creation of a supra-national polity are rather vague. This is different for questions regarding specific policies; with regard to the question at which political level (supranational, national, and/or sub-national) policies should be dealt with, the positions are usually clear and stable.

The most stable attitudes can be confirmed for the CDU (pro-European) and the *Republikaner* (sceptical), to a more limited extent for the SPD (pro-European) and the PDS and its successor parties (sceptical). In general, there is some volatility, sometimes even quite high, as for example with regard to the variables on national identity (see above).

There is certainly a left–right dimension in the attitudes. However, this finding has to be qualified better in two respects: first, the finding is relatively strong, as soon as attitudes regarding certain policy issues are concerned. For example, when evaluating what the main decision-making level for social policy should be, there is a clear gap between left- and right-wing parties. (This also holds for the other policy fields.) Second, when it comes to more general questions on European integration, this left–right dimension strongly overlaps with the dimension of mainstream and radical political parties. It goes without saying that the right-wing populist party of the *Republikaner* are the most clearly Eurosceptical actor in the sample. However, even in this case, the statements are not exclusively anti-European. While mainstream and radicalism do play a role, there is hardly any effect of government incumbency. In general, government incumbency does not seem to be such an important factor in the German system: first, five out of the seven political parties (not the PDS and not the *Republikaner*) were part of the federal government at a certain point in time during the period of analysis; second, the possibility of alternation has always been given during the period of analysis[2] so that even non-incumbent actors were potential new parts of a subsequent government; third, the German federal system with its very strong second chamber also contributes to the fact that 'incumbency' is not even easy to be defined.

It is certainly the case that – apart from tipping points such as the Treaty of Maastricht – German electoral manifestos for the European elections are overshadowed by national political needs. This is also due to the fact that the attitude towards the European Union and European integration has not been important an issue for debate in Germany during the period of analysis. Explicitly anti-European parties have never been strong. (This is also connected to the general weakness of party-based right-wing radicalism in Germany.) Also, despite all political differences, there is the 'elite consensus' between the most important political parties in government (CDU, CSU, SPD, FDP, and Greens) that European integration is a good thing (although the CSU sometimes qualifies this statement in its political propaganda). Also, times of crisis seem to confirm this consensus on European integration: the German Parliament has usually taken decisions on 'rescue packages' for EU countries in crisis with very broad majorities, overcoming the usual gap between the government and the opposition (on the role of parties in office versus parties in opposition, see also Conti 2012).

In brief, while different attitudes can be confirmed, these differences are more visible with regard to the margins of the political spectrum. Many specific positions are rather erratic, while a general friendliness towards European integration can also be seen.

Notes

1 As we will see later on, these changing results also continue over the subsequent two waves of analysis, although to a smaller extent. Between 1999 and 2004 a low level of change exists. However, while this low level of change can also be confirmed for the period between 2004 and 2009 for the question on national identity, the change with regard to the question on national culture is again extremely erratic between 2004 and 2009: all values (but the one for the CSU) change.

2 A victory of an alliance of CDU, CSU, and FDP in the 2002 federal elections was not excluded; finally, the SPD and the Greens could renew their alliance. A much higher result for CDU and CSU was expected for the federal elections in 2005; finally, CDU and CSU were forced into a Grand Coalition with the SPD. Only the result of the 2009 federal elections (a victory of CDU, CSU, and FDP) was not very surprising.

58   *C. Wagemann*

References

Bartolini, Stefano (1993) 'On Time and Comparative Research', *Journal of Theoretical Politics*, 5, 2: 131–167.

Conti, Nicolò (2012) 'The EU in the Programmatic Statements of Domestic Parties', in Heinrich Best, György Lengyel and Luca Verzichelli (eds), *The Europe of Elites: A Study into the Europeanness of Europe's Economic and Political Elites*. Oxford: Oxford University Press: 192–207.

Conti, Nicolò and Vincenzo Memoli (2012) 'The Multi-Faceted Nature of Party-Based Euroscepticism', *Acta Politica*, 47: 91–112.

De Vries, Catherine and Erica Edwards (2009) 'Taking Europe to Its Extremes: Extremist Parties and Public Euroskepticism', *Party Politics*, 15, 1: 5–28.

Feist, Ursula and Hans-Jürgen Hoffmann (1999) 'Die Bundestagswahlanalyse 1998: Wahl des Wechsels', *Zeitschrift für Parlamentsfragen*, 30, 2: 215–251.

Gibowski, Wolfgang G. (1995) 'Election Trends in Germany: An Analysis of the Second General Election in Reunited Germany', *German Politics*, 4, 2: 26–53.

Helms, Ludger (2006) 'The Grand Coalition: Precedents and Prospects', *German Politics and Society*, 24, 1: 47–66.

Hilmer, Richard and Rita Müller-Hilmer (2006) 'Die Bundestagswahl vom 18. September 2005: Votum für Wechsel in Kontinuität', *Zeitschrift für Parlamentsfragen*, 37, 1: 183–218.

Hooghe, Lisbeth, Gary Marks and Carole J. Wilson (2004) 'Does Left–right Structure Party Positions on European Integration?' in Gary Marks and Marco Steenbergen (eds), *European Integration and Political Conflict*. Cambridge: Cambridge University Press: 120–140.

Pappi, Franz Urban and Susumu Shikano (2003) 'Schröders knapper Sieg bei der Bundestagswahl 2002', *Zeitschrift für Politik*, 50, 1: 1–16.

Pierson, Paul (2003) 'Big, Slow-Moving and … Invisible: Macrosocial Processes in the Study of Comparative Politics', in James Mahoney and Dietrich Rueschemeyer (eds), *Comparative Historical Analysis in the Social Sciences*. Cambridge: Cambridge University Press: 177–207.

Reif, Karlheinz and Hermann Schmitt (1980) 'Nine Second-Order National Elections: A Conceptual Framework for the Analysis of European Election Results', *European Journal of Political Research*, 8, 1: 3–44.

Roberts, Geoffrey K. (2003) ' "Taken at the Flood?" The German General Election 2002', *Government and Opposition*, 38, 1: 53–72.

4   Great Britain

Giacomo Benedetto and Diego Varela

For our country the European Community presents an opportunity to influence world events once again by acting in consultation with all the most powerful nations in Western Europe. The best hope for Britain's future lies in continued and successful membership of the European Community. We know that changes are needed, but we are more likely to achieve them if we seek allies within the Community rather than making enemies.

(Conservative Party 1979)

Too many in the EU remain stubbornly wedded to some of the dogmas of the past: to the concept of ever closer union; to the centralisation of power; to a focus on the EU's internal structures rather than the world between its borders. And these people are determined to press ahead with the renamed European Constitution. This is not the right approach for tackling the big issues of today – too inflexible, too bureaucratic, too out of touch with the spirit of the age.

(Conservative Party 2009)

In our view, the European Assembly cannot constitute a proper instrument of democratic control. The basis of democratic control, we believe, must continue to be vested firmly in the right of the European peoples to govern themselves, as far as possible through their own national parliaments.

(Labour 1979)

We in the Labour Party are proud to be strong and influential Europeans. We also know that being part of an EU of 27 members makes us stronger in the world. We know that the challenges we face today – ranging from climate change to cooperating across borders to detain and arrest criminals – can only be solved in partnership.

(Labour 2009)

Introduction

The quotations above reveal a remarkable change in the pro- and anti-European integration positions of the British Conservative and Labour parties during the

30 years between 1979 and 2009. This chapter analyses the evolution of party position-taking in European Parliament (EP) election manifestos in Great Britain during that period.[1] We find that the two largest parties in British politics have indeed reversed roles on the pro- and anti-integration scale. While Conservative pro-integrationism was couched in the language of British influence on other European partners as well as market access, Labour's later pro-European discourse revolved around public investment and collective action on issues such as climate change. In displaying Eurosceptic opinion, Labour in 1979 and 1984 and the Conservatives since 1999 have each used the language of democratic connection with the nation state and protection of national parliamentary sovereignty.

During the same period, we find that the steadiest party in terms of attitudes displayed in EP election manifestos has been the Liberal Party and its successor the Liberal Democrats. The Greens, the Scottish National Party (SNP) and the Welsh nationalist Party of Wales/Plaid Cymru (PC) have also moved from Euroscepticism towards pro-integrationism. We agree with the analysis offered by Clarke (1995) of the Conservative, Labour and Liberal manifestos for the elections of 1979 to 1994. He found that economics, agriculture and position on European integration were the most frequent themes, with Conservative emphasis on free markets and Labour emphasis on job creation. By 1994, all the parties were mentioning social and environment policies, which had become more notable policy areas over time. Finally, before 1994, the Labour Party had the most hostile manifestos towards European integration. This was soon to change.

Since the late 1980s, there has been a pattern of the party of government losing the EP elections and losing all the more the longer that it is in office. The Conservative losses of 1989 were exceeded by those of 1994. Meanwhile, the vote for Labour and for other parties increased. Following Labour's election to government in 1997, the vote share of the Labour Party rapidly declined at EP elections. In 1999, the Conservatives enjoyed the largest share of the vote. In 2004, Labour declined further and the United Kingdom Independence Party (UKIP) enjoyed a significant boost. Although the Conservatives remained the largest party, their vote share declined consistent with the Reif and Schmitt (1980) observation that large parties (including large opposition parties) perform badly at EP elections. In 2009, Labour's decline accentuated while the Conservative and UKIP vote shares were almost unchanged compared to 2004. Throughout this period the Liberal Democrats failed to capitalise from a second-order effect, gaining a lower vote share than in national parliamentary elections despite their outsider status.

In the sections that follow, we contrast the manifestos of parties that in general secure seats in the EP or are relevant within the party system. For this reason, we include the Liberal Democrats and their predecessors the Liberal and Social Democratic parties for all elections since 1984. The Conservative Party, Labour Party and Liberal Party contested EP elections throughout Great Britain (England, Wales and Scotland). In 1984, the Liberals were joined in an alliance with the Social Democratic Party (SDP). By 1989 the Liberals and SDP had merged to form the Liberal Democrats. Elections throughout Great Britain were gradually contested also by the Green Party of England and Wales (GPEW)/ Scottish Green Party (SGP), UKIP and the British National Party (BNP). The GPEW and UKIP won seats for the first time in 1999. The BNP won two seats only in 2009. Besides these Great Britain-wide parties, the SNP has contested and won one and then two seats in Scotland since 1979, though manifestos are available only since 1989, and PC has contested seats in Wales, winning one or two seats in elections since 1999. In terms of placement in the organised party politics of the EP and the European Union (EU), the Labour Party, Liberal Democrats and Greens have, when elected to the EP, joined forces respectively with the groups of the European Socialists, Liberals or Greens. The SNP and PC have since 1999 also been part of the Green group in the EP. The Conservatives had more difficulty in coalescing with a Europe-wide ideological group. They sat in a small group with the Danish Conservatives from 1979 to 1992. Between 1992 and 2009, they allied with the mainstream Christian Democrats and secular Conservatives from the rest of Europe. Since 2009, the British Conservatives established a more Eurosceptic group further to the right known as European Conservatives and Reformists. Since 1999, UKIP has been aligned with other radical Eurosceptic parties (Benedetto 2008), while the BNP since 2009 has had insufficient allies to form a group. To what extent do issues in EP election campaigns have a bearing on the content of manifestos? Campaigns differ from manifestos and this book is looking at manifestos. An observer of the 2009 EP election campaign in Great Britain could be forgiven for thinking that the parties were fighting an election whose content was entirely second-order. After all, speeches by politicians and the focus of the media were dedicated to a recent scandal on the abuse of expenses of members of the British parliament or to the unpopularity of the incumbent Labour government. It therefore seems plausible that the content of the British party manifestos for the EP election of 2009 would also be second-order. Instead, much of their content focuses very precisely on matters concerning the EU that are far from second-order. The same is true for the manifestos during the period before 2009.

Euroscepticism is now part of European politics (Brack and Costa 2012) and of British politics in particular. However, other dimensions remain relevant in the campaigns and manifestos of British parties in competition for seats in the EP. Those dimensions include left–right politics (Hix and Noury 2009), the government–opposition divide (Conti 2012), the mainstream–radical divide (Marks and Steenbergen 2004), interests and identity (Sitter 2001), all of which are detected in British party manifestos for EP elections. Euroscepticism has not operated in isolation; it has interacted significantly with social and economic concerns for radical left-wing parties, or concerns of national identity for the right. In the 1970s, British Euroscepticism was located within the centre-left and marginal extreme-right. Left-wing Euroscepticism was an extension of leftist opposition to western capitalism. However, just as West European communist parties came to reform, democratise and become less Eurosceptic (Benedetto and Quaglia 2007), the same has happened to the non-communist left that previously had misgivings about capitalism, such as the Labour Party, the Greens and the Welsh nationalists.

Euroscepticism and pro-Europeanism are conscious choices (Neumayer 2008; De Vries and Edwards 2009), even if strong pro-Europeanism appears scarce in Great Britain. The pro-Europeanism of the Conservatives in 1979–94 coincided with being in government as well as their economic objectives. The government–opposition divide in Great Britain has been an unreliable guide to the likelihood of Euroscepticism adopted. The only neat switch in British party politics between pro- and anti-EU policy and position in government came with the Conservatives who moved from presenting a pro-integration manifesto in 1994 to a strongly Eurosceptic one in 1999, having been ejected from national government in 1997. Labour, the Greens and the SNP and PC became pro-European while in opposition, while the Liberal Democrats always remained pro-European despite being in opposition. This pro-integrationism is to be found in the parties' manifestos only and not necessarily in their campaigns.

The chapter is chronological. Its analysis of party manifestos begins in 1979. It looks at election results and the dimensions of issues presented in the manifestos. Explanatory factors include the politics of left and right, whether a party is in government or opposition, the role of sub-state nationalism in the politics of Wales and Scotland. We shall look at the appearance of identity, representation and the desired scope of governance when analysing the manifestos. At the end of the chapter, before we conclude, we offer an analysis of word counts in the 2009 manifestos as a measure of the salience of policy issues in the contents of the manifestos. We view this material as complementary to the more qualitative content of the rest of the chapter.

The Euromanifestos of 1979 and 1984

The Conservatives enjoyed a huge victory in the EP elections of 1979, gaining 51 per cent of the vote one month after Margaret Thatcher's election as Prime Minister in May 1979. With a lower turnout and a falling away from the polls by disillusioned Labour supporters, the Conservative percentage share increased while that of Labour declined compared to the British parliamentary election. Usually governing parties do badly in European elections except during their 'honeymoon' period (Reif and Schmitt 1980). In 1984, the Conservatives were relatively untainted by long years in office and gained a plurality of the vote with 41 per cent, but still fell back compared to the EP election of 1979 and the British parliamentary election of 1983. The Labour Party gained some support increasing its vote share compared to the EP elections of 1979 and the British parliamentary election of 1983. The Liberal/SDP Alliance declined compared to its performance in the British parliamentary election of 1983. In 1979 and 1984, the Labour manifestos were negative in their attitude to European integration, citing economic reasons alongside concerns for national parliamentary sovereignty. Meanwhile the Conservatives were positive, using a discourse about British influence in the world and the benefits of market integration. This position was shared in 1984 by the Liberal/SDP Alliance. PC was, like Labour, critical on European integration in 1984. By 1999, the European integration positions of all these parties except the Liberal Democrats would be reversed.

The Conservatives wished for Britain to be a leader of Europe and to influence in 1979 and 1984, the attitude of the Labour Party was rejectionist in 1979, but more cooperative by 1984. The Liberal/SDP Alliance was cooperative in 1984. The Conservative manifesto favoured a mix of intergovernmental and supranational decision making in 1979 and 1984, while Labour was intergovernmental in 1979 and in favour of specific national preference in 1984. The Liberal/SDP Alliance manifesto favoured a mix like the Conservatives in 1984. Nobody mentioned European identity.

In terms of policy areas, we find the Conservatives favoured a mix of supranational and national management of foreign, social and environment policies, and supranational management of defence policy. The 1984 manifesto of the Conservatives spoke very favourably of market integration and interdependence:

> Conservatives recognize that the member states of the European Community are today more dependent upon one another than they have ever been. The more Community member states work together to promote them, and the more we exploit the potential of a common market of 270 million consumers, the greater will be the benefits. That is why Conservatives believe that the greatest single contribution from the Community need cost no money at all – it is to make a reality of the common market.
>
> (Conservative Party 1984)

In 1984, the Liberal/SDP Alliance supported market integration and interdependence as much as the Conservatives but also emphasised the social market and job creation in the context of global competition:

> Only by working on a European scale can we establish the high-technology industries which hold the key to the future, and without which Europe will become increasingly dependent on Japan and America. The creation of new jobs and the attack on unemployment is far more effective on a continental scale.
>
> (Liberal/SDP Alliance 1984)

In 1979, Labour favoured national control of social policy, moving to a mix of national and supranational control by 1984 though still highly critical of the perceived impact of European integration on unemployment:

> Labour demands new policies for Europe – for an end to mass unemployment and industrial decline. Labour demands a break with the past in the European Community. Membership has helped to speed up our economic decline. It has cost Britain jobs.
>
> (Labour 1984)

In 1984, Labour also favoured national control for defence policy and a mix of national and European control in environment policy. The Liberal/SDP Alliance manifesto favoured a mix of national and European control of foreign and social policies, but mainly European control of defence and environment policies.

The Conservative manifestos of 1979 and 1984 linked the European Economic Community (EEC) to democracy, with the 1984 manifesto particularly praising the democratic role of the EP: 'Since 1979 the directly-elected European Parliament has established for itself a position of real influence at the centre of the Community's decision making. Over the next five years, the Parliament must consolidate its influence' (Conservative Party 1984). The Liberal/SDP Alliance manifesto questioned the lack of democracy despite its support for European integration. Nevertheless it went further than the Conservatives in urging specific increases in the legislative and revenue powers of the EP: 'The first urgent reform is that Parliament and the Council should jointly exercise legislative authority in the Community. The powers of the parliament over expenditure of the Community should be extended to the revenue side' (Liberal/SDP Alliance 1984).

Labour was worried about democracy. Its position on the EP contrasted significantly with that of the Conservatives and it reaffirmed its Euroscepticism and sense of national democracy:

> We do not believe that the European Parliament should be given more powers – for this would take power and decision making even further away from ordinary people. Labour believes that the institutions of the Community must be made fully accountable to the people through their own Parliaments.
>
> (Labour 1984)

The Welsh nationalist PC played a critical card on EEC democracy and emphasised the democratic needs of Wales:

> The crisis of the EEC gives new hope for Europe: at last people can understand our slogan 'Europe Yes, EEC No'. But there is no answer in totally rejecting Europe and retreating to fortress Britain which is the official policy of Labour party. The answer is a new treaty to reshape the European Community, but when a new treaty is negotiated the voice of Wales must be heard.
>
> (PC 1984)

The manifestos of 1979 and 1984 were drawn up during a period of Conservative popularity when British membership of the EEC was likewise popular. Together with the Liberal/SDP Alliance, the two parties enthusiastic about European integration reached a combined share of the vote of 60 percent in 1984. The Conservative position was based on British leadership in the world and the market, important priorities for a right-wing free market party. The Liberal/SDP

Alliance shared some of these concerns but also emphasised social and environment policy, in particular addressing the unemployment crisis. The Liberals and SDP also offered some criticism of EEC democracy. The Labour Party manifestos were hostile in 1979 and still highly critical of the EEC in 1984. The election of 1984 took place shortly after the election of Neil Kinnock as party leader, who oversaw a gradual change in the party's attitude to Europe. Labour Euroscepticism took the form of a criticism of capitalist economic policy and defence of national parliamentary democracy. In this period government or opposition status made little difference. The most Eurosceptic manifesto was that published by Labour in 1979, probably drawn up when the party was still (just) in government. Labour's manifesto of 1984 was less Eurosceptic. Meanwhile the Liberal Party, permanently in opposition, presented the most pro-integration manifesto in 1984.

The Euromanifestos of 1989 and 1994

The year 1987 saw the ratification of the Single European Act, the Conservative Party's third successive national election victory and the decision of Neil Kinnock's Labour Party to engage in a policy review that would lead to the party becoming more moderate and pro-European. In the autumn of 1988, Margaret Thatcher's speech at the College of Europe in Bruges signalled the start of the Conservative move towards Euroscepticism or at least scepticism of social and environmental regulation. Meanwhile, the Labour Party's outward Euroscepticism was weakening. Did this critical juncture affect the content of manifestos in the EP elections of 1989 and 1994?

In the EP elections, in 1989 the pro-integration Conservatives declined from their level in the 1984 election and the British parliamentary election of 1987. Following the merger of the Liberals and SDP and many party divisions in 1988, the Liberal Democrats declined to just 6 per cent compared to 19 per cent in 1984 and 23 per cent in 1987. The Labour Party's share of the vote increased to 40 per cent (gaining the plurality for the first time). The combined score for the three pro-integration parties, now including Labour, was 81 per cent. In 1994, the Conservative decline and Labour increase continued, the Liberal Democrats recovered their support to 17 per cent. Conservative pro-integrationism present in the Conservative manifesto means that the pro-integration parties shared 93 per cent of the vote in 1994.

Conservative Euroscepticism at this time was detected by the media but did not appear significantly in the party's EP election manifestos, which continued to speak favourably of the opportunities afforded by European integration. The 1989 manifesto emphasised British leadership, support for the principles of the Schengen Area and continuing integration:

> In order to make it easier to reduce and simplify frontier checks we are committed to more effective European action against international crime. Improved intelligence work and closer collaboration between member states

police and judicial authorities are crucial … We hold the door wide open to co-operation on all the other issues covered by the Helsinki accords – trade, economic co-operation, human rights, the exchange of information and ideas, free movement of people, the environment and security.

(Conservative Party 1989)

By 1994, the Conservatives remained pro-integration while reserving some criticism for Brussels though no more than Labour would display once in government after 1997:

We are clear that our national interest lies in Europe. Millions of our jobs depend on Europe. So we want it to be a success. We will fight for the kind of Europe we want – not a European superstate, but a Europe of nation states working together. We want less interference from Brussels not more.

(Conservative Party 1994)

The contents of the Labour, Liberal Democrat, SNP and PC manifestos were more reserved though not Eurosceptic. Only UKIP, standing for the first time in 1994, was more negative. The Conservatives continued to profile themselves as leaders in Europe and, in this, they were joined by Labour and the Liberal Democrats in 1994, the latter stating: 'This country has great potential – we could be leaders in Europe. We reject the "opt out mentality". Instead we would play a full part in shaping a European Union that benefits Britain' (Liberal Democrats 1994). The SNP and PC manifestos adopted a consensual tone profiling their parties as cooperative in Europe. Previously in favour of integration and intergovernmentalism, the Conservatives joined Labour and the Liberal Democrats in demonstrating intergovernmentalist language in 1989 before becoming more integrationist in 1994. In 1994 the SNP and PC adopted significantly more integrationist language than in the past. In 1989, the Conservatives spoke of defending British national interests and in 1994 this fell to the Conservatives and UKIP. Labour offered no view on the matter. In 1989, the Liberal Democrats spoke of defence of a common European interest, not mentioned by any of their competitors.

In 1989 references to European or British culture or identity were absent. Sub-state identity was cited by the SNP and PC in 1989 and 1994, while in 1994 Labour made references to European values.

In terms of policy areas, the Conservatives in 1989 continued to call for national and European level control of defence, social and environment policies, extending this call in 1994 to foreign, justice and immigration policies. By 1989, Labour had moved in a more integrationist direction also favouring national and European responsibility for defence, social and environment policies, for example, 'We want to see rapid progress on the social dimension and on environmental co-operation' (Labour 1989). In 1994, the party linked social policy to monetary and fiscal policy: 'Labour will press for co-ordinated monetary and fiscal policies designed to promote investment, growth and employment' (Labour 1994). This extended to foreign and justice policies but not immigration in 1994. In 1989, the Liberal Democrats displayed less enthusiasm for the integration of policy areas, urging national and European responsibility for only foreign, defence and environment policies, extending to justice and social policies in 1994.

The SNP and PC favoured integration in social and environment policies in 1989 and in foreign and defence policies by 1994, while underscoring their support for sub-state nationalism, for example:

> The political construction of Europe must be built on the diversity of European experience and tradition on the decentralisation of power and the active involvement of the individual. We believe in a Wales as well as in a European Union of the peoples in a national culture which includes and celebrates the different cultures within the nation.
>
> (PC 1994)

In 1994, UKIP favoured national control in all policy areas, affirming that: 'Europe is a democratic and economic disaster' (UKIP 1994).

On the subject of legitimacy and the democratic deficit, the Conservatives, Labour, Liberal Democrats, SNP and PC all supported greater competence for the EU in 1989. By 1994 with the passage of the Maastricht Treaty, all parties expressed support for the legitimacy and democratic values of European integration apart from UKIP.

The Euromanifestos under the Labour government of 1997–2010

The 1994 EP elections had taken place at a time of maximum Conservative unpopularity when the Conservatives were also showing divisions in their approach to European integration. The leadership of the Conservative Party under Prime Minister John Major had taken the step at the time of the Maastricht Treaty of negotiating opt-outs for the United Kingdom (UK) from monetary union and social regulation. Despite this, the Conservative manifesto for the EP elections of 1994 had remained relatively pro-integration, as discussed above, in fact rather more so than the Labour Party's manifesto.

In the national election of 1997 the Conservatives were defeated. Labour had profiled itself as a pro-European party, which would opt into social regulation but remained sceptical of monetary union. Apart from the elections of 1979, EP elections have been held at least one year after the previous national election, at which the governing party is losing popularity (Reif and Schmitt 1980; Schmitt 2005). This was the case with the 1999 EP elections. Although Tony Blair remained popular in the opinion polls, the Conservatives received a plurality of the vote in 1999. The Conservatives' campaign of 1999 was their most Eurosceptic, while the Labour and Liberal Democrat campaigns were shy in their commitment to the EU. The campaign of 1999 also differed from its predecessors in another important respect: it was held under a new electoral system that offered improved prospects for smaller parties. The 1999 election saw a defeat for Labour, a rather underwhelming victory for the Conservatives on 36 per cent and a decline in votes for the Liberal Democrats. The Greens with 6 per cent and UKIP with 7 per cent were the beneficiaries of stray votes. Given the Conservative turn to Euroscepticism, the 1999 election saw that Labour, Liberal Democrats, SNP and PC as pro-integration parties shared a combined vote of 54 per cent. This combined total reached only 40 per cent in 2004. In 2009, including the newly pro-integration Greens, it reached only 41 per cent. Euroscepticism in public opinion was beginning to coincide with the vote share of parties with Eurosceptic manifestos in EP elections.

Labour was re-elected to national government in 2001 and 2005, being eventually defeated in 2010. In the EP elections of 2004 and 2009 Labour continued to lose support to 23 and then just 16 per cent respectively, yet the Conservatives did not perform as strongly as might be expected, falling to just 27 per cent in 2004 and to 28 per cent in 2009 because of the stronger role of UKIP. On the left, the Greens retained a vote share of between 6 and 9 per cent. What was the effect on the content of the manifestos in 1999, 2004 and 2009 given the proportional electoral system, the long period of Labour government, rising Euroscepticism and the strengthening of more marginal parties like UKIP, the Greens and, in 2009, the extreme-right BNP?

In 1999, for the first time, the Conservative manifesto expressed a negative view of the effect of European integration on the UK, consistent with the party's shift into opposition and towards the right. In 2004, this changed to a mix of negative and positive. Labour, the SNP and PC moved in the opposite direction with a positive view of European integration in 1999, 2004 and 2009, following more negative views before 1999. During this period the Liberal Democrats and the Greens expressed mixed views of the effects of European integration. UKIP and the BNP expressed exclusively negative views.

In terms of the desired level of national action within Europe, the Conservatives displayed an attitude of national defence against European integration for the first time in 1999, having previously advocated a positive British leadership role: 'It [the Conservative manifesto] is the manifesto of a proudly British party, which believes that our national identity, institutions and ability to govern ourselves are priceless assets, and will not see them sacrificed' (Conservative Party 1999). The Conservatives' attitude modified in 2004 when leadership re-emerged as a theme. The Labour Party's attitude was cooperative in 1999 and leadership-oriented in 2004. In 2004, Labour condemned the Conservatives' perceived isolationism and defended its commitment to Europe's market in a statement that could have appeared in the Conservative manifesto of 1984 (though not that of 2004):

> Isolation and withdrawal is not only undesirable it is unthinkable if we are to remain a strong and successful nation. That's why being a leading member of the European Union is so crucial to our national interests, to our

future prosperity and security. Far from diminishing British sovereignty, the EU – as a union of independent sovereign states – increases our power to deliver real benefits to British people on issues that matter. We are better off as a result of being a member of the largest single market in the world.

(Labour 2004)

The Liberal Democrats displayed leadership or cooperative preferences for Britain's role in the EU:

We would see the European Union for what it is: a way of tackling shared problems, upholding shared values, settling disputes between traditionally fractious neighbours and applying the rule of law to agreements that have been entered into. Through the EU Britain can exercise real influence over the global economy and over international problems we can't deal with alone.

(Liberal Democrats 2004)

The preferences of the SNP in 2004 were largely cooperative, demonstrating both soft Euroscepticism and support for monetary union:

The SNP believes in the European Union as a confederation of states. And we believe that issues such as our national constitution, and our taxation system should be retained under national control. The SNP believes that the euro offers significant economic benefits to Scotland and would be preferable to sterling.

(SNP 2004)

In terms of the desired level of EU decision making, the Conservatives' preference in 1999 was for national decision making and in 2004 and 2009 for intergovernmentalism. In terms of their view on European integration, this was a significant change from before 1999 when the Conservatives favoured either supranationalism or a mix of supranationalism with intergovernmentalism. In 1999, Labour, the Liberal Democrats, the Greens, SNP and PC all had preferences for a mix between supranational and intergovernmental decision making. Again, this showed that all of these parties had become pro-integrationist in terms of public policy pronouncement at exactly the same time that the Conservatives had become less so. The view of the Greens in 1999 was internationalist but anti-EU due to Green criticisms of EU institutions and market integration: 'The Single Market, the Maastricht Treaty and Monetary Union have followed one after another. Each puts profits before people and the environment. With every step economic control has been centralised' (GPEW 1999). References to European identity, values or culture were made in 1999 by the Conservatives, Labour and Greens, and in 2004 by the SNP. In 1999, Labour supported the Charter of Fundamental Rights as a means to promote identity, something from which Tony Blair would later seek an opt-out in 2007:

In order to develop a stronger European identity we propose that the fundamental civic, economic, social and cultural rights which have been won by
citizens throughout the European Union, including access to public services,
should be set out in a European Charter of rights.

(Labour 1999)

References to British identity, values or culture were made in 1999 by the
Conservatives, Labour and UKIP, and in 2004 by the Conservatives only. References to sub-state nationalism, values or culture were made by the SNP and PC
in 1999 and 2004. For the Welsh nationalists, the Charter of Fundamental Rights
was a means to protect Welsh and other sub-state identity:

Our vision is a just Wales, where all citizens are equal and Wales' unique
contribution to linguistic diversity in Europe is promoted. Europe and the
European Charter on Fundamental Rights are your ultimate guarantee of
your rights no matter who you are. The Welsh language is a unique cultural
expression in a Europe of many cultures.

(PC 2004)

At which level should different policy areas be decided? The Conservatives and
Labour favoured a mix of European and national management of defence and
foreign policies and justice and police matters in 1999. In the same year, the
Conservatives continued to support European and national management for
immigration, social and environment policies but with strong Euroscepticism
expressed, a real departure compared to just five years earlier:

All these risks make the balance sheet for membership much less favourable
for Britain than for her partners. That is why Britain should not consider
joining the single currency until it has been tested in bad times as well as
good, and its economic and political consequences have been properly
assessed.

(Conservative Party 1999)

In 2004, the Euroscepticism of the Conservatives was less pronounced:

Working with other nations we can solve problems that we cannot tackle
successfully on our own. So Conservatives believe that Britain cannot and
should not turn its back on Europe. The vision we deliver is what British
people want from Europe: freedom, stability and prosperity.

(Conservative Party 2004)

This was matched by Labour's commitment to social and economic reform: 'We
pushed for agreement of the "Lisbon Agenda" for economic reform to create
more and better jobs – working towards full employment in Europe' (Labour
2004). The Liberal Democrats, Greens, SNP and PC also favoured European and

national management of environment policy. UKIP favoured national management for all policy areas. Despite the Conservative move in 1999 towards significantly more Eurosceptic positions, this was not the case when it came to specific
policies. In 2004, the Conservatives reserved a stronger national preference for
managing foreign policy but supported a mix of national and supranational intervention in defence, justice and police matters, immigration, social and environment policies. In almost all these policies, Labour, Liberal Democrats, Greens,
SNP and PC supported a mix of national and European solutions. The consensus
between all parties other than UKIP on preferences for the level of governance
for managing areas of important policy is remarkable given the polarising potential of Euroscepticism in the election campaign if not the manifestos of 2004.
The Conservatives of 2004 nevertheless expressed significant Euroscepticism in
terms of opposition to regulation versus the desirability of free markets: 'European Business is over-regulated and over-taxed, thanks in large part to the European Union. European jobs are being lost because firms cannot compete with
overseas companies operating in more flexible markets' (Conservative manifesto
2004). For immigration and social policies, Labour and the Liberal Democrats
favoured mixed national and European intervention, while the Greens favoured
exclusive European or international management. The Liberal Democrats were
keen to link employment to market access: 'The EU enhances trade within the
European single market. That is good for British jobs and British industry'
(Liberal Democrats 2004).

The Greens were critical of EU handling of social and environmental issues
rather than being Eurosceptic. The problem was that the EU was not doing
enough: 'Greens see the EU's response to climate change as woefully inad-
equate' (GPEW 1999). 'EU legislation designed to protect us from hazardous
chemicals is totally ineffective – currently we have little or no human health or
environmental safety information for more than 95% of the chemicals we use'
(GPEW 2004). And yet: 'We applaud the environmental, judicial and safety
legislation that has come out of Europe', while on immigration policy, the
Greens supported a different type of European integration: 'The Green party
works for a significant reduction in immigration control and the protection of the
rights of migrant workers regardless of their economic value' (GPEW 2004).

PC had the most pro-integration manifesto, favouring exclusive European
management of foreign, defence and social policies, with a mix of European and
sub-state (Welsh) management of immigration and environment policies. In
1999, it stated its support for monetary union: 'The Party of Wales believes that
the single currency can bring significant benefits for industry and competit-
iveness given a strengthened regional economic policy and a commitment to
employment, for building up a Welsh financial sector' (PC 1999). The SNP supported European approaches to the environment, social rights and justice matters:
'Environmental protection, citizens' rights, equal opportunities, measures to
guard against illness and poverty, the protection of children, and tackling international crime are all issues that require action across national boundaries' (SNP
2004). Concerning the state of EU democracy, all parties except for the neutral

SNP expressed negative views in 1999. The issue was not addressed in the manifestos of 2004 except by the SNP, which expressed a mixed view.

The chapter now turns to the election manifestos of 2009 in cases where they differed from 2004.

The Euromanifestos in 2009

In 2009, the Conservative manifesto contained positive and negative views of European integration. Both the Conservative and Labour manifestos emphasised a mix of preferences including the desire for leadership in Europe, cooperation and defence. At the same time, the Greens were taking a critical, left-wing, pro-European line in favour of a different form of European integration:

> Our vision for Europe seeks to replace the unsustainable economics of free trade and growth with the alternative of local self-reliance. There are essential matters – safeguarding basic rights, peace and security achieved through mutual understanding, environmental protection, the spread of culture and ideas, regulation of the financial system – where we agree that EU action is appropriate.
>
> (GPEW 2009)

The position of the Welsh nationalists was also distinctly cooperative, left-wing and pro-integration:

> There is no other region in the world in which half a billion people can move freely between states to work and live. Yet while we are entirely committed to the ideals for which the countries of Europe came together to create a Union – peace and economic partnership – Plaid Cymru also believes that it is time to reform the EU so that it is able to protect the people of Europe against the threats of the climate crisis, globalisation and the credit crunch.
>
> (PC 2009)

UKIP and the BNP were resolutely rejectionist:

> A vote for UKIP is a vote to say 'No' loudly and clearly. It may be the last chance you get. UKIP is committed to a free, democratic, independent Britain which is governed not by the faceless bureaucrats in Brussels but by our own people through our elected Parliament at Westminster.
>
> (UKIP 2009)

'We will campaign for Britain to withdraw from the EU' (BNP 2009).

In 2004, Labour, the Liberal Democrats and the Greens had favoured intergovernmentalism, while the SNP and PC favoured a policy mix. This changed in 2009 amid the economic crisis, with Labour, the Liberal Democrats and SNP favouring a mix of supranational and intergovernmental decision making and the Greens and PC becoming the only parties to favour an explicitly supranational preference for decision making.

References to European identity, values or culture were made in 2009 by the Liberal Democrats, PC and the extreme-right BNP. All parties except the Greens, SNP and PC referred to British identity, values or culture. The Liberal Democrats, SNP and PC also referred to sub-state nationalism, its values or culture.

In 2009 compared to 2004, we find a Conservative manifesto that is more Eurosceptic and Liberal Democrat, Green and PC manifestos that are more integrationist in terms of policy management. The Conservatives favoured national management of foreign, defence and social policies, with mixed management for justice and immigration, and supranational management for environment policy. Labour, the Liberal Democrats and the Greens favoured a mix of European and national management of foreign and defence policies, with environment policy to be managed exclusively at supranational level. Labour's commitments to social rights in the 2009 manifesto are more significant for their left-wing content than for their commitment to European integration, a notable observation given Labour's impending defeat in 2010 and the tendency of parties to adopt more ideological positions as they head towards opposition:

> The EU, thanks to the hard work of Labour MEPs, has helped deliver stronger rights at work and a better deal for British consumers and families. Labour MEPs will continue to stand up for hard-working people in Europe whether through campaigning for lower prices and better standards for British consumers or calling for improved working rights. As we have shown, we will act to prevent the unfair treatment or exploitation of workers across Europe, including safety at the workplace, decent minimum standards for holidays, meal breaks and working hours, maternity leave, and protection against unfair discrimination. As we face the current economic crisis we will retain our strong international alliances to secure the action needed to create jobs, fight climate change and build a fairer world.
>
> (Labour 2009)

Meanwhile, the Liberal Democrats moved further to the right on employment under the leadership of Nick Clegg, favouring integration yet opposing the 48-hour week:

> Labour MEPs often fail to support British workers and businesses, for example by voting against their own government and backing damaging plans to scrap the UK's opt out of the 48 hour week limit in the Working Time Directive. Too often Labour has used EU rules as an excuse to enact burdensome and centralising regulations. Liberal Democrats would put an end to this so-called 'goldplating' of EU rules.
>
> (Liberal Democrats 2009)

At the same time, PC moved further towards left-wing pro-integrationist positions on foreign, social, immigration and environment policies:

> We believe that we share a duty to uphold and defend people's right to seek asylum and we will work to ensure Europe's proud tradition of offering refuge to the persecuted continues.
>
> We will continue to work to end discrimination and worker exploitation through the adoption of stricter laws and improved workers' rights throughout Europe. If it's easier and cheaper for companies to sack workers in Wales than in other countries, that's exactly what will happen. We believe in a Europe where wages and jobs are protected; a Europe where conditions are equal all over the continent. We believe in a Europe of harmonised working conditions, where employers cannot drive down pay by exploiting cheap labour in another country. We believe that European funding should be channelled into a substantial investment programme to fight climate change, which will create sustainable jobs and sustainable economic growth.
>
> (PC 2009)

In 2009, the Conservatives, Labour, Greens, UKIP and BNP expressed negative views of EU democracy, the Liberal Democrats expressed a positive view, PC expressed a mixed view and the SNP expressed no view.

We end this chapter with a short investigation as to whether word count methods could shed further light on the interpretation of Euromanifestos, using those presented by British parties in 2009. We use data mining techniques to analyse the most common issues dealt with by parties. First we prepared the data by tokenising the manifestos, transforming all the tokens to lower case, filtering prepositions and other stopwords, filtering words of fewer than two characters, and generating n-grams (terms) of up to three words. The results are reported in Table 4.1.

Table 4.1 shows the list of the most frequently used words in the 2009 EP election manifestos. The first point to note is that the words 'EU, 'European', 'Europe' and 'MEPs' are the most common words, with between 201 and 570 occurrences each. This finding, which might seem obvious and unimportant at first sight, contrasts with the predictions of the second-order election model that depicts EP elections as second-order national contests, which are mostly beauty contests about the popularity of the national government and therefore deal with national not European issues (Reif and Schmitt 1980; Schmitt 2005). The results of the statistical analysis seem to contradict this hypothesis, at least as far as EP election manifestos are concerned.

The second finding we can draw from the table is that Euromanifestos pay a great deal of attention to the economy and employment ('work', 'economic', 'jobs', 'economy', 'working', 'worker') and energy and the environment ('energy', 'green', 'climate', 'climate change', 'carbon', 'emissions' 'environment'). They also pay some attention to trade, development and global issues

Table 4.1 List of most common words in the 2009 Euromanifestos

Term	No. of occurrences	No. of manifestos
EU, European, Europe, people, Britain, MEPs	201–570	6–8
UK, green, support, countries, Scotland, work, British, world, energy, government, jobs, labour, economic	137–171	5–8
help, change, ensure, liberal, make, economy, believe, working, trade, climate, parliament, Wales, action, climate_change, rights, union, continue, policy, conservative, future, party	79–121	4–8
Scottish, democrats, including, SNP, development, liberal_democrats, European_Union, want, national, deal, international, co, global, year, businesses, social, investment, European_Parliament, free, system, create, financial, million, services, fair, carbon, conservative_meps, take, time	58–78	1–8
crime, part, standards, years, workers, strong, use, emissions, communities, market, states, interests, conservatives, put, common, crisis, citizens, environmental, measures, Plaid, power, protect, rules, money, country, environment, policies, promote, secure, security, single, stronger, developing, families, fight, food, further, legislation, level, member, challenges, committed	43–56	1–8
Total	10,033	8

Source: authors' own calculation with RapidMiner.

('world', 'trade', 'international', 'development', 'global') and finance ('financial', 'crisis', 'money').

Finally, it is important to note that regional issues also play an important role in EP manifestos ('Scotland', 'Wales'). Not in vain, the EP is the main EU institution through which sub-state nationalist parties can bypass the national governments' control of the Council and the Commission, and are keen to use this option to make their demands heard.

Although EP election results and campaigns are second-order, the content of the Euromanifestos is not second-order. As these word counts demonstrate, the manifestos focus on policy and institutions at the EU level.

Conclusions

This chapter has reviewed the contents of Euromanifestos of British parties for EP election campaigns since 1979. The analysis was undertaken chronologically, comparing the manifestos of each party at different stages in time and looking at the policy emphases, including questions of identity and preference in policy. We evaluated the positions of each party according to position on the left–right spectrum, status in government or opposition and preferences towards or against European integration.

The role of Euroscepticism in British party politics has remained significant since the 1970s. As Szczerbiak and Taggart (2008) explain, one of the ways in which Euroscepticism manifests itself is through factions in larger mainstream parties. These factions were present in the Labour Party once most of the party had accepted European integration. Since the 1990s, Euroscepticism at the level of party leaderships seems to be a right-wing phenomenon in Great Britain, particularly in 2009, going against the assumptions of those who say that Euroscepticism and left–right politics cross over (Neumayer 2008; De Vries and Edwards 2009; Conti 2012). Indeed the correlation of Euroscepticism with centre-right and radical right politics in 2009 seemed to be far more significant than either the government–opposition or radical–mainstream divides.

When the Conservatives favoured European integration until the 1990s, it was defended in terms of strategic interest, influenced by concerns for the UK's diminished power in the world and the advantages of economic integration. The centrist Liberal Democrats shared these positions and maintained them until 2009, also favouring environmental regulation and action against unemployment. The pro-integration positions of the Labour Party and, more recently, of the Greens and PC have been motivated by support for social and environment regulation, although Labour has also emphasised aspects of free trade. When Labour, the Greens and PC were more Eurosceptic in the past, this was motivated by an (anti-capitalist) economic critique. The more recent Conservative Euroscepticism targets economic 'over-regulation'. Both Labour and the Conservatives, at different times, have emphasised the danger of European integration to British parliamentary sovereignty.

The role in government or opposition does not tend to have much effect except for the Conservatives. The latter lost government power in 1997. The EP manifestos of the Conservatives until 1994 were pro-integration, while those afterwards were profoundly Eurosceptic. The Liberal Democrats' manifestos were also in favour of integration despite being permanently in opposition. The manifestos of Labour, the Greens, SNP and PC became pro-integration while the parties were in opposition.

A final contribution of this chapter has been the preliminary word count analysis for the manifestos of 2009. In the future, this analysis could be extended. The data which we have analysed have shown that beyond the sense gained from the qualitative reading of a manifesto, the content of the manifestos is very far from second-order and is focused on policy matters for which the EU and the EP are responsible. The content of British party manifestos for EP elections is therefore quite different from the second-order nature of the EP election campaigns or results themselves.

Note

1 The United Kingdom consists of Northern Ireland and Great Britain (England, Scotland and Wales). Northern Ireland has an entirely separate party system in which the British parties do not compete. This chapter is looking at the party manifestos from Great Britain only.

References

Benedetto, G. (2008) 'Explaining the Failure of Euroscepticism in the European Parliament', in Szczerbiak, A. and Taggart, A. (eds) *Opposing Europe? The Comparative Party Politics of Euroscepticism* 2, Oxford: Oxford University Press.

Benedetto, G. and Quaglia, L. (2007) 'The Comparative Politics of Communist Euroscepticism in France, Spain and Italy', *Party Politics* 13(4): 479–500.

Brack, N. and Costa, O. (2012) 'Beyond the Pro/Anti-Europe Divide: Diverging Views of Europe within EU Institutions', *Journal of European Integration* 34(2): 101–111.

Clarke, S. D. (1995) 'An Analysis of Britain's Party Manifestos for Europe, 1979–94', in Rallings, C. and Thrasher, M. (eds) *British Elections and Parties Yearbook 1995*, London: Frank Cass.

Conti, N. (2012) 'The EU in the Programmatic Statements of Domestic Parties', in Best, H., Lengyel, G. and Verzichelli, L. (eds) *The Europe of Elites: A Study into the Europeanness of Europe's Economic and Political Elites*, Oxford: Oxford University Press.

De Vries, C. and Edwards, E. (2009) 'Taking Europe to its Extremes: Extremist Parties and Public Euroskepticism', *Party Politics* 15(1): 5–28.

Hix, S. and Noury, A. (2009) 'After Enlargement: Voting Patterns in the Sixth European Parliament', *Legislative Studies Quarterly* 34(2): 159–174.

Marks, G. and Steenbergen, M. (2004) *European Integration and Political Conflict*, Cambridge: Cambridge University Press.

Neumayer, L. (2008) 'Euroscepticism as a Political Label: The Use of European Union Issues in Political Competitions in the New Member States', *European Journal of Political Research* 47(2): 135–160.

Reif, K. and Schmitt, H. (1980) 'Nine Second-Order National Elections: A Conceptual Framework for the Analysis of European Election Results', *European Journal of Political Research* 8(1): 3–44.

Schmitt, H. (2005) 'The European Parliament Election of June 2004: Still Second-Order?' *West European Politics* 28(3): 650–679.

Sitter, N. (2001) 'The Politics of Opposition and European Integration in Scandinavia: Is Euro-Scepticism a Government-Opposition Dynamic?' *West European Politics* 24(4): 22–39.

Szczerbiak, A. and Taggart, P. (eds) (2008) *Opposing Europe: The Comparative Party Politics of Euroscepticism*, Oxford: Oxford University Press.

5   Italy

Nicolò Conti and Vincenzo Memoli

Introduction

Although it is one of the founding members of the EU, for a long time Italy was characterised by the polarisation of the Italian party system, a phenomenon that also involved the issue of European integration. The country was characterised by fervent Europhilia on the side of government parties as opposed to hard Euroscepticism on the side of the Italian communist party, the second largest party and main opposition force in the country (it was never in government). However, since the 1980s, Italy has become one of the most pro-European member states, with broad support coming from all main parties. Consensus on the European issue developed after a long process of realignment lasting several decades, when fierce opposition to the Common Market from the left gradually evolved into more supportive and pragmatic attitudes (Conti and Verzichelli 2005). Such development was the result of a reduced polarisation of the system which occurred over several decades as left-wing parties shifted from the extreme to the core of the party system. Alberta Sbragia (2001, 93) described the phenomenon as follows: 'once the PCI [Italian communist party] changed its position and supported Italian participation in the European Community, it became difficult to find anyone who questioned the appropriateness of Italian participation in the process'.

In the beginning of the 1990s, the end of the so-called first republic coincided with the disappearance of the old parties, a de-polarisation of the party system and with the creation of a new party system based on bipolarism and alternation in government. At the same time, negotiations for the European Monetary Union were taking place. In the past, few voices were heard outside the two positions of principled support and principled rejection of the Common Market, since any pragmatic approach to the issue of European integration was scantly represented in the Italian party system, but, since 1994, all positions – from hard Euroscepticism to fervent pro-Europeanism – are represented. Indeed, in the 1990s, after a period of consensus in the final years of the first republic, a new tendency towards divergence over EU issues developed. In particular, the first discontinuity to note is that the major parties of the centre-right show some clear signs of Euroscepticism. Their political discourse has been described as moving back and forth from soft Euroscepticism to vagueness to broad un-specific pro-Europeanism (Conti 2009). On the other side of the political spectrum, several analyses show that the Italian centre-left has Europe at the centre of its programme more than the right does, and it has developed the traditional commitment of the Italian governments of the first republic towards the idea of a united Europe (Conti 2006, 2009). It is worth noting that several authors maintain that across Europe, parties have swapped their positions on the EU, so starting from the 1990s the left has become more pro-European than the right (Gabel and Hix 2004; Ladrech 2000). In line with this trend, Italy's left has also become more pro-European than the centre-right. On the other hand, at the extremes of the political spectrum, hard Euroscepticism has been a remarkable feature, though not a stable one. The small Communist party *Rifondazione comunista* has shown signs of strong opposition to European integration, for example by voting in parliament against the ratification of the Maastricht Treaty, the Treaty of Nice and the Treaty establishing a Constitution for Europe.[1] At the other extreme of the political spectrum, the *Lega Nord* has also criticised the achieved results of European integration and voted against the ratification of the Treaty establishing a Constitution for Europe (yet voted in favour of the Lisbon Treaty).

On the whole, the picture of contemporary Italian parties could be seen in the light of two points of view proposed by the comparative literature. The first one concerns the European vocation of social democrats (Hix *et al.* 2007; Ladrech 2000; Ray 1999) that has clearly emerged in Italy. The second one concerns the Eurosceptical attitudes of parties on the flanks of the political spectrum (Szczerbiak and Taggart 2008) that has found some ground also in the Italian situation. Starting from these two theoretical arguments, this chapter explores patterns of contestation of the EU issue in Italy. We make use of the Euromanifestos of the Italian parties collected from 1989 to 2009 and coded under the common framework of the INTUNE project. The data allow the in-depth analysis of many dimensions of the European issue on which, as we will document, parties take a stance and express their preferences. Specifically, party attitudes will be described with respect to three main dimensions of the EU process and of its impact on the member states (described in the Introduction): identity, representation and policy scope. First, we will document how these three dimensions have structured the parties' programmatic offer on the EU and how this structure has changed over time. Second, we will analyse the preferences of the individual parties along these three dimensions so as to document their attitudes towards the EU. Finally, we will conclude by explaining the attitudes of the Italian parties in the light of the main theoretical arguments available in the literature.

The structure of the programmatic offer of the Italian parties

In this section, we analyse how the programmatic supply on EU issues was structured by the Italian parties in the period between 1989 and 2009. Certainly, this is a crucial period of time: European integration has not only experienced substantial intensification with decisive developments in deepening and widening the EU, but the Italian party system has also changed, through a deep trans-formation that marked the disappearance of the traditional parties born in the first half of the past century, and through the creation of a completely new party system. Hence, we start our analysis moving back to 1989, the year when the last European elections in the first republic took place. The years from 1994 on refer to the new party system of the so-called second republic, through the trans-itional period of the mid-1990s and up until the greater maturity achieved by the system in more recent years. Therefore, in this section, we will be able to docu-ment how the structure of the programmatic supply on the EU has changed over time, from the first to the second republic and within the new party system across fifteen years.

According to Budge (1994, 45), any process of policy change induced by parties coincides with their strategic choice to give more or less emphasis to political subjects and to programmatic positions. In order for a party preference to become a programmatic stance, it is necessary to have a reiterated political discourse on that preference. Through reiteration of programmatic positions, citizens become acquainted with the party preferences to which they cognitively and normatively adapt or, otherwise, react. In any case, the emphasis given to subjects and to programmatic positions is a key factor in the formation of popular legitimacy and in support for parties (Jacquot and Woll 2003). Follow-ing this line of reasoning, we start our analysis by investigating how widespread some EU issues are in the programmatic supply of the Italian parties. Informa-tion on the structure of contents will allow us to understand the weight of differ-ent dimensions in the formation of a contested space of EU issues. In Figure 5.1, we offer a representation of how the different dimensions figure in the

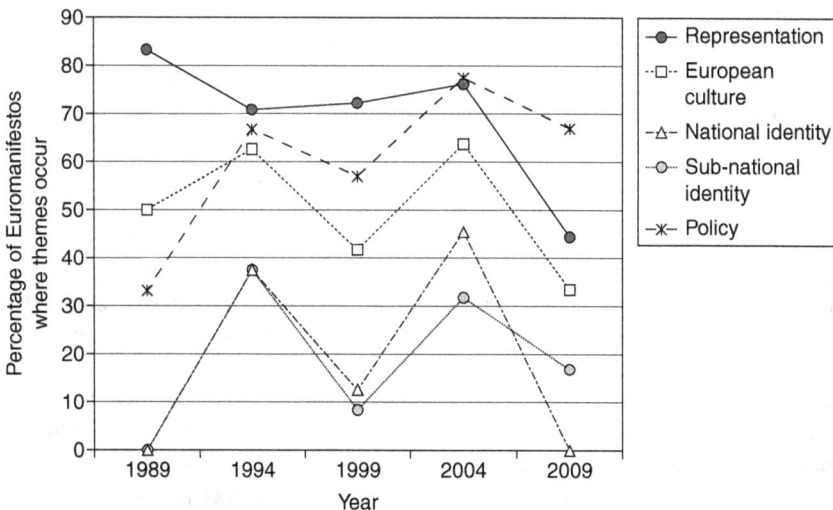

Figure 5.1 The content structure of Euromanifestos.

Euromanifestos. Many of the analysed themes are so specific that they only appear in small fractions of texts. However, it is our purpose and, more broadly, it is the goal of the INTUNE project, to document the most specific preferences of parties on the EU process. So, in this part of the analysis, we show whether or not the selected themes are present in the Euromanifestos, regardless of how many times they appear in the same document.

In order to reduce the wide range of indicators considered in the analysis (see Appendix to this volume), we built four indexes, respectively, for representation,[2] policy scope,[3] national[4] and sub-national[5] identity. We used only one indicator of European identity.[6] Trends show that, over time, several of the analysed issues (policies, but also national and sub-national identity) have become more recurrent in the party manifestos, although somewhat intermittently. Particularly, moving from a broad discourse on the EU, symbolised here by the dimension of representation, to more specific themes such as those concerning policies, party positions have become more informed and recurrent. Indeed, in the late 1980s, less attention was paid by parties to the specific problems (notably to *policies*) of the debate on a *closer Union* than in the following years. Certainly, many observers agree that, at the time, particularly in Italy, focus on the European field depended less on the party than on the initiative of various individuals such as prime ministers or ministers of foreign affairs. This resulted in an episodic presence of the Italian parties, particularly of the Christian Democrats, who led the government for almost fifty years, in matters of foreign policy in general, and in European affairs in particular. Their activism was mainly linked to the individual initiative of some of their officers within the executive, but, on the whole, it revealed a lack of strategy and policy initiative at the EEC level (Bull 1996), as well as a lack of attention to the EEC impact on domestic policies (this dimension is only salient in 33.3 per cent of the Euromanifestos of 1989, but it is salient in 77.4 per cent of those of 2009).

As Bull (1996) argued, in the first republic the Italian government was more characterised by *flawed* than by *genuine* Europeanism. In the most critical junctures of the integration process – such as the Single European Act and the Maastricht Treaty – Italian technocrats really became the main guarantors of country loyalty to the EEC/EU and, with their work, they filled the gap of the absence of a genuine European dimension in the programme of the national government (Dyson and Featherstone 1996). Furthermore, technocrats and other national opinion-leaders found the solution that they considered necessary to stop the distributive laxity of the Italian government in the European external constraint (Cotta and Isernia 1996). In other words, the choice to be 'saved by Europe' was mainly made by other actors rather than parties, and even against the abuse in public spending made by parties (Ferrera and Gualmini 1999). But over time, the political discourse of the Italian parties has become more rich and specific on European policies, a phenomenon that could be considered obvious given the deepening of the integration process, but, in reality, the fact is that it does not occur in the same way in all countries, as it is documented in this volume. So, although we could expect a greater salience of policy after the deepening of

European integration, the phenomenon is certainly substantial in the Italian case and it shows a clear pattern of change in the structure of the party programmatic offer.

Passing from the first to the second republic, another relevant change relates to identity issues. With the break-through in the early 1990s of a regionalist party – the *Lega Nord* – characterised by a radical stance in favour of local self-determination, the issue of sub-national identity has permeated in the Italian party system. Since then, although with some discontinuities, local identity has become one of the issues structuring the party discourse on the EU (it became salient in 37.5 per cent of Euromanifestos in 1994, Figure 5.1). The appearance of the sub-national layer of identity in the Italian political scene certainly marks an important phenomenon, one that has changed political discourse as well as the fabric of identity in the country (Rusconi 1993). But it is interesting to note that the theme of national identity also made its appearance after 1989. It is the result of an attempt of the new parties of the second republic to politicize national identity, after a long period of marginalisation by the parties of the first republic which associated reference to national identity with the fascist dictator-ship. Indeed, nationalism was perceived as a stigma by the anti-fascist party bloc that emerged after the Second World War from the ruins of the fascist regime, so with the only exception being that of the extreme right, it was virtually suppressed from the political discourse of the first republic. Finally, the salience of European identity is of great relevance. Figure 5.1 shows that it has always been a rather salient issue in the discourse of the Italian parties, one that overall exceeds any reference to the other layers of identity. This result could partially be due to the nature of the analysed documents: Euromanifestos may show a natural tendency to emphasise reference to this layer of identity. However, it should be noted that Italy is a country of diffuse Europhilia where, since the early days of the integration process, membership in the EU not only is perceived as an economic opportunity, but also as a choice for the West and for its system of values (Conti and Verzichelli 2005). Since the downfall of the Italian fascist regime during the Second World War, the rejection of nationalism and the subsequent identification with various supranational communities (the Euro-pean and Transatlantic communities for the Christian democrats, the Warsaw Pact and then a Third Force Europe for the left) became predominant in the country. This made the Italians very supportive of the idea of a supranational identity (Isernia 2008). Also in these years when national identity has become a more salient issue, European identity has not vanished in the programmatic supply. In fact, the opposite is true. As the three layers of identity show similar trends, an increase in the references to one layer does not occur at the expense of another layer. As was shown by Isernia (2005), the reason is that in Italy, the citizens who are more attached to the nation also tend to be more attached to Europe. Our analysis shows that the same holds true for parties as well: the greater the salience of national/local identity in the party system, the greater the salience of European identity. This is a different pattern from in other member states where, as we document in this volume, national and European identities are often represented as opposite faces of the identity dimension. In the following section we will more closely investigate how the three layers of identity correlate instead in the Italian case.

As Figure 5.1 shows, representation themes are less frequently referred to after 1989 (with a heavy decline in 2009). This is the broadest of our analysed dimensions. For this reason, it is largely the most recurrent one in the Euromanifestos of the first republic, where the broad Europhilia of the Italian parties was displayed along the following lines: membership was represented as a necessity for the country; the delegation of competences to the European institutions was broadly supported; an acquiescent conduct of the Italian government within the European arena was endorsed. The decrease in the salience of this dimension over time may denote the emergence of more critical attitudes: the principled pro-Europeanism displayed by the parties of the first republic in 1989 is slowly evolving into a more cautious approach. But the decrease could also reveal a specialisation of the discourse on the EU, from broad and principled to a more specific policy-oriented one (as shown by a remarkable increase of reference to policies). In the following section, we will explore whether the change in the structure of the political discourse on the EU really has developed together with the emergence of more critical stances on the integration process for which, as was discussed above, no evidence could be found in the final years of the first republic.

Finally, the analysis of the dimensionality of the party programmatic supply on the EU shows that since the beginning of the second republic in 1994, parties have expressed more specific positions on the EU. Although there are some discontinuities (and a relevant decline in 2009 that will be discussed later), they have made reference both to functional aspects (representation and policies) and symbolic ones (identity). Overall, the functional aspects are those that occur more systematically, while the reference to identity issues grows particularly in the transition from the first to the second republic. It shows that after the Maastricht Treaty, parties have defined their positions on Europe in a more precise and, at the same time, complex way. It should be added that the party system created in the second republic marks a total break with that of the first republic both in terms of format and mechanics, a discontinuity that is unique in the context of the old member states. The European arena has become a point of reference for the new parties to gain legitimacy. For example, these newly born parties made use of their affiliation to transnational party federations in order to gain legitimacy domestically as well as internationally. This is particularly true for the post-communists on the one hand and post-fascists and the personalistic party created by Berlusconi on the other hand who, after ideological realignment, affiliated respectively with the European Socialist Party and with the European People's Party. At the same time, after a consensus in the final years of the first republic, parties have made the European issue one for party competition. Hence, EU issues have become particularly salient during the 1990s. So far, the analysis does not inform us of the direction of the party positions, but only the multidimensional nature of the party stance on the EU. In the following section, we analyse in more depth the party stance on Europe. Moreover, we will show that parties take pro-European but also Eurosceptic positions, making Europe a relatively contested issue.

The party positions in 2004

Since the Italian party system was extremely fluid starting in the early 1990s and, as it was shown by other studies (Conti 2006, 2009), it was characterised by the creation of many new parties whose ideology and stance on the EU changed a great deal over time, in this and in the following sections we concentrate on the most recent EP elections, in order to depict a situation that is, at the same time, mature and the closest to the actual reality. However, in 2013 a new radical anti-EU party that did not contest any nationwide election before, the Five Star Movement, made a breach in the party system, but its medium- and long-term impact are difficult to assess at the time of writing. For this reason, in this and in the following section, we depict a scenario that actually reflects the pre-2013 Italian context.

Throughout the analysis we attempt to answer the following questions. Is the EU a relevant issue in the party programmatic supply of the Italian parties? Is it a contested issue? How do parties divide over such an issue? Has the content structure of the programmatic supply changed over time?

In this section, we make use of a principal component analysis (PCA) based on content analytic measurements of the Euromanifestos of 2004. The PCA allowed us to reduce the wide range of indicators considered here (and reported in the Appendix to this volume) into a more limited number of factors. Using the SPAD N software, we calculated the relationship among the two indexes of representation and policy scope and the three layers of identity presented in the previous section. The result was the reduction of so many variables into a bi-dimensional space with two factors that explain 66.4 per cent of the total variance. In the graphical representation (Figure 5.2), these two factors translate into two distinctive axes. The first factor (horizontal axis) explains 39 per cent of the total variance and the second factor (vertical axis) 27.4 per cent.[7] In Figure 5.2, the size of the arrows tells us how much they contribute to the definition of the axes. In particular, the longer arrows define the axis more than shorter arrows. Hence, those that define the horizontal axis more are national and European identity. It is interesting to note that these arrows follow the same direction, meaning that positive references to national identity are strongly correlated to positive references to European identity. Also, as it is shown by the more limited size of the arrow, they correlate, although less intensely, to positive references to the EU as an actor of representation. As already discussed in the previous section, and contrary to the widespread expectation that defence of national identity constitutes a challenge to the making of a European identity (Bartolini 2007, 212–222), Italy is a case where positive reference to national identity overlaps with support for European identity. Indeed, those who defend Italian identity also see Europe as the natural context where this identity can flourish. Under this

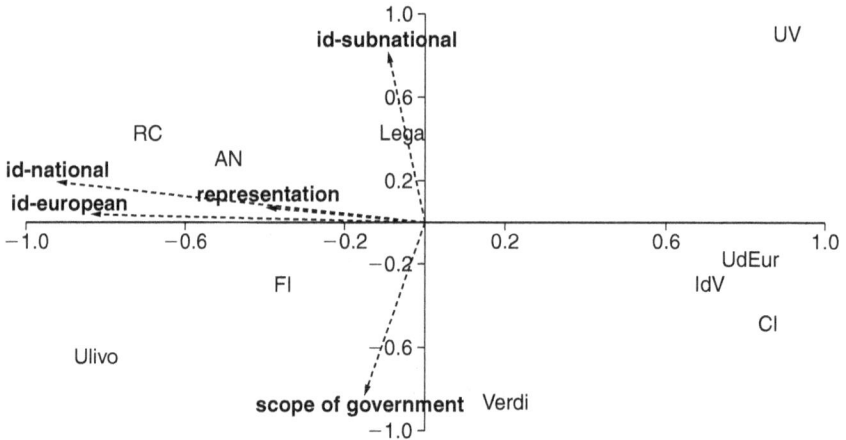

Figure 5.2 Italian parties in a bi-dimensional space (2004).

perspective, Italian identity is not seen as separate from the identity of the other member states. Even less often, it is seen in opposition to the other member states. Instead, the strong correlation between these two layers shows that Italian identity is often represented as one inner phenomenon of a broader European identity. As a consequence, it seems appropriate to label this horizontal axis the *Euro-national identity factor*.

The vertical axis is, instead, characterised by reference to sub-national identity and to policies. In this case, the relevant arrows move in opposite directions. It shows that supporters of local identity are also more negative about the EU as a policy-maker. Thus, our evidence shows that sub-national identity and the EU competence in policy are negatively correlated. It follows that the vertical axis expresses a conflict between localism and supranationalism, and for this reason we can label it the *supranational vs local factor*.

In Figure 5.2, the arrows mark distinctive spaces of attitudes along the two axes. When we charted parties in our bi-dimensional space, we found the following results: the two main forces of the Italian system, the *Ulivo*[8] and *Forza Italia*,[9] respectively a centre-left and a centre-right party, have different positions on the EU. The *Ulivo*, far ahead all other parties in these elections with 31.1 per cent of votes, is very high in the Euro-national axis, so it is a political force strongly characterised by a connection of national and European identity and by the support for the EU as a level of representation (although, as already said, representation characterises this axis less than identity). As to the vertical axis, the *Ulivo* is high in the policy pole but opposite to sub-national identity, hence it is a party that strongly supports European policies and the EU as a level of government, but not local identities. Ultimately, as the data and past research show (Conti 2006, 2009), this is the party that more intensely supports the EU process in its different dimensions (identity, representation, policy), thus it is the most Europhile party.

The other main political force of the Italian system, *Forza Italia* (FI), in 2004 the party of Prime Minister Berlusconi and second party in these elections with 21 per cent, instead shows more cautiousness towards the EU. First of all, it should be noted that in 2004, it was a deliberate decision of *Forza Italia* to present a Euromanifesto that is, for the most substantive part, the platform of the European People's Party (EPP). This is a rather unique case in the Italian system and very rare in Europe,[10] as parties tend instead to produce their own manifestos and make their stance more explicit than it would be in the platform of a transnational federation – by definition a lowest common denominator agreement among the different national components. Consequently, we can consider the positions expressed in this document as just an approximation of the positions of *Forza Italia*. The party is relatively supportive of the EU competence in policy and it shows a limited support for Euro-national identity. In the end, consistent with past analyses, whereas the centre-left confirms to be the most Europhile camp within the Italian party system and to have inherited the broad but omnipresent Europhilia of the Italian governments of the first republic, *Forza Italia* seems less influenced by the traditional pro-European roots of the Italian government. This party shows levels of support for the EU corresponding, at best, to the position of the EPP, a party that over time has shifted into more cautious attitudes after the accession of new members of non-Christian democratic and of more Eurosceptic ideology. *Forza Italia*'s assertion that it shares the same roots as the Christian democrat party family and, for this reason, has a right to be part of the EPP, has long been used as an argument to gain domestic and international legitimacy after its creation in 1994, especially after its alliance with more radical right-wing parties in the domestic scene. This has certainly contributed to the party's characterisation as a (conditional) supporter of the EU in general and of a Euro-national identity in particular. However, the centre-left more than *Forza Italia* seems to have inherited the solid pro-Europeanism of the Italian Christian democrats, who were also among the founders of the EEC/EU.

Although on the two opposite sides of the political spectrum, *Alleanza Nazionale* (right, AN, third force in these elections with 11.5 per cent) and *Rifondazione comunista* (extreme left, RC, 6.1 per cent) show some similarities when it comes to their position on the EU. Both parties are positively oriented in the Euro-national identity axis (although less than the *Ulivo*). They also express a relatively strong defence of sub-national identity and they oppose the EU in policy-making at the same time. Their stance on the EU is mostly rooted in an identity appeal. National identity is the layer that they endorse more, but in their view, the other two layers can co-exist with the national one. The identity appeal of these two parties is mainly addressed to mark a distance from more global phenomena –of an economic, political or cultural nature – which are perceived as a threat to the European peoples and to Europe at large. However, because they represent different ideologies, the cultural roots these parties want to defend within and throughout Europe clearly are of a different nature. *Alleanza Nazion-*

ale is a conservative party of nationalist (even post-fascist) origins. As for *Rifon-dazione comunista*, it is well known that in their opposition to globalisation and to European integration, communists often take a nationalist stance. Regardless of whether their platforms consist of a defence of traditional values (family, religion and the nation) or defence of social justice (the welfare state), they lead to the same result: a Euro-nationalist discourse based on the defence of national/European culture from external threats, defined as global economic forces, international finance, immigration or secularisation. At the same time, these parties voice firm criticisms against the policies of the EU, because they do not defend the national interests or because they are too restrictive and socially unresponsive, a stance that is confirmed by their position with respect to the vertical axis in Figure 5.2. Interestingly, these parties voice a particular kind of Euroscepticism that is policy-oriented, although they are pro-European in the identity dimension. Thus, our findings show that attitudes towards the EU can be multifaceted and that it is correct to define Euroscepticism as a continuum of stances (De Vries and Edwards 2009, 11) that cannot be locked into one static definition of categorical or typological nature. Although for different reasons these two parties tend to share similar positions in the bi-dimensional space that we present in Figure 5.2, their conduct on the EU is not identical. *Rifondazione comunista* is a radical party whose only time in government was in the period 2006–07. It is a party with an overall radical platform that has actively voiced its opposition to the EU on several occasions, for example, by voting in Parliament against the ratification of the Constitutional Treaty, the Nice Treaty and the Maastricht Treaty. This is not the case of *Alleanza Nazionale*, a conservative party often in government that has moved far from its radical neo-fascist ancestor of the first republic, and whose voting behaviour in the national parliament has always conformed with the mainstream conduct of ratification of the EU treaties.

As could easily be expected, the *Lega Nord* (5 per cent of votes), a regionalist party with a populist radical stance, is the one most associated with the defence of sub-national identity, but it is also the most opposed to the EU policies. While this is the most Eurosceptic party of the Italian system, once in government it tends to adopt a pragmatic strategy more than an effective anti-system tactic (Albertazzi and McDonnell 2005).[11] It tends to take a more moderate stance on the EU as well, so the *Lega Nord* has never proved to be a serious threat to Italian membership in the EU. The party played the double role of EU opponent in its rhetoric addressed to the electorate and of acquiescent legislator within the institutions (Conti and De Giorgi 2011). The Eurosceptic rhetoric that was voiced by the party in 2004 consisted of opposition to the European system of governance in the vertical axis, requests for re-nationalisation of powers in the EU and no support (it is close to the zero point) in the Euro-national identity axis. For instance, surprisingly for a regionalist party, in their Euromanifesto of 2004 they wrote that 'politics should be back in the hands of the people' and for this reason 'national parliaments and assemblies should be able to fully ensure the European Union's acknowledgement of national sovereignty' and 'oppose the adoption of bills and regulations that, even incidentally, could violate the principles and values expressed in the national constitutions' (4). As to the EU policies, they firmly criticised the building-block policies of the EU:

> The Euro, the uncontrolled opening of the markets ... the abolition of duties, the lack of control of borders ... the inadequate protection of the typical products as well as of the intellectual property, the enlargement to East, the stubborn restrictive interpretation of the Stability and Growth Pact, the rules on state financial aids to enterprise that are much too restrictive, the over-regulation: these are the main causes of the disaster that the European Union has caused to the enterprise in the territories of *Padania*,[12] many of which are obliged to dismantle.
>
> (11)

In the end, although it is a regionalist party, the *Lega Nord* has a clear populist radical right character with respect to the EU.

Finally, a considerable number of parties do not characterise their Euromani-festos by the analysed dimensions. In other words, they do not express any stance on the analysed themes. These are, however, minor parties whose ideo-logy is often not very articulated and whose programmatic stance is minimal. So, it should not come as a surprise that they fail to produce a programmatic supply as developed as those of the larger parties. For example, a small Christian demo-cratic party (UDC) that was in government in 2004 certainly shares broad support for the EU that is typical of this party family. However, as shown by another study (Conti 2009), it is a minor party of limited programmatic purpose-fulness – particularly with reference to the EU – that did not produce a proper Euromanifesto that we could analyse. Other minor parties such as the Greens (*Verdi*) characterise only for one dimension of pro-Europeanism, namely support for EU policy competences, and hence for the empowerment of the EU in the multilevel system of governance (vertical axis). The *Partito repubblicano* shows moderate support for the EU in Euro-national identity axis, as well as for EU policy competence in the local vs supranational axis. Finally, three other small parties (*Italia dei Valori* [IDV], UDEUR, *Comunisti italiani* [CI]) show a mild support for EU policy competence, but they have no stance in identity or repres-entation issues, so they fluctuate in rather undetermined positions opposite to the relevant arrows, just as ambiguously as their lack of pronouncements. It is rather surprising to find a communist party (*Comunisti italiani*) within this group of mild Euro-supporters, but we see a similar tendency in some other countries ana-lysed in this volume as well. It is the sign of a slow and uneven realignment of the radical left on EU issues. The tiny ethno-regionalist party *Union Valdotaine* (UV) is very supportive of sub-national identity but not of EU policies or of Euro-national identity that is absent from its Euromanifesto. However, any ana-lysis of the attitudes of these parties could be of little use as, with the only excep-tion being that of *Italia dei Valori*, these parties are very small and have now disappeared from the Italian parliament as well as from the EP, consequent to their failure to reach the 4 per cent threshold that is now applied to both elections.[13]

To conclude, the Italian party system shows a structure of positions and preferences on the EU that is rich in diversity. The EU could easily become an issue for highly intensive competition among parties if only it was as salient in the public debate as it is in the Euromanifestos. The main division is indeed the one opposing a Europhile centre-left to a more cautious centre-right. Moving towards the extremes, in 2004 the *Lega Nord* was the most Eurosceptic party of the Italian system, while *Rifondazione comunista* was only partially Eurosceptic and about to the same extent as other political forces of much less radical stances, such as *Alleanza Nazionale*. We have also seen that another communist party of even smaller size, *Comunisti italiani*, does not even qualify as Eurosceptic in 2004. So, Euroscepticism characterises the radical right (*Lega Nord*) more than the radical left.

The party positions in 2009

In 2009, we find some similarities as well as some differences compared to 2004. First of all, in Figure 5.1 we noticed a massive decrease in the salience of all the analysed dimensions. In 2009 the EP elections took place on the same day as the local elections. This was not new, as in the past the local and the EP elections have overlapped in Italy. However, this time the electoral contest for the local government gained much greater visibility than that for the EP. Indeed, turnout was greater for the municipal (76.7 per cent) and province (69.2 per cent) than for the EP elections (65 per cent).[14] Additionally, the contents of the electoral campaign were literally monopolised by the sexual scandals involving Prime Minister Berlusconi that had just been revealed.

The quality and quantity of the documents influence the results of our analysis, as the depth of the programmatic statements often depends on the length of the documents. So, since in 2009 the focus of the electoral campaign concentrated almost exclusively on national and local issues and the Euromanifestos were much shorter in content, reference to our analysed themes was consequently vaguer. In particular, it was difficult to analyse the attitudes of those parties that did not make reference to the examined issues, as the information was simply lacking in these cases. As we will see, this problem also affected some major parties more than in 2004.

Applying the PCA to the Euromanifestos of 2009, the bi-dimensional space that has emerged shows the following structure: the horizontal axis explains 59.4 per cent of the total variance and the vertical axis 26.8 per cent (Figure 5.3).[15] Interestingly, national identity has disappeared from the programmatic platforms of 2009. For a long time, in Italy (as well as in the other South European member states, see Conti *et al.* 2010) the political discourse has represented Europe as a national goal, in order to anchor the nation to the highest standards of civilisation, democracy, social harmony and economic stability, but this kind of discourse was lacking in 2009. This is a sign of the times: Italy has achieved the

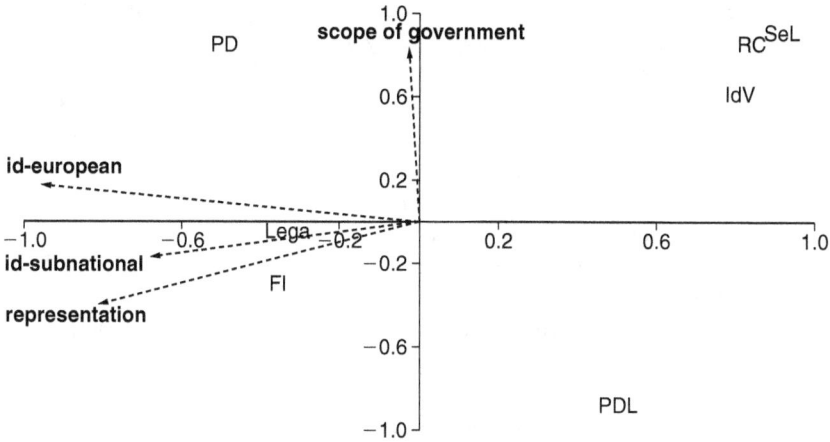

Figure 5.3 Italian parties in a bi-dimensional space (2009).

major goals of joining the euro since its first stage and until 2009 to avoid the financial turbulence involving the other South European member states; moreover it has avoided a national implosion in spite of the centrifugal pressures of the secessionist *Lega Nord*. As a consequence, the representation of a nation in danger and being saved by Europe has become less recurrent over time. In terms of identity, only the European and the sub-national layers were salient in 2009. Differently from 2004, these two identity layers, together with representation, now characterise the horizontal axis. As we will show below, this major change has been influenced, most of all, by a new stance taken by the *Lega Nord*. The vertical axis is instead characterised by policy.

When we charted parties in the bi-dimensional space, we found that the two major political forces, the newly created centre-right *Popolo della libertà* (PDL, incumbent since 2008, 35.3 per cent of votes in these elections) and centre-left *Partito democratico* (PD, 26.1 per cent), took opposite positions. Actually, the PDL is located in the bottom-right area of the graph, the area of the most uncertain positions and lack of salience of Europe. As a matter of fact, the Euromanifesto of the PDL only partly referred to the EU and it was not characterised by any of our analysed themes (representation, policy, identity). So, one could say that the party shows attitudes that are implicitly negative or, following the analysis of Budge (1994) of the phenomenon of lack of salience, attitudes that are in favour of conservation of the status quo. It is interesting to note that if in 2004 *Alleanza Nazionale* showed a Euro-nationalist stance and *Forza Italia* embraced the stance of the European People's Party, in 2009 after they merged in the PDL they show only lack of salience. The reasons for such an undetermined attitude could be questioned. Certainly, this is largely due to the influence of *Forza Italia*, whose leader Silvio Berlusconi became the leader of the PDL too. *Forza*

Italia was a party increasingly characterised by a lack of programmatic dedication to the EU, consequent also to its uncertain ideological roots. This party originated outside the Christian democrat party family and some of its founding figures were rather Eurosceptic. Membership of the EEP was indeed a source of legitimacy for the party, especially in the mid-1990s when it made alliances with more radical parties (the post-fascist *Movimento Sociale Italiano*, the nationalist *Allenaza Nazionale* and the radical right regionalist *Lega Nord*). Maybe for this reason, *Forza Italia* did not take an open Eurosceptic stance and did not challenge the EU overtly, although relations were not always that harmonious.[16] Another explanation could also be found in the organisational nature of the PDL that so much mirrored *Forza Italia*, a highly personalistic party whose central and public offices were very much subject to the party founder Berlusconi (Paolucci 2007). Also the PDL is a party that delegates its main political choices and programmatic positions to the party leader, who every time decides without necessarily formalising them in a programmatic platform.

We have already seen that in 2004 *Forza Italia* did not issue its own Euromanifesto. In the same way, in 2009 the newly created *Popolo della Libertà* did not produce a real manifesto, but only a short list of priorities that only partially referred to the EU. To be more precise, the focus of this document was mainly on the following themes:

- the rebuilding of the *Abruzzi* region after a disastrous earthquake with partial use of EU funds;
- the involvement of the EU in the fight against illegal immigration;
- a broad sharing of the values and ideas of the EEP.

Otherwise, this list of priorities dealt with other subjects unrelated to the EU, such as pledges in favour of strengthening the cooperation between Italy, Russia and Libya and to over-pass – thanks to Italian mediation – the resistance of Turkey in the appointment of the Secretary General of NATO.

On the contrary, in 2009 the *Partito democratico* issued a proper Euromanifesto that was characterised by the highest standards of Europhilia of the whole Italian party system. Such a broad attitude was also visible in 2004 in the *Ulivo*, so it can be considered the sign of an established posture. Their programmatic platform was characterised in particular by the following contents:

- open support for the delegation of powers in many policy areas from the state to the EU, including those of the ex-Second and Third pillar and social policy;
- defence of the Lisbon Treaty;
- support for the reinforcement and direct legitimisation of EU institutions, particularly through the direct election of the President of the Commission.

Another peculiar feature of the programmatic supply of 2009 concerns the *Lega Nord* (10.2 per cent of votes). Contrary to 2004, this time the party issued only one manifesto for both EP and local elections. Actually, the contents of this document mostly refer to the domestic arena, so it was a more relevant platform for the local election contest. However, the few sections that were dedicated to the EU are quite assertive and rather distinctive from a normative point of view. In 2009, the opposition to the EU of the *Lega Nord* was mainly voiced through open opposition against:

- the democratic deficit of the EU;
- any delegation of power from the state to the EU;
- any project of constitution for Europe;
- enlargement to Turkey.

Beyond these themes, as it was easy to expect from a regionalist party, the *Lega Nord* supports a preservation and self-determination of local identities. However, its identity discourse becomes local-European. The European continent is represented as a meta-culture rooted in Christianity and apart from the other cultures. Over time, this reference to shared identity roots among the Europeans, based on the common heritage of Christian culture, has become a central point in the discourse of the party, one that is actually used to justify another theme on which the party exerts a sort of issue-ownership: a rejection of non-EU citizens (particularly Turks) considered as alien and enemies of the European civilization. Actually, xenophobia has become a main component of the party stance and electoral appeal, one that has acquired as much prominence as the original stance of this regionalist party, i.e. the self-determination of the North of the country from the rest of Italy. On the contrary, the party does not make explicit reference to our selected policies; this is a major difference compared to 2004 and a sign of the under-developed nature of the programmatic platform of this party (with reference to the EU). As for representation, the party takes a broad critical stance, but not one that is too radical. The *Lega Nord* expresses a preference for intergovermentalism, the Council as compared to the supranational institutions, and the defence of national interests in the EU. Moreover, it makes a negative evaluation of the effects deriving to Italy from EU membership. Overall, the party position is manifest with reference to the horizontal axis of the bi-dimensional space, where an interaction between the party (positive) stance on identity and (negative) posture on representation is at play, but it is close to the zero point in relation to the vertical axis.

Other smaller parties had a limited programmatic supply in 2009. For example, the Euromanifesto of *Italia dei Valori* (8 per cent of votes), a single-issue party led by the ex-judge Antonio di Pietro and specialised in the fight against public corruption, is a list of twelve priorities, most of which are in support of the EU-isation of justice and defence. However, the themes of the horizontal axis are lacking, so the position of this party in the bi-dimensional space clearly reveals its support for the EU in some policy areas, as well as a lack of salience in relation to the themes of the horizontal axis.

As in 2004, the UDC did not issue its own Euromanifesto in 2009, but only a list of priorities that highlight the main traditional values of this small Chistian democratic party, none of which directly referred to the EU. So, we did not analyse this document.

Finally, the communist and the green-alternative-libertarian left did not pass the threshold of 4 per cent necessary from 2009 in order to get seats in the EP. Contrary to 2004, *Rifondazione comunista* (this time in a joint list with the *Comunisti italiani*) and the newly created *Sinistra e Libertà* (SEL) favour a shared national–EU competence in all the policy sectors that we have analysed, but they do not make any reference to European or sub-national identity themes (they declare to be more interested in cosmopolitanism), or to representation themes (apart from broad criticisms to the democratic deficit and the under-representation of the most disadvantaged citizens within the EU system). As their positions in the bi-dimensional space show, in spite of their broad criticism against the current trajectory of the EU, radical left parties do not show a prin-cipled opposition to the EU, on the contrary they trust future developments of EU policy.

In the end, the results of the analysis of 2009 show some points in common with 2004 and some differences. The centre-left (PD) has been confirmed as the most pro-European force of the Italian party system. The radical left, although increasingly irrelevant, show a level of conditional support for the EU that is remarkable and definitely higher than in other countries. The centre-right has become more ambivalent about the EU over time and definitely less enthusiastic than the centre-left. Finally, the Eurosceptic *Lega Nord* partly revised its posi-tions, by de-emphasising its critiques to the EU and, at the same time, embracing the concept of a European identity, although for instrumental use to challenge the non-Europeans, and although it still firmly defends national sovereignty vis-à-vis the EU.

Conclusion

In this chapter, we have analysed the stance on the EU of the Italian parties through the analysis of Euromanfestos. Trends of the salience of issues reveal a consolidation of a multidimensional stance over time. The discourse on the EU has become increasingly multifaceted and issue-specific. Certainly, we do not assume that at the time of European elections citizens are exposed to an equally multifaceted discourse on the EU. Conversely, they are actually submerged by domestic issues, as is typical of second-order national elections. However, parties definitely have different preferences concerning the EU that, coherently, they could make the object of party competition.

Party positions have been analysed through principal component analysis. It shows that parties select from the rich European menu (which is variously related to the polity, politics and policy dimensions) on the basis of principles and ideals, but also instrumentally by accommodation of the EU issues to their domestic agenda and institutional position. The overall structure of contents shown through PCA changes accordingly, as a result of the changes in contents of the individual parties. We showed that in the Italian case, positions on the EU converge or diverge across the different dimensions *between* as well as *within* parties. The Italian centre-left has proven to be pro-European across the different dimensions, while the centre-right fluctuates between supportive, critical positions or silence across the dimensions. The extremes, notoriously more inclined to Eurosceptical stances, are also split between fierce criticism, silence or even support across the different dimensions, so even their Euroscepticism is not absolute. Those parties that are more stable in their attitudes have a principled approach to the EU (centre-left), while the other parties that fluctuate have a more instrumental approach (centre-right, *Lega Nord*), or maybe they are in a process of ideological re-alignment (radical left) that might even bring them to embrace more Europhile attitudes as was the case in the past with the left (Gabel and Hix 2004). This happens regardless of the government/opposition status of parties, as those right parties that were in government in 2004 were also in government in 2009, and the same is true for left parties that were in the opposition.

Finally, in the Italian case, the lines of division that characterise party contestation over the EU issue tend to overlap with the main cleavages at work in the domestic scene and do not produce a separate dimension of conflict. On the one hand, we have a competition between centre-left and centre-right, and on the other hand we have a competition between moderate and radical parties. Contrary to what happens in other systems, where the European issue tends to cut across the party system and to destabilise consolidated cleavages (Aylott 2002; Hubè in this volume), in Italy, divisions over the EU issue tend to overlap with the main lines of conflict that also determine political competition on the domestic front.

In theoretical terms, many studies confirm that mainstream parties tend to share an underlying support for the EU (Hooghe *et al.* 2004; Gabel and Hix 2004). Then, it has been argued that the centre-left has become more pro-European over the years as they see in the EU an opportunity to regulate the market (Hix *et al.* 2007; Ladrech 2000; Ray 1999). Both arguments hold true in the Italian case. With the sole exception being that of some cautiousness of the centre-right that, in reality, does not truly oppose any alternative trajectory to the EU. Until 2009, the underlying support for the integration process was not under question in Italy. Another theoretical argument that found wide recognition in the literature concerns the hard Eurosceptical nature of parties at the flanks of the political spectrum (Szczerbiak and Taggart 2008). On one hand, in the Italian system, until the outbreak of the Five Star Movement, the more pronounced form of Euroscepticism was that of the *Lega Nord*, but it has become more indulgent over time. On the other hand, the Euroscepticism of the radical left is not absolute as it does not show in all the analysed dimensions and it even becomes residual over time. Overall, the Euroscepticism of these two parties is tangible but it is not principled and it is even declining. This might explain why they have not produced any redirection of policy when they have taken part in

Italian government and on EU issues they have instead accepted to converge to the mainstream conduct (Conti and De Giorgi 2011).

In the end, the Italian case seems to have overstepped the exceptional consensus on the EU that emerged in this country by the end of the 1980s, and has joined a pattern of competition on the EU that opposes a pro-European centre-left to a more suspicious centre-right and, less intensely than elsewhere, to sceptical radical parties. Over time, citizens have also become more Euro-sceptical. Under the impact of the economic crisis and the austerity measures, the campaign for the Italian general elections of 2013 was characterised by an unprecedented Euroscepticism on the side of centre-right and radical parties and by the success of the Five Star Movement (the first party in the country in 2013 general elections) that proposed the exit of Italy from the Euro-zone. It is to be seen whether this radical party will converge on mainstream conduct once in Parliament. Certainly, the lack of consensus on the EU trajectory and the mounting Euroscepticism that were documented in this chapter are emergent phenomena that could rapidly become very prominent in Italy, once a Europhile country.

Although the chapter is the result of a joint effort, Nicolò Conti is particularly responsible for sections 1 and 3 and Vincenzo Memoli for sections 3 and 4, the conclusion was written jointly.

Notes

1 As from 2008, the party is not represented in the Italian parliament anymore, therefore it has not participated in the ratification process of the Lisbon Treaty.
2 The Index aggregates the variables on membership, national action in Europe and EU decision-making (MEMBERSHIP, NATACT, EUDEC) that are reported in the Appendix to this volume.
3 The Index aggregates the variables on foreign policy, defence, social policy, justice, immigration and environmental policy (SCFORE, SGDEF, SGSOC, SGJHA, SGIMM, SGENV).
4 The Index aggregates the variables national identity and culture (IDNAT, NACULT).
5 The Index aggregates the variables sub-national identity and culture (IDSUB, SUBCULT).
6 The variable is European cultural belonging (EUCULT).
7 The Eigenvalues of the first and second factors are, respectively, 1.950 and 1.370.
8 This was an alliance of parties that later in 2007 merged as the largest part in the newly created *Partito Democratico*, now the main left-of-centre party and a member of the Group of the Progressive Alliance of Socialists and Democrats within the European Parliament.
9 In 2008 this party merged with *Alleanza Nazionale* to form the People of freedom party, an affiliate of the European People's Party.
10 In 2004, only seven parties of all member states made use of the Euromanifesto of the transnational party federation. Among them, *Forza Italia* is the most relevant one in terms of size (Bressanelli 2009).
11 For instance, the party voted in favour of the ratification of the Lisbon Treaty while in government in 2008, although the party initially opposed the treaty and campaigned against it when it was in opposition.

12 It is the name given by the party to the North of Italy.
13 The *Union Valdotaine* has one Deputy and one Senator in the Italian Parliament.
14 The difference between turnout at local and EP elections was smaller on other occasions. For example, in 2004 turnout was 73.1 per cent in the EP elections, 78.8 per cent in the municipal and 75.5 per cent in the province elections. In 1999 it was 70.8 per cent in the EP elections, 77.2 per cent in the municipal and 73.3 per cent in the province elections. In 1994 it was 74.6 per cent in the EP elections and 79.4 per cent in the communal elections (data are from the Ministry of Interior and from the Cattaneo Institute; turnout in 1994 was calculated only for towns with more than 15,000 inhabitants and in 1999 only for towns that are also *capoluogo di provincia*).
15 The Eigenvalues of the first and second factors are, respectively, 2.377 and 1.073.
16 To make an example, since 2008 when he was Prime Minister, Berlusconi threatened to boycott the works of the EU by making use of its veto power any time that it was possible, if the Commission continued to criticize the policies of the Italian government, especially in the fields of immigration and freedom of information.

References

Albertazzi, D. and D. McDonnell (2005) 'The Lega Nord in the second Berlusconi government: In a league of its own', *West European Politics*, 28, 5: 952–972.
Aylott, N. (2002) 'Let's discuss this later: Party responses to Euro-division in Scandinavia', *Party Politics*, 8, 4: 441–461.
Bartolini, S. (2007) *Restructuring Europe*, Oxford: Oxford University Press.
Bressanelli, E. (2009) 'I Partiti Politici e le elezioni del Parlamento Europeo: un'Analisi Comparata dei Programmi nell'Europa Allargata', Paper presented at the Annual Conference of the Italian Political Science Association SISP, 17–19 September, available at www.sisp.it/files/papers/2009/edoardo-bressanelli-535.pdf.
Budge, I. (1994) 'A new spatial theory of party competition: Uncertainty, ideology and policy equilibria viewed comparatively and temporally', *British Journal of Political Science*, 24, 4: 443–467.
Bull, M. (1996) 'The Italian Christian Democrats', in J. Gaffney (ed.), *Political Parties and the European Union*, London, Routledge.
Conti, N. (2006) 'Party conflict over European integration in Italy: A new dimension of party competition?' *Journal of Southern Europe and the Balkans*, 8, 2: 217–233.
Conti, N. (2009) 'Tied hands? Italian political parties and Europe', *Modern Italy*, 14, 2: 167–182.
Conti, N. and E. De Giorgi (2011), 'L'Euroscetticismo a parole: Lega Nord e Rifondazione comunista, tra retorica e comportamento istituzionale', *Rivista Italiana di Scienza Politica*, 41, 2: 265–289.
Conti, N. and L. Verzichelli (2005) 'La Dimensione Europea del Discorso Politico: Un'Analisi Diacronica del Caso Italiano (1950–2001)', in M. Cotta, P. Isernia and L. Verzichelli (eds), *L'Europa in Italia*, Bologna: Il Mulino.
Conti, N., M. Cotta and P.T. de Almeida (eds) (2010) 'Citizenship, the EU and Domestic Elites', special issue of *South European Society and Politics*, 15, 1.
Cotta, M. and P. Isernia (1996) *Il Gigante dai Piedi d'Argilla*, Bologna: Il Mulino.
De Vries, C.E. and E.E. Edwards (2009) 'Taking Europe to its extremes: Extremist parties and public Euroscepticism', *Party Politics*, 15, 1: 5–28.
Dyson, K. and K. Featherstone (1996) 'Italy and EMU as a "Vincolo Esterno": Empowering the technocrats, transforming the state', *South European Society and Politics*, 1, 2: 272–299.

Ferrera, M. and E. Gualmini (1999) *Salvati dall'Europa*, Bologna: Il Mulino.

Gabel, M.J. and S. Hix (2004) 'Defining the EU political space: An empirical study of the European election manifestos, 1979–1999', in G. Marks and M. Steenbergen (eds), *European Integration and Political Conflict*, Cambridge: Cambridge University Press.

Hooghe, L., G. Marks and C. Wilson (2004) 'Does left/right structure party positions on European integration?' in G. Marks and M. Steenbergen (eds), *European Integration and Political Conflict*, Cambridge: Cambridge University Press.

Hix, S., A. Noury and G. Roland (2007) *Democratic Politics in the European Parliament*, New York: Cambridge University Press.

Isernia, P. (2005) 'L'Europa vista dagli italiani: vent'anni dopo', in M. Cotta, P. Isernia and L. Verzichelli (eds), *L'Europa in Italia*, Bologna: Il Mulino.

Isernia, P. (2008) 'Present at creation: Italian mass support for European integration', *European Journal of Political Research*, 47, 3: 383–410.

Jacquot, S. and Woll, C. (2003), 'Usage of European integration: Europeanisation from a sociological perspective', *European Integration Online Papers* (EIoP), 6, 7, available at http://eiop.or.at/eiop/texte/2003-012a.htm.

Ladrech, R. (2000) *Social Democracy and the Challenge of European Union*, London: Lynne Rienner.

Paolucci, C. (2007) 'Forza Italia', in L. Bardi, P. Ignazi and O. Massari (eds), *I Partiti Italiani*, Milan: Bocconi University Press.

Ray, L. (1999) 'Measuring party orientations towards European integration: Results from an expert survey', *European Journal of Political Research*, 36, 2: 283–306.

Rusconi, G.E. (1993) *Se cessiamo di essere una nazione*, Bologna: Il Mulino.

Sbragia, A. (2001) 'Italy pays for Europe: Political leaders, political choice and institutional adaptation', in M.G. Cowles, J. Caporaso and T. Risse (eds), *Transforming Europe: Europeanisation and Domestic Change*, Ithaca, NY: Cornell University Press.

Szczerbiak, A. and P. Taggart (eds) (2008) *Opposing Europe: The Comparative Party Politics of Euroscepticism*, Oxford: Oxford University Press, vol. I–II.

6   Spain

Rafael Vázquez-García, Santiago Delgado
Fernández and Aleksandra Sojka

A friend in need is a friend indeed.

Spanish proverb

Introduction

After Franco's death in 1975, the starting of a successful transition proved unmistakably the extended desire of a majority of Spaniards to rejoin the family of Western democratic nations, especially the increasingly successful European Community (EC) (Díez-Nicolás 2003, 119–120; Avilés 2004). While the Franco regime was isolationist, authoritarian and highly centralized, repressive of national minorities, the new Spain would be European, democratic and decentralized (Richards 1999). In this sense, the Spanish Constitution, approved in December 1978, reflects these aspirations and compromises.

> The democratization of Spain was a preparation for entry into Europe and, at the same time, the prospect of Europeanization was a powerful stimulus towards democracy. Most Spaniards at the time of Franco's death were very keen to reconnect with the rest of Europe and wished to put the past behind them.
>
> (Loughlin and Hanley 2006: 5)

Europeanism became the officially sanctioned national project, defended by the leading political figures of the transition period (Bassols 1995). Even before the accession, national political elites identified the national interest with European interests. As some historians and scholars have remarked, the newly created social democratic state was constructed in part around the notion of the myth of Europe, which epitomized everything that was modern (Farrell 2005, 215).

Entry into the EC in 1986 was supported by key sectors of Spanish society: the Army, the Church, the trade unions and especially by political parties. Thus, Spain's European vocation exerted a powerful unifying influence over political life. "Throughout the years since its accession to the European Union, Spain was both an ardent supporter of integration and a major beneficiary of its largesse, largely through the Structural and Cohesion Funds" (Farrell 2005, 215).

Regarding the positive and high consensus on the EU among citizens, percentages of support for the EU have been consistently higher than EU averages (Díez-Nicolás 2003; Ruiz 2007; Szmolka 2007; Ruiz and Egea de Haro, 2011). Some findings derived from the survey conducted by the *Centro de Investigaciones Sociológicas* in April and May 2009 confirm this expectation. There is a clear majority (54.3 per cent) who think that belonging to the EU has mainly benefited Spain, while 70.4 per cent hold very favourable, quite favourable or somewhat favourable attitudes towards the EU.

Spain has presented until now a comparative lack of debate within Spanish society on the question of European integration. However, and very probably because of the economic crisis and its dramatic effects, it is also evident that in the last three or four years Euro-critical attitudes towards different aspects of the integration project are becoming more frequent among citizens and parties. This type of criticism mainly refers to the EU's economic policies. In this sense, Spanish political parties seem to be adopting a new stance from 2009 onwards that is more focused on the defence of national interest, partly because of a still soft, but increasing, Euroscepticism among the population, the economic crisis and the climate of austerity.

Spanish political parties and Europe through Euromanifestos

The aim of the analysis is to present a description of the relationship of Spanish parties with the European integration project through the analysis of Euromanifestos. For this purpose, we have distinguished between the state-wide (PSOE, AP-PP, PCE-IU) and regionalist parties (CiU and PNV).

Taking the last election as an example, the agenda of issues for the Spanish 2009 elections to the European Parliament was to a great extent non-European. The lack of focus on European issues, the fragmentation of the issue agenda and the low saliency of the most prominent topics put forward by the political actors reinforce an image of the European elections as a true second-order event in the Spanish political system. Instead, parties and media focused on other issues, particularly those generating disagreement and polarised policy stances, and those where party competition did not focus on distinct policy positions but on images of credibility and competence in handling specific political problems (Casal Bértoa *et al.* 2010).

The non-European character of the issue agenda in Spain is a paradoxical consequence of a very high consensus on the virtues and benefits derived from belonging to the EU, and of a notable lack of differentiation regarding European stances on the supply side of the political spectrum. Europe is good, and everybody seems to agree on that. This consensus has a correlate on the supply side of the electoral dynamic. Without exception, all parties compete in the pro-European range of the spectrum. Moreover, the group of particularly pro-Europe parties located in this common space is quite diverse in terms of socio-economic and regional orientation. This shows that agreement on European issues clearly cuts across other axes of competition. In this group one can find green alternatives (IC-V), social-democrat national parties (PSOE), regionalist Catalan parties (ERC and CiU) and conservative parties (PP). However, within a context of underlying support, the defence of the national interests in the first place and the conception of Europe and the future of the EU in the second have also become (low intensity) issues (Vázquez 2012).

It is also important to note that Spain remains a country of geographical contrasts which overlap with nationalist/linguistic/cultural cleavages, specifically in the Basque Country and Catalonia. An important part of the population of both regions, at elite as well as mass level, considers themselves to be "stateless nations" and not simply part of the Spanish nation. Regionalist parties in Spain (mainly CiU, PNV and ERC) support two interconnected goals. On one hand, they look for more Europe in order to weaken the Spanish state. On the other hand, the development in Europe of a new model of nation-state of a smaller scale is supported with the aim of making Catalonia or the Basque Country independent.

The attitudes of national parties

The Spanish Socialist Worker's Party

The *Partido Socialista Obrero Español* (PSOE) (Spanish Socialist Worker's Party), as well as the rest of national democratic socialist organizations, supported the idea of European membership from the beginning, even during the exile period. The PSOE adopted very soon a positive vision of European integration derived from the historical experience of opposition to the Franco regime and linked to the idealism of Ortega y Gasset (Gillespie 1996, 160). The Spanish socialists have always kept a clear idea that the national interest of Spain and the European or EU's interest go hand in hand:

> the national interest has never been inconsistent with the European interest, not only because Europe forms a part of our project for this country, but also because we remain convinced that the further Europe progresses the better we will be able to defend our interests.

> (2009)

When referring to identity, the PSOE has always supported the idea of creating a European cultural dimension, strengthening cultural exchanges in order to build a genuine *Europe of the People*. EU identity is presented as diverse in cultural terms, but with unique values (something that should be reinforced). The Socialist Party has developed a strong pro-European identity, specially focused on elements such as peace, democracy and human rights defence. "European integration is a successful event without precedents in our history. Peace, democracy, prosperity and solidarity … great achievements in our common European trail" (2004). "Deeply rooted in our national constitution as traditional values, the EU also improves them: pluralism, no discrimination, tolerance, justice, solidarity and gender equality" (2004).

In the sphere of representation, the Spanish socialists maintain that the Council, formed by national government representatives, should have more respect for the supranational spirit of the European treaties, and consider that there is no opposition between the national and the European interests. Power sharing is a matter of particular relevance to PSOE, specially because "a debate on the principles underlying the mechanisms by which power is shared between the EU and the member States could spread to the issue of power sharing between regional and central government within Spain itself" (Closa 2001: 20). The party maintains the need for making community decisions easier and closer to citizens and, at the same time, respect the principle of subsidiarity that is also defined in article 5 of the Treaty of Lisbon,

> to ensure that decisions are taken as closely as possible to the citizen and that constant checks are made as to whether action at Community level is justified in the light of the possibilities available at national, regional or local level.
>
> (1999)

The democratic deficit in the EU is actually a concern for the Spanish socialists along all the Euromanifesto series. They affirm that more democracy is absolutely necessary in order to make the European project work. More democracy means more efficacy and efficiency, as well as more transparency and closeness to citizens in the policy-making.

> The roll-out of European citizenship and the extension of democracy must remain priority objectives of our party, as well as how to enrich the concept of citizenship that is a key component of cultural and democratic cohesion within the process of European integration.
>
> (2009)

"Socialists consider that the only way to improve the way towards a genuine European Union, as the Single European Act (SEA) established, is giving citizens and their representatives the opportunity to participate in policy-making processes" (2004). As is well known, the loss of sovereignty of national institutions has not produced an equivalent increase of responsiveness by European institutions, most notably by the Parliament. However, the PSOE positions are far from being in support of a renationalization of competences; on the contrary they maintain a preference for federalism and delegation of power. In the 2004 Euromanifesto a revealing statement appears: "Spain must strongly support the project of a political Union, becoming a real federation of states and citizens" (2004). Historically, the PSOE has always put forward some ambitious expectations from Europe. From 1982 to 1996, Gonzalez's policies were clearly pro-European, with more emphasis on economic modernization and social cohesion in Europe than on a federal construction and institutional change (Quintanilla 2001, 82–107). Overall, the PSOE Euromanifestos have always been focused on economic policy and foreign and security policy primarily. The dilemma of how to balance pressures of European economic liberalism and a more traditional social democratic emphasis on public investments in welfare and social cohesion was acute at the beginning. Indeed, Spanish socialists clearly support large EU involvement in social policy and an ambitious European Social Charter: "In fact, we are increasingly more concerned about the current period of globalisation: the only way to preserve our national singularities and the European social model consists in reinforcing the integration path" (2004); "The role of social actors – clearly defined by the European norms and laws – gives member states the chance to develop faster the field of social rights" (2004).

Another important chapter for the Socialists is cohesion policy. The PSOE emphasized it very clearly, particularly in 2004 and 2009, extending the principle of cohesion to all policies. Ideally, every policy should include reference to cohesion and help to less advanced member states (Closa 2009, 515):

> we need to take proactive action to transform the economy – through investments in key priorities – in order to secure a prosperous and sustainable future for everyone.... We can re-launch Europe's economy and create a fairer and safer society for all in a New Social Europe.
>
> (2009)

Beyond economic policy, European integration had a remarkable influence on the PSOE preferences in foreign and security policies. As Esther Barbé has outlined, "the common foreign policy (as well as European security/defence) was an important tool in the process of Europeanization initiated by the socialist government with all that it entailed" (1995, 119). In addition, the party proposed to bring justice and home affairs under the Community sphere of competence as well. After the 2004 socialist electoral victory, changes in the international choice of the Spanish government became evident in the field of transatlantic relations. The socialist government radically departed from the *Partido Popular* policies towards the US. The PSOE clearly re-established privileged relationships with other European countries, most notably France and Germany, and renewed support for the deepening of the European integration process. The party was also an enthusiastic defender of the integration of Western Balkans and Turkey into the EU. Finally, the PSOE attempted to develop Spain's relationship with its two traditional areas of influence, the Mediterranean and Latin America, through EU policy and most notably cooperation policy: "The EU is currently leading international cooperation worldwide, especially in geographic areas such as South America, the Mediterranean countries of North Africa and many other countries which have deposited their hopes in the EU values" (2004).

With respect to security policy, thanks to its efforts when in government to guarantee Spain's membership in the EU and in the Western defence system, could the PSOE transcend its historical international isolation. "With Spain's entry into the Western European Union in 1988, the PSOE had brought the country's security arrangements in line with EU norms, enabling Spain to participate fully in the framework of European security" (Kennedy 2006, 69). In the last years, the party has developed a discourse focused on EU-promoted pacifism and multilateralism: "the Common Foreign and Security Policy (CFSP) demands a set of accurate mechanisms and instruments, leading to create the elements to let the EU participate in peacekeeping operations abroad, always with the supervision of the United Nations" (2004).

> A new European progressive agenda is essential to enhance the EU's role as a partner for peace, security and development, for the sake of our own future development and security, as well as of solidarity with other countries and peoples.
>
> (2009)

The Popular Party

Alianza Popular (AP) (later *Partido Popular* – Popular Party) was the closest group to Franco's ideas after the dictator's death. Unlike PSOE and the rest of the main parties, the PP only partly shares the mythical belief in Europe that is the underlying theme of the Spanish scene. However, and despite its origins, over time the party assumed the defence of European integration and the inclusion of Spain into the European Economic and Monetary Union as a priority.

To be more precise, according to the PP Euromanifestos, the EU must remain a union of national states and not a federal construction. It is quite clear that among all Spanish parties, the PP shows the least favourable attitude to a federal model for Europe and has repeatedly and openly expressed distrust for a European "federation". The recovery of a more nationalist, but pragmatic, discourse since 1996 that concentrates on the defence of the national interest has been described as a part of a process of "normalisation" of the party (Torreblanca 2001). Particularly, the aim of the PP is not to reject the EU, but rather to increase the role of Spain by becoming more active in proposing specific public policies that meet Spanish interests: moreover, by giving Spain institutional representation in accordance with its size, a principle that might be put under question by the various enlargements.

> In so doing we must Hispanize Europe while we Europeanize Spain. We have made much progress in both endeavours since 1986. Today the European Union is much more responsive to Spanish interests than it was ten years ago. As the Popular Party leader, José María Aznar said, the best European policy is a good national policy. For the Popular Party, the constructive and responsible support for Spanish objectives cannot be reached without Europe.
>
> (1994)

The PP, which has been in power from 1996 to 2004, and again from 2011 to today, has strongly supported the Union on the basis of a pragmatic discourse.

Transfers of competence to transnational institutions should be limited to those fields that cannot be managed at the national level and that could reinforce member states if managed instead at the European level (Avilés 2004, 412). On the other hand, fears of European interference in national matters emerged within the party during the pre-accession period and resurfaced when AP became PP in 1989 under the new leadership of José María Aznar. As he stated "the design is that of a Europe formed by strong and stable national states.... the Europe that has arisen is not a post-national Europe, but a EU constituted by consolidated nation states" (Aznar 2004, 233).

However, the idea of Europe of Spanish conservatives is also one of a community with shared beliefs, characterized by the main principles of freedom and solidarity and Christian humanism.

> The PP, which is sharing the same inspiring principles of the European Community foundations, supports the idea of deepening the relationship between states and citizens. The EU construction is an original, flexible and dynamic form of integration, based on common institutions and public policies, in order to produce and guarantee more freedom, security and prosperity for every European person.
>
> (2004)

Regarding the representation dimension, the PP underlines the idea that the European Union is the sum of the entire set of national states with clearly recognized national rights for citizens (Rodríguez-Aguilera de Prat 2008, 94). In this sense, integration should not remove the role of states in what are currently national decisions, neither should it nullify the sense of state authority, because most public spending and political decisions should continue to lie in the hands of states. The PP Euromanifestos from 1987 to 2009 are those most favourable to an intergovernmental model for the EU. Member states should be given the last word in important decisions. As national governments should keep a decisive role in the European game, it was considered crucial by the party to struggle for a voting weight in the EU that would favour Spain. As in the case of the socialists, also the PP supports the idea of improving the quality of democracy in Europe. This can be done though improvement of the existing double legitimacy channel: the representation of the will of member states on the one hand and of citizens through their representatives in the European Parliament on the other hand.

> The main purpose will be trying to maintain the institutional equilibrium among the Council, the Commission and the European Parliament, and at the same time, to increase the role of Spain and its capability to be influential within the European institutions.
>
> (1999)

"[O]ne of the main objectives of the Spanish conservatives is to go beyond the democratic deficit and make European institutions more transparent and democratic" (2004).

In terms of preferences on public policies, there are not major differences between PP and PSOE. Both parties have developed an "uncritical commitment to the EU, the single market and economic and monetary union, while pledging to defend Spanish interests" (Loughlin and Hanley 2006, 42). Until 1993 the PP was mainly focused on the defence of national competence and an underlying opposition to political integration. Henceforth, its stance became more optimistic about European affairs and the important benefits deriving to Spain from the fact of being a Euro-zone country. By 1996, the goal of Spanish economic convergence for the purpose of monetary union served as a justification for cuts in public expenditure and budgetary austerity. Overall, a shared position with the PSOE on European affairs exists, although the PP emphasizes more the defence of Spanish interests, such as those in agricultural and fishery policies. In the last Euromanifesto of the PP (2009), we found as well a clear advance in the defence of a more social Europe (a prominent theme of PSOE). When dealing with foreign policy the supranational sphere is clearly preferred. Known for having a strong Atlanticist position, the Popular Party fostered stronger ties with the United States as well, in an effort to combine pro-Europeanism and Atlanticism, and in contrast with the much more cautious stance of the Spanish socialists towards the United States.

> There will be no possibility to generate a political union in Europe without a common foreign and security policy. For the rest of policies, and despite the possibility of coordinating and collaborating, the first option is always the responsibility of national governments to look for solutions.
>
> (1994)

For the PP, "the European Union could reach its final development just in case of designing an authentic common foreign and security policy, to be complemented by a shared defence policy led by the Western European Union" (2009).

The Communist Party of Spain

Similar to the Italian communists (see Conti and Memoli in this volume), the Spanish communists have defended the adhesion of Spain to the EEC since their VIII Congress in 1972. Even before Franco's death, the *Partido Comunista de España* (the PCE that later merged in a radical left alliance called *Izquierda Unida*) marked a distance from Moscow and was among the first of the European communist parties to develop the theory of "Euro-communism", an alternative path to the one of the Soviet world to promote communism within the framework of Western democracies.

Although critical of the economic and monetary union project, the party discovered soon that rejection of the European project would virtually mean electoral suicide. IU's strategy in opposing Maastricht in 1992 and the EU Constitution in 2005 should not be considered as principled Euroscepticism (Benedetto and Quaglia 2007, 493). Opposition to the Maastricht Treaty formed a part of IU's strategy, including the use of soft, economics-based Euroscepticism and it should be seen as a tactical ploy to distinguish the party from the PSOE, which was its nearest ideological rival (Benedetto and Quaglia 2007, 492). In principle, "the European Union is a strategic objective for the left ... the future of Spain is intrinsically linked to the economic and political integration inside the Union" (1994). This idea should be compatible with the existence of multiple nations, formed by different regions and cities, that is, a multicultural and multiple European identity.

> the Single Market should replace the traditional concept of citizenship, based on the official nationality, by a new one focused on the residence criterion. This will be contributing to offer new social and political rights to immigrant minorities, while respecting their national and cultural identity.
>
> (1989)

When analysing representation in the EU, the Council is criticized for being the main institution with legislative and executive power.

> Decisions are made without taking into account the EP positions, nor the interests of citizenship. Therefore, all the competences which have been transferred by each country to the EU are controlled by the Council, without real guarantee of democratic accountability.
>
> (1989)

Izquierda Unida supports the idea of a federal EU with a single voice in the international sphere. The Spanish leftists support indeed the Europeanization of a majority of public policies or, at least, they have a clear interest in sharing their management among different levels, with special attention at the local level that they consider closer to citizens and communities. In fact, most parts of their Euromanifestos refer to the necessity of bringing the European decisions closer to people.

> The European unification process has been built without taking into account national public opinions and citizens' real problems, so maintaining the so-called democratic deficit. This is something tremendously important and it means that the EU integration is not fully democratic.
>
> (1994)

For IU, it will be necessary to give a larger role to citizens to strengthen the democratic dimension of the European project. Particularly, the EP should increase its capabilities for political action:

> In order to create a political space for everyone who lives in Europe, the European Parliament should exercise a full right of legislative initiative. In addition, the EU must develop some mechanisms of direct popular

participation to the policy-making process, including referenda in the EU
and in the member states.

(2009)

Similarly to other leftist forces, *Izquierda Unida* demands that Europe should
become a peace promoter in the international scene and that its economies
should be more socially and ecologically sustainable, with inclusive employment
policy able to integrate new demands such as those stemming from migration
and demographic change. "Creating the European Social Space is a way towards
full employment and to improve its quality. The EU must defend a genuine
social employment policy with specific programmes and funds" (1989). IU supports the idea that credit must be redirected to the productive sectors of the
economy and to employment, social and environmental priorities. Corporate
social responsibility should imply that companies – especially major local
employers – listen to and work with their local partners to achieve harmony. IU
has adopted a much more critical position than PSOE and PP, defending the idea
that the Union needs to tax financial transactions and income in Europe and to
abolish tax havens and introduce taxation for speculative capital.

Regarding the Common Foreign and Security Policy, IU thinks that global
and regional crises, as well as developments within the EU, created new pressures for the EU's external activities. As a global actor, the EU should actively
be involved in many regions, in close cooperation with its partners but with
important degrees of independency from the United States and NATO. Unlike
most Spanish parties, IU thinks that military engagements with NATO should be
replaced with an alternative concept of security based on peace, dialogue and
international cooperation. "IU will claim in favour of a European multicultural
identity, based on solidarity and peace, and against the Atlantic hegemonic inten-
tions" (1994).

To articulate a pan-European defence of the European social model, which
is at the heart of a European identity. To free the European integration
process from "Euro-Atlanticism" and from President Bush's calls for "a
united Europe under an expanded NATO".

(1999)

It can be concluded that IU believes that the EU should be oriented towards construction of an integrated and independent economic and social space able to
promote Europe's own universalistic values against processes of globalization
and economic liberalization.

The attitudes of regionalist parties

Regionalist political parties have been supportive of European integration precisely because the EU threatens national sovereignty (Marks and Wilson 2000).
Furthermore, the EU may be a friendlier environment for sub-national groups

because the European Union is multicultural, with no single dominant or pan-European identity (Lynch 1996, 15). Although there are important differences among minority nationalist parties on EU issues, commitments to post-sovereignist conceptions of power sharing involving EU, state and sub-state authorities, many of those parties sustain common demands (Keating 2001, 72–83; Bourne 2008, 290). European integration implies a variety of changes that induce the emancipation of "nations without states" and the expansion of the main representatives of their demands, the ethno-regionalist parties.

CIU

Catalonian nationalists of *Convergència i Unió* (CiU) defend the Union as a whole, as well as its economic developments through the Economic and Monetary Union (EMU). In the same line as other regionalist and nationalist parties in Europe, CiU observes the process of European integration as positive, since the process is perceived as eroding the sovereignty of the member states and, in this way, to open new opportunities for the sub-national level of government. It has been said that Catalan demands for greater territorial autonomy are reinforced by the idea of a Europe that exists over and above the configuration of its states (Laitin 1997, 293). Indeed, an important component of the contemporary Catalanism is that of pro-Europeanism. The vision of a "Catalanised Spain" shared by the conservative Catalan party of the early twentieth century, *Lliga Regionalista*, was transformed during the Franco regime into that of a "Europeanized Catalonia". Catalonia has "acted as a bridge between Spain and Europe" (Dowling 2005, 109) and the pro-Europeanism of contemporary Catalanism echoes a long tradition in Catalanist discourse that sees Catalonia as an integrally European culture. "[T]he interest of Catalonia will be firmly defended in Europe, showing in this sense, that it is possible and necessary to put together the regionalist interests and the European goals" (1994). "We strongly support the recognition of the Catalan language as an official language of the EU. It will be the ninth language spoken in the EU ahead of other languages as Portuguese, Hungarian, Swedish, Bulgarian or Danish among others" (2009).

Thus, CiU has always been a strong supporter of European integration and the Catalan government, the *Generalitat*, has been at the vanguard of the European regionalist movement. Catalan identity is represented by the party as a collective sentiment, a vision of the world, a language, a culture, a lifestyle of a particular polity. Together with the people from the rest of the Catalan countries, the Catalan people have formed a culturally independent region in Western Europe. In the opinion of CiU, the Catalan identity benefits from the opening-up of Europe, becoming less local and more open to new forms of expression and recognition.

Our people must inevitably participate in the European construction, but without losing their cultural, linguistic and political identity. This is because we will defend in Europe the respect and even the promotion of our respective peculiar situations. In this sense, we'll be especially focused on the importance of our linguistic reality.

(1994)

Catalonia's status as a powerful region is considered to have been enhanced by the EU: the region has had its own embassy in Brussels since 2004 and directly lobbies the European Commission and the European Parliament, particularly to secure changes to the law that are beneficial to its cause and seeks regional funding from the EU budget. Such funds, worth billions of euros a year, are directly managed by the Catalan Parliament and government. CiU has demanded that Catalan ministers (*consellers*) are allowed to participate in the EU Council of Ministers meetings and won the right for Catalonian authorities to participate in some European Commission committees and, most importantly, to participate in the drawing up and revision of EU treaties. CiU also demands the right of direct access to the European Court of Justice in order to protect its own interests, but at present it needs the backing of the Spanish government to go to court. Catalan nationalists are also looking for Barcelona to become the headquarters of the EU's Union for the Mediterranean project, a regional bloc intended to improve links with the countries of North Africa.

When dealing with public policies, *Convergència i Unió* is in favour of the most advanced programme for European integration, including the single currency and a common foreign and security policy, but accompanies this with demands for a strict application of subsidiarity in policy-making. Therefore, CiU supports the idea of "shared sovereignty between the various levels of government in Europe, with equal respect for the language and identity of all the nations of the EU whether they enjoy the condition of statehood or not" (2004).

At the practical level, CiU has been very active in playing a role in EU policy-making, especially in those areas of competence of the regions such as the management of the European Social Fund and promotion of economic and social cohesion.

> In order to get a full economic, social and territorial cohesion inside the EU, it is absolutely necessary to reduce the inequalities and development differences among regions, nations and member states. Because of that, CiU has always considered the European Regional Development Fund (ERDF), the European Social Fund (ESF) and the Cohesion Fund as essential financial tools with the aim of developing an effective European Regional Policy.
>
> (2009)

PNV

The PNV's position is more radical, since the mainstream Basque nationalists consider the concepts of nationhood and the indivisibility of the Basque people to be fundamental and non-negotiable, together with their demands for sovereignty, self-determination and, finally, independence. Early Basque nationalism

was rooted in local particularism with a remarkable racist element rejecting outsiders of all sorts and especially Spaniards (Keating 2000, 35). A pro-European
discourse has had less resonance in the Basque Country than in Catalonia, since
there is a weaker historic basis here for it. However, the Basque Nationalist Party
(PNV) was converted to the cause of European integration thanks to its contacts
with Christian Democratic International and since 1949 has modified its independence policy to call for national autonomy within a federal Europe.

> We are Basque people, millenary people who want to be developed in a
> changing world, but keeping our basic roots. We conceive ourselves as a
> historical realty in evolution, able to adapt itself to different political con-
> texts, but integrated in a common and specific culture. Euskadi is, therefore,
> our nation and our culture, and the full sovereignty is the main and the last
> aim.
>
> (1999)

> It is absolutely imperative move forward a new demos, a *European demos*,
> through the construction of a European public sphere, where citizens will be
> allowed to freely discuss about common affairs that concern all the Euro-
> peans and generate a truly European identity.
>
> (2009)

The Basque Country, with its long tradition of participation from the outset of
the construction of Europe, has constantly worked to contribute to this European
"ideal". The identity construction should not be seen as a function of nation-
states only. Instead, nations and peoples of Europe beyond the state, such as the
Basque people, are main ingredients and should be considered as main actors
who can with their participation improve the democratic legitimacy of the Union.
The final objective is building a Federal Union of European Peoples based on
principles of equality, responsibility, justice and solidarity. "The European cultural identity cannot be understood as a homogeneous culture, but as a wide
culture space integrating a vast number of cultures. This diversity is the main
resource of richness in Europe" (1989). The PNV has long demanded direct
representation of the Basque government in the European Union and is indeed a
strong supporter of the subsidiarity principle within the EU. Precisely, direct
participation should involve the following processes: the early warning system
at a pre-legislative stage; subsidiarity control; participation to the Council of
Ministers; appeals to the European Court of Justice.

> The European Union must ensure the survival of this diversity in a natural
> way, without impositions, but also without enforced homologations. The
> development and application of the principle of subsidiarity to respect diver-
> sity, not only of the States, but also of all the people that make up Europe, is
> vital.
>
> (1999)

Once again, but not last, it is clearly proved that Europe is not the problem but the solution. It means that obstacles towards the direct participation of Euskadi in the European processes are coming from Madrid and not from Brussels.

(2009)

The Spanish government has not supported the capability of autonomous regions in Spain to defend their own competences in the Court of Justice of the EU. At the same time, it has neglected the possibility to establish relationship procedures between the regional parliaments of Spain and the European Parliament.

(1999)

For PNV, in order to obtain a minimum level of efficiency in common action within the EU, the principle of unanimity and the veto power of member states should be abandoned. At the same time, the active involvement in European decisions of other bodies than the *strictu sensu* state organizations – such as regions – should be a key factor to allow the EU to move forward and its construction be legitimized. Many policies should be integrated at the European level and the competence of both the EU and regions increased, particularly in the fields of welfare, sustainable development, energy, immigration policy, R& D investment, joint security and defence. "The regions should play an increasingly important role and mechanisms should be put in place from a community level to support the rights of the regions to act in European decisions within the sphere of their competence" (2004).

The creation of a European identity may and should become a central element in its external projection. European foreign policy will hardly be able to achieve a minimum significance, thereby enabling Europe's voice to be heard in the world, unless there is a common identity for all Europeans.

(1999)

Conclusions

After centuries of isolationism Spain finally accepted European integration as a great chance to develop democracy and liberal economy. The transition to democracy in Spain was based on an unwritten agreement which included, among other matters, a tacit consensus regarding accession to the EU. For a variety of reasons virtually all Spanish political parties openly accepted accession so a European *cleavage* or deep inter-party divergence have not really emerged as in other countries.

Thus, there is a quite homogeneous attitude towards most European issues within the Spanish party system. Minor differentiations of low intensity can be explained through the working of domestic cleavages and the need of parties to qualify their stance and demarcate from each other, such as the traditional left–right cleavage (opposing PSOE to PP) or radical mainstream (opposing IU to PSOE and PP) and centre-periphery (with PP confronting regionalist parties as CiU, PNV). Thus, while the PSOE has developed more engaged and unconditional pro-EU values, the PP maintained some suspicions at least until the mid-1990s, and now is a convinced but more conditional supporter of the EU that pays greater attention to safeguarding national sovereignty. The communists of IU have been quite critical about the free market and the lack of democratic legitimacy in the decision-making process of the EU. Finally, regionalist CiU and PNV have seen Europe as an opportunity to hollow-out the nation-state and obtain recognition as nations of a united Europe.

Finally, the Spanish party system as a whole, and individual parties in particular, have expressed a high level of pro-Europeanism, due in part to the fact that they perceive Europe as a guarantee for democracy and economic development. At the same time, although the EU issue is not one of intense political contestation, and therefore it is not very salient for party competition, to some extent, the historical cleavages of the Spanish party system still affect the party stance on the EU. On the whole, the European issue has been absorbed by the Spanish party system without any particular disruption in a context of widespread party Europhilia.

References

Avilés, J. (2004) "España y la integración europea: partidos y opinión pública, 1977–2004", *Espacio, Tiempo y Forma*, 16: 409–423.

Aznar, J.M. (2004) *Ocho años de gobierno: Una Visión personal de España*, Barcelona: Planeta.

Barbé, E. (1995) "European political cooperation: the upgrading of Spanish foreign policy", in R. Gillespie, F. Rodrigo and J. Story (eds) *Democratic Spain: Reshaping External Relations in a Changing World*, London: Routledge.

Bassols, R. (1995) *España en la Unión Europea: Historia de la adhesión a la CEE*, Madrid: Política Exterior.

Benedetto, G. and L. Quaglia (2007) "The comparative politics of communist Euroscepticism in France, Italy and Spain", *Party Politics*, 13: 478–499.

Bourne, A. (2008) "Europe, constitutional debates and the Spanish state of autonomies", *Perspectives on European Politics and Society*, 9, 3: 283–300.

Casal Bértoa, F., M. Ferrín and S. Pardos-Prado (2010) "Spain", in Wojciech Gagatek (ed.) *The 2009 Elections to the European Parliament: Country Reports*, Florence: European University Institute.

Closa, C. (2001) "The domestic basis of Spanish European policy and the 2002 presidency", Groupement d'Études et de Recherches Notre Europe, Paper 16.

Closa, C. (2009) "Much ado about little: continuity and change in the European Union policy of the Spanish socialist government (2004–8)", *South European Society and Politics*, 14, 4: 503–518.

Diez-Nicolás, J. (2003) *Framing Europe: Attitudes to European Integration in Germany, Spain, and the United Kingdom*, Princeton, NJ: Princeton University Press.

Dowling, A. (2005) "Convergència i Unió, Catalonia and the new Catalanism", in S. Balfour (ed.) *The Politics of Contemporary Spain*, London: Routledge.

Farrell, M. (2005) "Spain in the new European Union", in S. Balfour (ed.) *The Politics of Contemporary Spain*, London: Routledge.

Gillespie, R. (1996) "The Spanish socialists", in J. Gaffney (ed.) *Political Parties and the European Union*, London: Routledge.

Keating, M. (2000) "The minority nations of Spain and European integration: a new framework for autonomy?" *Journal of Spanish Cultural Studies*, 1, 1: 29–42.

Keating, M. (2001) *Plurinational Democracy: Stateless Nations in a Post-Sovereign Era*, Oxford: Oxford University Press.

Kennedy, P. (2006) "The Spanish Socialist Party", in D. Hanley and J. Loughlin (eds) *Spanish Political Parties*, Cardiff: University of Wales Press.

Laitin, D. (1997) "The cultural identities of a European state", *Politics and Society*, 25 3: 277–302.

Loughlin, J. and D. Hanley (2006) "The emergence of the Spanish party system: historical background and contemporary realities", in D. Hanley and J. Loughlin (eds) *Spanish Political Parties*, Cardiff: Univesity of Wales Press.

Lynch, P. (1996) *Minority Nationalism and European Integration*, Cardiff: University of Wales Press.

Marks, G. and C. Wilson (2000) "The past in the present: a cleavage theory of party response to European integration", *British Journal of Political Science*, 30, 3: 433–459.

Quintanilla, M.A. (2001) *La integración europea y el sistema político español*, Madrid: Congreso de los Diputados.

Richards, A. (1999) "Spain: from isolation to integration", in R. Tiersky (ed.) *Europe Today: National Politics, European Integration and European Security*, Boulder, CO: Rowman & Littlefield.

Rodríguez-Aguilera de Prat, C. (2008) *Partidos políticos e integración europea*, Barcelona: Institut de Ciències Polítiques i Socials.

Ruiz, A.M. (2007) 'The European Identity of Spanish Citizens: Trends, Meanings and Consequences. A Quantitative Analysis', Working Paper Online Series, 72, Madrid, Universidad Autónoma de Madrid.

Ruiz, A.M. and Egea de Haro, A. (2011) "Spain: Euroscepticism in a pro-European country?" *South European Society and Politics*, 16, 1: 105–131.

Szmolka, I. (2007) *Veinte años de pertenencia de España a la Unión Europea: actitudes de los españoles ante el proceso de integración comunitaria*, Cuaderno Opiniones y Actitudes, 57, Madrid: Centro de Investigaciones Sociológicas.

Torreblanca, I. (2001) "La europeización de la política exterior española", in C. Closa (ed.) *La Europeización del sistema político español*, Madrid: Istmo.

Vázquez, R. (2012) "The Spanish party system and European integration: a consensual Europeanization", in E. Kulahci (ed.) *The Domestic Party Politics of Europeanisation*, London: ECPR Series.

7   Portugal

José Santana Pereira and
Edalina Rodrigues Sanches

Introduction

Portugal accessed the European Economic Community (EEC) in 1986, twelve years after the Revolution of the Carnations, which put an end to the authoritarian regime known as *Estado Novo* (New State). Portugal's integration was a result of an elite-based negotiation process that started immediately after the transition to democracy, and through which political elites sought to break with the dictatorial, isolationist and colonialist past (Pinto and Teixeira 2003). The first constitutional government of the democratic era (elected in 1976) defined a new foreign policy, based on European relations, and viewed European membership as means for democratic consolidation, but also as a condition for economic development and modernization (Pinto and Teixeira 2005; Teixeira 2012; Lobo 2007). Portugal's formal request for EEC membership was submitted in 1977 but conditioned by the community's decision of negotiating the Iberian countries' accession simultaneously. The double accession was not possible before the mid 1980s due to the political and economic turmoil that both Portugal and Spain experienced during this period. The Treaty of Accession was signed in Lisbon on 12 June 1985 and Portugal became a full member on 1 January 1986 (Teixeira 2012, 13–14).

After almost thirty years of membership, Portugal is nowadays one of the twelve most ancient European Union (EU) member-states in a community composed of twenty-eight countries, being also a member of the more restricted Euro-zone. In recent times, Portuguese scholars have shown a strong interest in the history and impact of the country's presence in the EEC/EU (e.g. Lobo 2003a, 2003b, 2007; Freire 2005a, 2005b; Jalali, 2005; Pinto and Teixeira 2005; Sanches and Santana Pereira 2010; Ruivo *et al.* 2012; Teixeira and Pinto 2012). One of the topics that received more attention from political scientists is the attitudes of citizens and political elites towards European integration.

For the average citizen, entry into the EEC/EU is generally seen as a good thing, an event that benefited the country. In fact, Eurobarometer survey results tend to display the Portuguese citizens as one of the most Euro-enthusiastic national groups. The levels of support are slightly decreasing since the 1990s, but the attitudes towards Europe were still largely positive in the 2000s (Lobo 2003b, 2007, 2011).

Portuguese accession was supported by the two main political parties – the Socialist Party[1] (PS) from the centre-left and the Social Democratic Party[2] (PSD) from the centre-right – and also by a minor party from the right – the Democratic and Social Centre-Popular Party[3] (CDS-PP). Only the Communist Party[4] (PCP) opposed the integration of Portugal in the EEC (Pinto and Teixeira 2005; Lobo 2007). Nowadays, PCP continues to be the least Euro-enthusiastic party in Portugal, while PS and PSD maintain an overall positive view of European integration. The CDS-PP went from being supportive of the EEC/EU to Euroscepticism in the early 1990s, joining the Communists in their opposition to the Maastricht Treaty. However, the party reassumed its initial stance on Europe in the last decade (Lobo 2003a; Freire 2005b). Lastly, the new player Left Block[5] (BE) has tended to demonstrate a diffuse Eurosceptical position since 1999.

In sum, taken as a whole, the positions of the Portuguese parties seem to be consistent with an inverted U-shape relationship between the position of parties in the left/right dimension and their support of the European Union (Hooghe *et al.* 2002). In other words, mainstream parties are more supportive of European integration than extreme parties. On the one hand, parties placed closer to the extreme left or extreme right of the ideological spectrum share a higher degree of Euroscepticism, but for different reasons. While left-wing parties seek to preserve the economic autonomy of the country, the right-wing scepticism of CDS-PP in the 1990s is based on national identity and sovereignty issues (Lobo 2007). On the other hand, parties placed closer to the centre of the political arena – in this case PSD and PS – are generally more supportive of European integration. Those parties perceive EEC/EU membership as beneficial for the country, since it is believed to have had a positive impact both for democratic consolidation and economic development (Pinto and Teixeira 2005; Lobo 2007).

Yet, our analysis of Portuguese Euromanifestos produced between 1987 and 2004 (Sanches and Santana Pereira 2010) revealed other interesting patterns within this general rule. We focused on three party-level variables – left–right divide, government/opposition status and ideological polarization – to explain variation in party attitudes towards the EU. Our expectations, derived mainly from Hooghe *et al.* (2002) and Sitter (2001) were, generally speaking, proven to be correct in the analysis of the Portuguese landscape of party attitudes on Europe. As expected, mainstream parties held more positive views on the outcomes of EEC/EU membership than more extreme parties; moreover, the ideological extremity was more important to explain differences in terms of attitudes towards Europe than left–right placement. Left-wing and right-wing parties do not have significantly different views on the modes of decision-making or opinions about which role Portugal should adopt in the European Union, but the ideological divide was important in terms of more general attitudes towards Europe. However, besides ideological extremity, the situation of a party at the time of the European election helped explain its positions on Europe, since, for instance, incumbent parties have a more positive account of Portugal's inclusion in the EU (Sanches and Santana Pereira 2010). In other words, context matters.

This chapter aims to contribute to the understanding of the parties' stances on Europe by introducing time as a relevant factor. We wish to analyse the dynamics behind the attitudes of Portuguese political parties towards EU integration with a longitudinal perspective. The main goal is to understand whether general attitudes towards identity, representation and policy scope of governance,[6] three central domains of European integration, vary according to the different phases of Portugal's membership in the EEC/EU and the political and economic panorama. We also want to see whether ideology, status (government/opposition) and ideological polarization have different impacts on the parties' attitudes towards the EEC/EU in distinct national and European contexts.

The analysis reported in this chapter includes recent data on the 2009 Euromanifestos' content. We have a particular interest in the analysis of these programmes, since they are not only the most recent documents of the kind, but also because they were produced in a particular moment of the country's political and financial cycle. On the one hand, the European elections of 2009 were the first of three elections scheduled in that year, opening a rather competitive electoral cycle. After three years without national elections, the Portuguese voters were asked to elect their representatives at the European Parliament (June), a new legislature (September) and their local administrators (October). On the other hand, 2009 is significant due to the fact that the first strong symptoms of a deep economic crisis were being felt (Santana Pereira 2010; Freire and Santana Pereira 2011).

Drawing on the INTUNE Euromanifestos dataset for Portugal,[7] our analysis covers all European Parliament (EP) elections that took place in this country (1987, 1989, 1994, 1999, 2004 and 2009) and includes the political parties who managed to gain parliamentary representation at the EU level.[8] For the purpose of our analysis, the manifestos were clustered in three slots: 1986–1991 (including the programmes of 1987 and 1989), 1992–2000 (including the programmes of 1994 and 1999) and 2001–2009 (including the programmes of 2004 and 2009). With this division, we aim at testing the hypothesis that the general attitudes towards the EU, as displayed in parties' Euromanifestos, reflect the different phases of the EU integration process and national political competition.

In Portugal, the period between 1987 and the late 1990s is usually regarded as a golden era characterized by "economic growth, rising incomes and social change in an optimistic atmosphere of modernization" (Ruivo *et al.* 2012, 35). However, in terms of developments in European integration, it is possible to draw a line dividing the years before the Treaty of Maastricht was signed, and the years from 1992 to the establishment of the single currency. We expect that, after a general panorama of optimism in the first years of integration, general enthusiasm will decay, with government and mainstream parties displaying optimistic views in their manifestos, while more polarized political parties will have more Eurosceptical positions.

The third period ranges from 2000 to 2009. At the EU level, this period is marked by several facts: the introduction of the single currency, the signature of the Nice Treaty, the eastern enlargement, the institutional crisis opened by the rejection of the Constitutional Treaty and the signature of the Lisbon Treaty under the Portuguese Presidency. At the national level it is marked by changes in the patterns of competition among political parties (as ideological polarization increased after the emergence of the BE), political instability (with three governments falling before completing the full mandate) and an international financial crisis from 2008 onwards. In this period, we expect that the parties' general attitudes will be less enthusiastic about the EU project, and this should be particularly true for those in the opposition. Therefore, ideological polarization of parties is expected to be more relevant in the first years of Portuguese membership in the EEC/EU than in the subsequent years.

The structure of this chapter is as follows. First, we describe the Portuguese context, presenting the major political parties, and discussing the European election results in Portugal. Following this, we present the results of the Euromanifesto content analysis, trying to establish a connection between the content of the programmes, the political parties' characteristics and the political/economic context in the country.

Portuguese parties and European elections

The parties

In Portugal, the political sphere is dominated by six parties: the centre-left PS, the centre-right PSD, the left-wing PCP and PEV[9] (which have formed an electoral coalition since the mid 1980s), the new left BE and the right-wing CDS-PP. These political actors present not only distinct ideologies, but also different electoral and legislative strengths; in addition, their strengths varied substantially over the last three decades. For instance, between 1987 and 2005 Portugal had a two-party system, with PSD and PS as the main parties. The average number of parliamentary parties (ENPP) during this period is 2.6, while in the previous period (1975–1985) parliaments were far more fragmented (average ENPP = 3.6) due to the political instability and ideological polarization experienced in the first years after the democratic transition.

In addition, the levels of fragmentation verified between 2009 and 2011 are higher than in the previous period, this being mainly due to short-term factors such as the economic retreat and the successful campaign strategies of more polarized parties, namely the CDS-PP, which is now trying to capture the centre-right electorate.

Now let us focus on the history and nature of each one of these parties in more detail, starting with the centre-left Socialist Party. Despite its name, the PS is not a traditional socialist party, but it is actually closer to the ideal-type of a social democratic party. It was created in 1973, just one year before the Revolution of the Carnations. From 1976 onwards, the PS ruled the country for about eighteen years – approximately half the duration of the Portuguese Third Republic. In 1976–1979 and 1983–1985, this party formed post-election coalitions with the right-wing parties CDS-PP and PSD (essentially due to the anti-system attitude of the second most relevant left-wing party at the time – the PCP; see Lobo 2007), but between 1995–2002 and 2005–2011, the PS governed alone. However, on both occasions the party was not able to conclude the mandates initiated in 1999 and 2009. In 2002, the prime minister resigned after a strong defeat at local elections, whereas in 2011 the head of government resigned after not being able to pass in parliament an austerity package to deal with the deep economic crisis affecting Portugal (Freire and Lobo 2002; Freire and Santana Pereira 2011; Freire 2012).

In turn, PSD is not a social democrat party, as its name would suggest, but instead a moderate right-wing liberal party. This party is the most important competitor of PS, and was in government for about twenty of the almost forty years of constitutional governments in Portugal (1979–1985, 1985–1995, 2002–2005, and 2011 to the present day). The PSD's natural coalition partner is CDS-PP (the second most important right-wing party, in terms of vote share). In fact, in the last decade the PSD was not able to replicate the astonishing electoral results that led to majoritarian governments in 1987 and 1991, and therefore had to form pre- or post-election coalitions with CDS-PP, renewing the alliance established between 1979 and 1983.

It is worth underlining that CDS-PP is actually a Christian democrat party, despite the fact that it includes the words 'centre' and 'social' in its name. In the mid 1990s, a new leader of the then-called CDS adopted the name *Partido Popular* (Popular Party) and the acronym CDS-PP, probably as a way of avoiding dissonance between the party name and its political agenda.[10]

The misleading names of these three political parties are a consequence of the pro-leftist bias that characterized the landscape in the 1970s. According to several studies (Lobo 1996; Jalali 2007; Stock 1985), this idiosyncratic feature reflects the nature of the Portuguese democratic transition, during which the political parties' choices, policies and ideologies were framed within the leftist space. In fact, this period was characterized by the radicalization of the political struggle due to the strong presence of parties and groups from the extreme left, as well as the dynamics of rupture with the authoritarian past (Bruneau 1997; Pinto 2006; Jalali 2007). The leftist bias was also accentuated because the right-wing parties (CDS-PP and PSD) founded in this revolutionary context did not openly assume the ideology that they really defended (Frain 1997).

On the left side of the political spectrum, we find PCP, the oldest political party in the Portuguese political landscape. The communist party was created in the 1920s and survived around fifty years of repression during the authoritarian regime. After the Revolution of 1974, the Communists were members of provisional governments, but since the Constitution of 1976 was passed, this party never reached the seat of power. Since 1987, PCP and the smaller green party PEV (founded in 1982) participate in national and European elections in a coalition named *Coligação Democrática Unitária* (CDU).[11]

The other relevant left-wing party is BE. It is a recent actor in the Portuguese arena, having been created in 1999 as a result of the fusion of three very small left-wing parties. BE is considered to be "new left" (in the sense that it adopts the agendas of social minorities that might not have space in the more morally conservative PCP).

The European elections

In the summer of 1987, more than one year after joining the EEC, the Portuguese citizens elected twenty-four representatives to the EP. Right from these first European elections, the majority of seats were disputed between the PS and the PSD. The social democrat PS won the European elections of 1994, 1999 and 2004, getting between 40 and 50 per cent of the seats at stake, whereas the PSD was the most voted party at the European elections in 1987, 1989 and 2009, winning around 40 per cent of the seats available for Portuguese representatives at the European Parliament.

The PSD formed a coalition with the CDS-PP for the 2004 EP election, mirroring the agreement between the two parties at the national level and trying to minimize damage resulting from their roles in government. However, as often happens to incumbent parties (Reif and Schmitt 1980; Schmitt 2005), these two parties had a disastrous result. In the same way, in 2009, in the most fragmented European election so far, the PSD won the largest share of seats, inflicting a very strong defeat to the incumbent PS. Nevertheless, incumbents were not always punished with a defeat in the European elections – in fact, in 1987, 1989 and 1999, the party in government was also the most voted for at the European election.

Both the CDS-PP and the Communist/Green coalition (CDU) never had more than four seats in the EP, and in the current Parliament their groups are composed of just two MEPs. The BE has been present at the EP only since 2004, having elected one representative in that election and three MEPs in 2009. In a way, this party capitalized on having assumed a very critical voice both towards the European project and the Portuguese government.

In terms of participation, the elections that took place in the 1980s were the ones where turnout was more expressive – 72 and 51 per cent, respectively. From 1994 onwards, however, abstention levels have been higher than 60 per cent, causing this to be a second-order type of election also in what concerns turnout.[12]

Attitudes towards Europe in Portuguese Euromanifestos

Party attitudes between 1986 and 1991: diffuse enthusiasm and specific pragmatism

In this section, we present the Portuguese parties' dominant views regarding representation, scope of governance and identity between 1986 and 1991, as expressed in the Euromanifestos of 1987 and 1989. In this period, it is possible to find a pattern of general enthusiasm and specific scepticism towards the European project – the elites tend to assess positively EEC membership and to propose a role of cooperation or leadership of Portugal within the EU, but at the same time are somewhat sceptical about giving up sovereignty in the decision-making process (Figure 7.1).

References to the impact that the EEC had on the country reflect a considerable degree of enthusiasm. In 1987 and 1989, 50 per cent of the manifestos mention that the EEC had mainly brought benefits to the country; interesting enough, all those manifestos were produced by right-wing parties. For instance, the PSD 1989 manifesto states:

> Three years after the accession, the "catastrophe" did not happen and the results achieved show clearly that we had no reason to fear … Portugal has left the tail of the Community countries … the Portuguese economy's development is faster than the community's average.[14]

In turn, the PS manifesto of 1989 includes a mixed assessment of the consequences of entry into the ECC, especially with regards to the Portuguese fisheries. This restrained enthusiasm expressed by a party that ruled the country at the moment of accession is probably due to the fact that in the late 1980s the PS was not in government and had a smaller number of MEPs vis-à-vis the incumbent PSD. Despite being a main supporter of the EU project, the PS decided to adopt a more moderate position while in opposition – a position that could give room for manoeuvre to challenge the incumbent PSD.

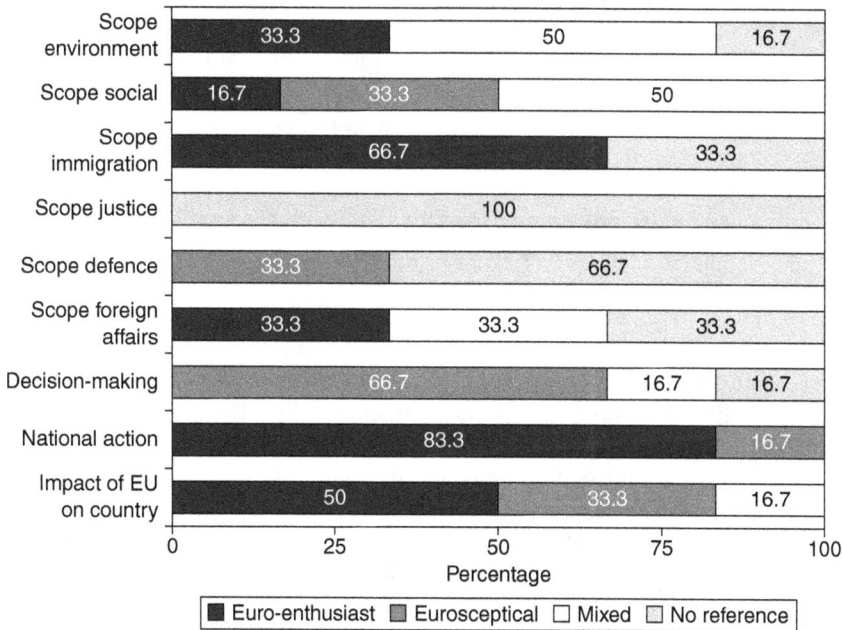

Figure 7.1 Party positions on representation and scope of governance, 1987/1989[13] (source: INTUNE Euromanifesto Dataset).

The PCP's perception of the accession consequences is completely different. Its two manifestos include a negative assessment of the Portuguese membership, exemplified by sentences such as "The central committee stresses the disastrous consequences that the EEC integration is having on the country: in the industries, in the agriculture, in the fisheries, in virtually every sector of the national economy" (1989 manifesto).

In these first years of European membership, a majority of manifestos displayed a preference for an active role for Portugal within the European framework (Figure 7.1). Half of the manifestos say that national action in Europe should be one of "cooperation/participation", whereas the PSD expresses a clear desire to influence and guide the European process. In fact, this is the only party that argues in favour of a leadership position for Portugal during this period. This makes sense if we consider that PSD's strategy for the first years of European integration, due to its status as incumbent party, was "focused on the credibility of full Portuguese membership, while at the same time seeking to profit from the economic and social advantages arising from EEC participation" (Teixeira 2012, 17). On the side of opposition parties, the PS and CDS-PP defended the paradigm of "cooperation/participation" in all manifestos, while the PCP expressed in 1989 the desire to cooperate and participate in the European decision-making process, abandoning momentarily the defensive posture towards Europe declared in 1987.

In what concerns the EEC decision-making process, the manifestos reflect some initial conservatism. During the first years, political parties predominantly prefer the national level (66.7 per cent of the manifestos). National preference is present not only in opposition and more extreme parties, such as PCP, but also in the programmes of the incumbent party – "The Community should not duplicate the functions exercised by the member states and that will not be transferred to the centre, as results from the principle of subsidiarity defined in the Treaties" (PSD 1989 manifesto).

In the late 1980s, positions about scope of governance are only identifiable within a minority of the manifestos under analysis. The favourite level of competence to handle each of the six policy fields in analysis clearly depends on the policy at stake, as Figure 7.1 shows, but the general panorama is (if one excludes immigration and the policy areas that were seldom mentioned) of preference towards mixed solutions. In the case of social and environmental policies, mixed solutions are the most frequently mentioned, whereas references to immigration usually favour supranational arrangements. In the cases of foreign policy and immigration, the incumbent PSD is keen on a supranational level of decision-making ("the European Communities shall, more and more, adopt a concerted foreign policy"; "definition of a European policy on Visa concession and immigration rights of foreign people coming from countries outside the Community"), but smaller parties prefer mixed strategies to deal with this issue. Defence policy is only mentioned by small parties (PCP and CDS-PP) defending an exclusively national level of decision-making regarding this issue.

Conversely, European identity has a very modest place within political parties' programmes during this period. References to European identity can be traced in only three out of six Euromanifestos under analysis. The PSD is the only party using this label consistently, presenting a positive view about the deepening of European identity, as this passage from early 1987 reveals: "We defend the construction of a Europe of citizens and not only of States." The left-wing parties (PS and PCP) did not mention this theme in their Euromanifestos at all.

In sum, in terms of representation and identity, in the late 1980s the manifestos from the right-wing parties PSD and CDS-PP are the most enthusiastic about the European project. Probably due to its opposition status, the PS mentioned both favourable opportunities and negative constraints that the EU created in the country, despite the fact that it called for more cooperation at the EU level and was open to mixed and supranational solutions for some policies. Fully fledged Euroscepticism is found only amongst the communist Euromanifestos. The PCP's stance is of open criticism towards the EU building-block policies, which are believed to have accentuated the peripheral status of the country, while promoting the interests of the main economic powers. Overall, the communists' Euroscepticism is quite strong, whereas the PS position is somewhat in between the open enthusiasm of the PSD and the anti-EEC posture expressed by the PCP. The attitudes found in the PCP Euromanifestos are rooted in the ideological basis of this party, whereas the restricted enthusiasm displayed in the 1989 PS manifesto is more contextual and due to its strategy as the main opposition party in the country.

Regarding scope of governance, the absence of expressed preferences in a considerable amount of the Euromanifestos does not allow us to track a specific pattern for each party or draw conclusions on the structuring effect of ideology, extremism and status.

Party attitudes towards the EU between 1992 and 2000: increased enthusiasm, but not for everyone

The period after Maastricht (1992–2000) is portrayed as being a moment of open Euro-enthusiasm and strong support for the EU project from government parties (Teixeira 2012), with the EP elections of 1994 and 1999 being particularly influenced by European issues, when compared to the previous elections (Lobo 2003a, 224). Moreover, Portugal has occupied the EU presidency on two occasions: 1992 and 2000 (Teixeira 2012, 7–18). This period was crucial in terms of EU integration, as several changes were underway. On the one hand, the Maastricht Treaty marked the beginning of Monetary Union in all the countries that managed to meet the economic requirements; on the other hand, there was a long debate about the institutional frame of the EU, which led to the signature of the Amsterdam Treaty in 1997. This period is also marked by the first signs of decay in terms of public opinion's support for the EU, which will be capitalized by the CDS-PP.

Looking at the eight Portuguese party manifestos from the 1990s, we see that the positions on Europe are not so different from those of the late 1980s. The major differences consist of intergovernmental decision-making being now a bit more popular than in the past, while the proposal of mixed solutions for governance in different policy areas is less recurrent (Figure 7.2).

It is interesting to note that, when running at the European elections as the major opposition party (1999), the PSD described the negative impacts of EU membership regarding the Common Agriculture Policy, making its Euro-enthusiasm more nuanced. At the same time, right before winning the legislative elections (1994) and already as an incumbent party (1999), the PS expressed its enthusiasm more strongly than in 1989, stressing the favourable opportunities brought by EEC/EU membership, defending cooperation with the EU and (in 1999) proposing a multilevel decision-making process:

> The European project must preserve the identity and the decision-making capacity of the member-States in areas that may be better dealt with at the national, regional and local levels. However, the Union must keep to itself the decisions about issues that cannot be tackled at levels that are closer to the populations.

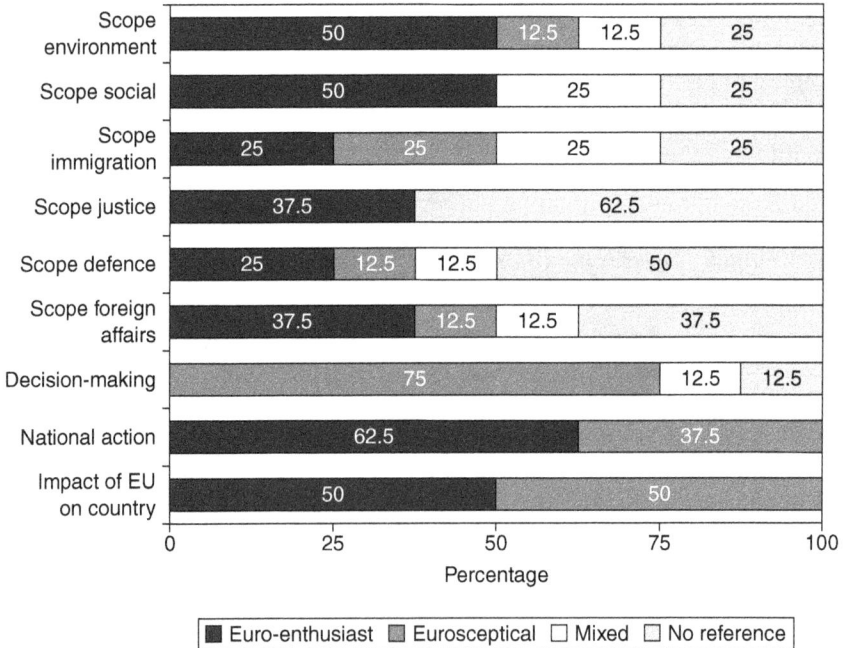

Figure 7.2 Party positions on representation and scope of governance, 1994/1999 (source: INTUNE Euromanifesto Dataset, Portuguese file).

The CDS-PP positions changed dramatically during this period. As noted earlier, CDS-PP was part of the group that supported EEC/EU membership (together with PSD and PS), but it became more critical and defensive as the EU process deepened. In the early 1990s, under the leadership of Manuel Monteiro, it refashioned itself as a Eurosceptic party and joined PCP's "chorus of criticisms" raising attention to the negative impacts of the Maastricht Treaty and EU policies in key national sectors, as this manifesto fragment illustrates – "In this environment of euphoria, entrepreneurs were not told that with the Accession to the Community, we would lose the right to autonomously defend our interests" (1994 manifesto).

This position was, nevertheless, more related to the CDS-PP position at the national level than with EU integration per se. After being elected, one of "Monteiro's goals was to prevent the end of the party, which in 1991 seemed like a distinct possibility" (Lobo 2003b, 109). The EU became a relevant issue because it allowed the CDS-PP to detach itself from PSD but also to openly capitalize on aspects of critical impact of the Single Market and the Maastricht Treaty on the Portuguese economy. The CDS-PP voted against the ratification of the Maastricht Treaty and this anti-European stance led to the party's suspension from the European People's Party (Lobo 2003b, 109). Although CDS-PP's momentary Eurosceptical position had costs at the EU level, it may have brought great benefits to the party at the national level, where public opinion's enthusiasm towards the European Project was decreasing. In fact, the number of parliamentary seats obtained by the CDS-PP in the 1995 legislative election tripled vis-à-vis the 1991 election results.

The PCP manifestos, now written with its coalition partner PEV, still displayed a strongly defensive and critical posture towards the European project, especially towards the consequences of a path that is believed to bring "evident disadvantages to the weaker productive structures, such as the Portuguese, which are therefore placed, in a sudden and defenseless way, in an open market facing unequal competition" (1999 manifesto).

In this period, support for supranational scope of governance is stronger than in the previous time frame. In fact, mainstream parties seem to be quite in favour of a supranational level of decision-making in areas such as foreign affairs – "the European Union needs to create organs to foresee and plan its foreign policy, and efficient and credible diplomatic instruments" (PS 1999 manifesto) – or immigration – essential and urgent that the Community develops a common policy of immigration and asylum" (PSD 1994 manifesto). Non-mainstream parties tended to defend national or mixed solutions for these policy areas.

European identity is seldom found in Portuguese manifestos during the 1990s. PSD is actually the only party that addressed it:

Our Portuguese-ness and our European-ness – two sides of the same political and cultural coin, with a complementary meaning – do not need to be explained. We do not have any problem with the European identity because we are sure of our Portuguese identity.

(1999 manifesto)

In the end, this period is characterized by a stronger divide between main-stream and non-mainstream parties regarding Europe, with CDS-PP joining the communists in their anti-EU posture. Even if the 1999 PSD manifesto stressed the negative impacts that EEC/EU membership brought to the country, this was mainly due to the PSD status as major opposition party. Otherwise, in general terms, the PSD position in the 1990s is of support for the European project, and therefore similar to the PS stances on Europe.

Party attitudes towards the EU between 2001 and 2009: diffuse scepticism and specific support

This phase of the EU membership is marked by the return of a discourse of moderation and pragmatism by the political elites (Teixeira 2012). At the EU level, several institutional changes are in progress after the signature of the Nice Treaty in 2001. Moreover, in 2004 and 2007, twelve new countries entered the EU; these enlargements affected Portugal in a negative way, both because Portugal was left behind in the competition for structural funds and because these new member-states were more "attractive to multinational corporations seeking to benefit from the lower wages and skilled labour" (Teixeira 2012, 23).

In addition to this, the EU process suffered an important setback after the rejection of the Constitutional Treaty by the French and Dutch electorates. The institutional crisis that followed was overcome in 2007 with the signature of the Lisbon Treaty under the Portuguese Presidency, but not for too long, as Irish voters said "no" to the Lisbon Treaty in the Referendum of June 2008. This issue opened an important political debate that opposed extreme-left parties – BE, PCP and PEV – to the government (PS) and the right-wing parties (CDS-PP and PSD).

In the 2000s, the Portuguese economy performed poorly,[15] the party system became more polarized ideologically with the emergence of the left-wing party BE, and parliament became more fragmented. As consequence of this economic and political context, three governments fell during this period – two PS governments (1999–2002 and 2009–2011) and the PSD/CDS-PP coalition government (2002–2005) (see Freire 2012).

As a reflection of the broad economic and political turbulence, the nine Euro-manifestos produced after 2000 display less enthusiastic attitudes towards the EU project, especially concerning the assessment of the EU's impact on the country and the desired level of decision-making. At the same time, this diffuse scepticism is accompanied by a stronger support for supranational governance in the six policy areas under study.

The proportion of manifestos stressing the positive benefits of EU integration for the country diminishes dramatically to less than 25 per cent in 2004 and 2009 (Figure 7.3). Concerning the main political forces PS and PSD, the assessment is usually dependent on the government/opposition status at the moment of the EP election, whereas negative and mixed references from smaller parties are less context-dependent.

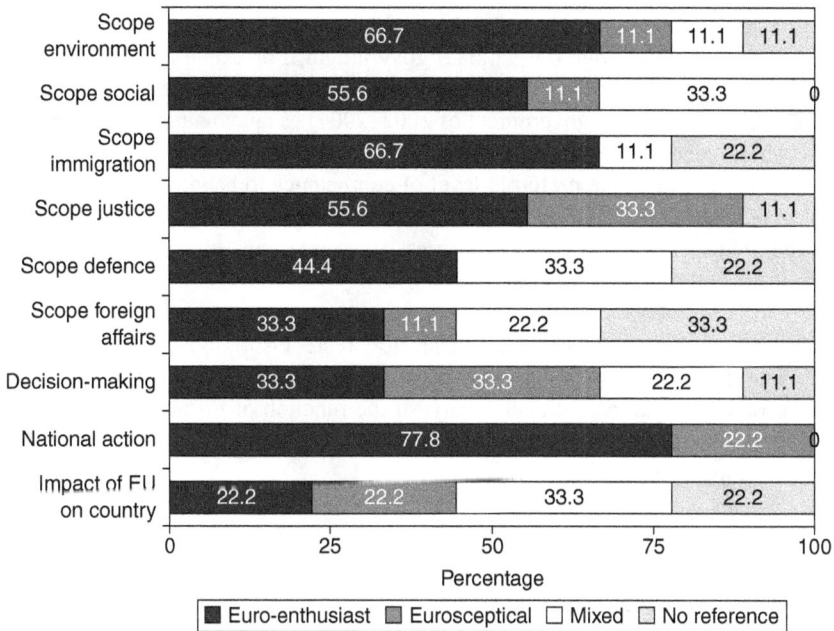

Figure 7.3 Party positions on representation and scope of governance, 2004/2009 (source: INTUNE Euromanifesto Dataset, Portuguese file).

In regard to the national action in Europe, cooperation is the most frequently preferred mode of action for the country. On the left side, the CDU systematically presents a defence of national interests and rejection of EU policies. This coalition's programme clearly states:

> the evolution of the European Union in the last five years is characterized by the accentuation of its central axis – federalism under the rule of the most powerful countries, a capitalism growing harsher and harsher in its forms of exploitation, and militarism. By their meaning, amplitude and consequences, these processes have a deep gravity for the workers and for the country.
>
> (2004)

Meanwhile the BE predominantly argues in favour of cooperation between member-states, despite being critical of the EU project. The PS prefers cooperation/participation at the EU level, whilst on the right side of the political spectrum the CDS-PP and PSD shift from a moderate position of cooperation/participation in 2004, to a position in favour of Portuguese leadership in the EU. This does not exactly mean that the PSD and the CDS-PP thought that Portuguese interests are threatened in the EU, but that the country's role in the EU should be enhanced. While in government, both parties expressed the desire to cooperate with other member states to achieve common goals, but when they shifted to opposition they started to demand a greater role for Portugal within the EU in order to challenge the national government. For example, they mention the role of the EC President Durão Barroso (the prime minister supported by the PSD/CDS-PP coalition government of 2002–2004) as an example of how Portugal can have a stronger role within the EU.

In what concerns the preferred level of competence to handle public policies, the trend in favour of the supranational level still holds, and is even stronger than in the 1990s (Figure 7.3). Parties express this preference by including in their manifestos affirmations such as:

> the European foreign policy needs to create institutions that will allow Europe to speak with a single voice. In this framework, the creation, proposed by the Constitutional Treaty, of the function of European Minister of Foreign Affairs, with connections both with the Council and the Commission, might be useful.
>
> (PSD 2004 manifesto)

Or

> in the field of immigration and asylum, we think that the assumption, at the EU level, of responsibilities able to tackle the current problems involves a European regulation and the application of a common policy (of which an integrated system to manage external frontiers is a crucial element) and also a common European system of asylum.
>
> (PS 2004 manifesto)

Once again, European identity is a more frequent label among right-wing parties – PSD, CDS-PP – while it is almost ignored on the left side of the spectrum, either by the mainstream party PS (only one reference) or the more polarized parties BE and CDU (completely absent): "European citizenship is not a replacement citizenship but a value added: a true second skin of national citizenship" (PSD 2009 manifesto); "If Europe is our cradle and the sea of our liberty, the European Union is a modern option for our national and international identity" (CDS-PP 2009 manifesto).

In sum, parties' manifestos reflect the broader context in which they are produced. Considering the previous period, political parties present less enthusiastic views about the consequences of the EU process in the country. Mainstream parties highlight favourable aspects while in government (PS in 2009 and PSD in 2004) and are more cautious (PS in 2004) while in opposition. In the case of the CDS-PP, incumbent/opposition status seems particularly relevant in what regards attitudes towards Europe. Consistency is found in the more extreme left side of the spectrum, with CDU presenting negative and critical positions in all manifestos and BE presenting a moderate (mixed) position in all manifestos.

Conclusions

In this chapter, the Portuguese parties' attitudes towards the EU have been mapped through a longitudinal reconstruction. Focusing on three domains of the EU project – identity, representation and policy scope of governance – our main goal was to observe whether party positions, as expressed in Euromanifestos, changed in different phases of the European integration process.

The first period (1986–1992) was characterized by overall enthusiasm and specific pragmatism. Supporters of the Portuguese accession – PSD and CDS-PP – highlighted the positive impact of EU membership on the country as well as the desire to cooperate and participate at the EU level, whereas PS tried to balance scepticism and enthusiasm due to its status of opposition party and its key role in the accession process in the late 1970s/early 1980s. In this scenario, the PCP was the only party with a clear anti-European integration agenda. Nevertheless, when we move from general to more concrete preferences, such as scope of governance for specific policies, we discern a more cautious and even sceptical posture and defence of national sovereignity. Left–right divide plays a modest role in this phase (the PS position is more strategic than ideological), but is visible when we trace positions on identity issues. European identity was mentioned only by right-wing parties – PSD and CDS-PP – while being completely ignored by left-wing parties – PS and PCP.

In the second period (1992–2000), mainstream and non-mainstream parties were more clearly divided regarding Europe. On the one side, we found the positions of mainstream parties – PSD and PS – which governed the country when Portugal held the EU presidency in 1992 and 2000. This was also a prosperous period, marked by the harmonization of national public policies and legislation with the EU. We found a clear Euro-enthusiastic stance, as well as preference for the supranational level to handle public policies in the Euromanifestos of these two parties. On the other side, the more polarized political parties – CDS-PP and PCP – pointed to the negative impact of the EU on national interests.

The third period (2000–2009) was characterized by lower levels of enthusiasm towards the EU project in general, but support for the EU level of governance. During this phase, the deepening of the EU integration process, the effects of the global economic and financial crisis, political instability and the emergence of a new and tendencially Eurosceptical political party, contributed to enhancing a negative vision of the EU project. In fact, the majority of the Euromanifestos referred to the negative or mixed consequences of EU integration in the country. Compared with the previous period, the CDS-PP moved closer to the mainstream parties (particularly in 2004), while the CDU and the BE presented more critical assessments of EU membership. Concerning the policies and scope of governance, the two main parties – PS and PSD – continued to prefer the supranational level to handle public policies, while the CDU and the CDS-PP were mainly in favour of a mixed solution involving the national and the supranational level. Although sustaining that the EU project should work differently, the BE viewed the supranational level as the best one to handle the great majority of policies. Economic context has played an impact on the overall stance of Portuguese parties on Europe. The EU is still considered a better policy-maker than the national government, even if the impact of Europe in the country is not seen as positively as in the past. The diffuse enthusiasm connected to the EU membership may have decreased, but a pragmatic preference for Europe seems to be thriving among Portuguese parties.

Notes

1 *Partido Socialista.*
2 *Partido Social Democrata.*
3 *Centro Democrático Social – Partido Popular.*
4 *Partido Comunista Português.*
5 *Bloco de Esquerda.*
6 In the first dimension – Identity – we analyse the reference to a European identity in the manifestos. In terms of Representation, three variables will be considered – the opinion about the consequences of membership of Portugal in the European Union (favourable opportunities, negative constraints, mixed), the opinion over about what should be the role of the country in Europe (leadership, collaboration/participation, defence/rejection) and which mode of decision-making would best serve the interests of Portugal (supranational, intergovernmental, mixed supranational and intergovern-mental and national). Lastly, Scope of Governance refers to the political party's pref-erences regarding the most appropriate level at which each of the following six policy areas should be addressed – justice, defence, foreign policy, immigration, environ-ment and social issues (employment included).
7 INTUNE collected several manifestos elaborated by the six most important Portu-guese parties for the six European elections that took place in Portugal since 1986. The selected parties are the ones that have representation at the European Parliament – PS, PSD, CDS-PP, BE, PCP and PEV (the last two under the coalition CDU). There are, however, some missing data issues that need to be addressed: for instance, for 1987, the PS and CDU manifesto was not available; for 1989, the CDU and CDS-PP manifestos were not available; for 1999 the manifesto for BE was not available. The decision to analyse the CDU coalition manifesto instead of the individual manifestos of PEV and the 1999 PCP programme is due to the fact we do not wish to enhance the weight of these documents. Including those documents would mean that the extreme, leftist and opposition stances on Europe would be artificially inflated and disguise the real patterns of competition in Portugal. The PCP manifesto is only used when the CDU manifesto was not available, i.e. for 1987 and 1989. Therefore, in the end, the analysis presented in this chapter is based on twenty-three Euromanifestos.
8 For the sake of precision, we need to say that there is one party that fulfils this cri-terion but is not represented in the INTUNE dataset, due to the fact that it had a very short history in the Portuguese party system. This party, known as PRD, or *Partido Renovador Democrático* (Democratic Renewal Party), elected an MEP in 1987, but in the 1990s lost representation at the national and European parliaments and vanished from the Portuguese political landscape.
9 Ecologist party "The Greens" (*Partido Ecologista "Os Verdes"*).
10 The Constitutional Court approved the new name in 1995. See the process at the Con-stitutional Court's website: www.tribunalconstitucional.pt/tc/acordaos/19950131.html.
11 Unitary Democratic Coalition.
12 This data is available at CNE (www.cne.pt).

13 Euro-enthusiast positions are represented by references to the EEC/EU as having had a positive impact on the country, the desire of Portugal to have a role of leadership or cooperation within the European institutions, and a preference for supranational decision-making and supranational scope of governance for the six policy areas presented in the graph. Eurosceptical positions are represented by the EU being seen as having had a negative impact on the country, references of defence/rejection of the EU, preferences for national or intergovernmental decision-making at the EU, as well as for national-only governance of the six policy areas. Mixed positions aggregate stances that are not clearly enthusiast or sceptical, or that defend multilevel solutions.

14 This and all the other excerpts of Portuguese Euromanifestos were collected from the INTUNE Euromanifesto Dataset, Portuguese file. Translation into English was made by the authors of this chapter.

15 Between 1999 and 2009 GDP rates dropped from 4.07 per cent to –2.91 per cent (source: PORDATA, www.pordata.pt/).

References

Bruneau, T. C. (1997) *Political parties and democracy in Portugal: Organizations, elections, and public opinion.* Boulder, CO: Westview Press.

Frain, M. (1997) "The right in Portugal: the PSD and CDS/PP", in T. Bruneau (ed.), *Political parties and democracy in Portugal: Organizations, elections, and public opinion*, Boulder, CO: Westview Press: 77–111.

Freire, A. (2005a) "As eleições europeias em Portugal", *Relações Internacionais*, 6: 119–125.

Freire, A. (2005b) "Eleições de segunda ordem e ciclos eleitorais no Portugal democrático, 1975–2004", *Análise Social*, 177: 815–846.

Freire, A. (2012) "European integration and party attachments: the Portuguese case as an example for new democracies", in N. S. Teixeira and A. C. Pinto (eds), *The Europeanization of Portuguese democracy*, New York: Columbia University Press: 183–224.

Freire, A. and Lobo, M. (2002) "Election report: the Portuguese 2002 legislative elections", *West European Politics*, 25, 4: 221–228.

Freire, A. and Santana Pereira, J. (2011) "Portugal, 2011: une victoire de la droite néoliberale et une défaite de la gauche", *Pole Sud – Revue de Science Politique*, 35: 157–166.

Hooghe, L., Marks, G. and Wilson, C. J. (2002) "Does left/right structure party positions on European integration?" *Comparative Political Studies*, 35, 8: 965–989.

Jalali, C. (2005) "As mesmas clivagens de sempre? Velhas e clivagens e novos valores no comportamento eleitoral dos portugueses", in A. Freire, M. C. Lobo and P. Magalhães (eds), *Portugal a Votos*, Lisbon: Imprensa de Ciências Sociais: 87–124.

Jalali, C. (2007) *Partidos e democracia em Portugal: 1974–2005*, Lisbon: Imprensa de Ciências Sociais.

Lobo, M. C. (1996) "A evolução do sistema partidário português à luz de mudanças económicas e políticas (1976–1991)", *Análise Social*, 139: 1085–1116.

Lobo, M. C. (2003a) "Legitimizing the EU? Elections to European parliament in Portugal, 1987–1999", in A. C. Pinto (ed.), *Contemporary Portugal: politics, society and culture*, New York: Columbia University Press: 203–226.

Lobo, M. C. (2003b) "Portuguese attitudes towards the EU membership: social and political perspectives", *Southern European Society and Politics*, 8, 1: 97–118.

Lobo, M. C. (2007) "A União Europeia e os partidos políticos portugueses: da consolidação à qualidade democrática", in M. C. Lobo and P. Lains (eds), *Em nome da Europa: Portugal em Mudança (1986–2006)*, Estoril: Principia: 78–96.

Pinto, A. C. (2006) "Authoritarian legacies, transitional justice and state crisis in Portugal's democratization", *Democratization*, 13, 2: 173–204.

Pinto, A. C. and Teixeira, N. S. (2003) "From Africa to Europe: Portugal and European integration", in A. C. Pinto and N. Teixeira (eds), *Southern Europe and the making of the European Union*, New York: Columbia University Press: 3–40.

Pinto, A. C. and Teixeira, N. S. (2005) "Portugal e a integração europeia, 1945–1986", in A. C. Pinto and N. S. Teixeira (eds), *A Europa do Sul e a Construção da União 1945–2000*, Lisbon: Imprensa de Ciências Sociais: 17–43.

Reif, K. and Schmitt, H. (1980) "Nine second-order national elections: a conceptual framework for the analysis of European election results", *European Journal of Political Research*, 8, 1: 307–340.

Ruivo, J. P., Moreira, D., Costa Pinto, A. and Almeida, P. T. (2012) "Portuguese political elites and the European Union", in N. S. Teixeira and A. C. Pinto (eds), *The Europeanization of Portuguese democracy*, New York: Columbia University Press: 27–59.

Sanches, E. R. and Santana Pereira, J. (2010) "Which Europe do the Portuguese political parties want? Identity, representation and scope of governance in the Euromanifestos (1987–2004)", *Perspectives on European Politics and Society*, 11, 2: 183–200.

Santana Pereira, J. (2010) "Portugal", in Wojciek Gagatek (ed.), *The 2009 elections to the European Parliament: country reports*, Florence: European University Institute (E-Book): 143–148.

Schmitt, H. (2005) "As eleições de Junho de 2004 para o Parlamento Europeu: ainda eleições de segunda ordem?" *Análise Social*, 177: 765–794.

Sitter, N. (2001) "The politics of opposition and European integration in Scandinavia: is Euro-scepticism a government/opposition dynamic?" *West European Politics*, 24, 4, 22–39.

Stock, M. J. (1985) "O centrismo político em Portugal: Evolução do sistema de partidos, génese do 'Bloco Central' e análise dos dois parceiros da coligação", *Análise Social*, 85, 45–85.

Teixeira, N. S. (2012) "Introduction: Portugal and the European integration", in N. S. Teixeira and A. C. Pinto (eds), *The Europeanization of Portuguese democracy*, New York: Columbia University Press: 7–26.

8   Greece

Susannah Verney with Sofia Michalaki

1994–2009: after Cold War polarisation and before economic crisis

This chapter examines the attitudes of Greek political parties towards the EU, as presented in their manifestos for the last four European Parliament elections. The 15-year period framed by the Euro-elections of 1994–2009 constitutes a discrete phase of the Greek European debate. By this point, Greece's relationship to European integration was no longer a source of polarisation, as it had been prior to the country's European Community accession in 1981. At that time, the parties of the right, centre and eurocommunist left had supported membership while the socialists and orthodox communists had adopted a hard eurosceptic line, entailing opposition both to integration as a matter of principle and to Greek participation in the process. In the country's first European Parliament election, held ten months after EC entry, the socialists and communists together won 52 per cent of votes and seats. However, the climate changed rapidly over the following decade. Domestically, Community membership became an accepted part of the environment within which Greek parties had to operate while externally, the Gorbachev period of perestroika in the Soviet Union inaugurated the cataclysmic shifts in the international system which culminated with the fall of the Berlin Wall in November 1989.

By the third Greek Euro-election in June 1989, 'it seemed that Greece's EC orientation was finally becoming a matter of national consensus' (Featherstone and Verney 1990 p. 96). The socialists, in power since 1981, after an initial period of ambivalence had accepted EC membership as a fait accompli that would be too costly to reverse, while insisting on the continued national right to veto. Subsequently, the socialist government's signature on the Single European Act marked a significant rapprochement with the deepening of integration, including the extension of qualified majority voting. The communist party retained a hard eurosceptic line much longer, but in Spring 1989 joined the former eurocommunists in the Coalition of the Forces of the Left and Progress (*Synaspismos*), whose programme included a recognition of the reality of Greece's EC membership in the context of a Europe undergoing rapid change. As a result, no significant party fought the 1989 Euro-election on a platform of opposition to membership. However, far from the start of a new era, 1989 was to prove the exception among the seven Greek Euro-elections to date. In the four subsequent Euro-elections – the contests which provide the material for this chapter – European integration was once again a contested issue.

By 1994, following a brief experiment with coalition government in 1989–90, the party system had adopted the form which it essentially retained throughout the period under consideration in this chapter. The basic characteristic of the system was its domination by the two major post-dictatorship parties, New Democracy (ND) and PASOK (Panhellenic Socialist Movement). At the national level, these two parties alternated in single-party governments (ND 1990–93, PASOK 1993–2004, ND 2004–09), while in the four European Parliament elections of 1994–2009, PASOK and ND together never won less than 68.8 per cent of the votes and 72 per cent of seats. Both parties during this period can be classified as Europhile. For ND, its historic role in leading the country into the EC had been a central element of the party's identity since the 1970s. Meanwhile, the socialists had now moved far from the radical positions of the pre-accession period.[1] By the time of the 1994 Euro-election – and even more after the 1996 leadership change, when party founder and former radical eurosceptic, Andreas Papandreou, finally retired – PASOK could be regarded as part of the mainstream West European centre-left.

The new shape of the party system, centred on two Europhile parties of power, stood in marked contrast to the previous period of polarisation, when the two major parties had faced each other from opposite sides on the question of European integration. Instead, in the period 1994–2009, euroscepticism became the exclusive preserve of the minor parties. After the brief interlude of coalition rule in 1989–90, the return to one-party government, confirmed by the national parliamentary elections of 1993 and 1996, meant the small parties found themselves in a position of permanent opposition. Thus, with the reconsolidation of the party system around two pro-integrationist forces, the Greek European debate had a quite different dynamic during this period.

First, as indicated above, political competition around Europe no longer had a strong left–right dimension but instead resembled the inverted U-curve noted by Hooghe *et al.* (2004), with a pro-integrationist centre-left and centre-right flanked by eurosceptic parties at the two ends of the political spectrum. Second, the content of the debate had changed. During the previous period of polarisation, underlying the debate had been the key existential question: 'to be or not to be in the European Community?' (Verney 1990). In contrast, from the early 1990s, with the reconsolidation of the party system around two pro-integrationist parties of power with such a dominant hold over the party system, it was clear that in reality – despite the communists' insistence to the contrary – Greece's EU membership was a fact of life. At the same time, with the advent of the post-Cold War era, European integration had entered a period of revolutionary change, with deepening and enlargement proceeding at an unprecedented scale and speed. The underlying question during this period, therefore, was no longer 'whether Europe' but 'what kind of Europe' did the Greek political forces want.

If the 1994 Euro-election came at the beginning of a new period, 2009 can be regarded as closing this particular chapter. After the outbreak of the Greek sovereign debt crisis, just a few months after this last Euro-election, the existential question of Greek participation in integration came back on to the political agenda. The Greek party system began a period of dramatic change, triggered by Greece's national bankruptcy and the ensuing policy of radical austerity linked to bailouts from the European Union and International Monetary Fund (IMF). These experiences resulted in the meltdown of the party system in the May 2012 parliamentary election and its partial reconstitution – on a different basis – in the repeat poll which took place six weeks later. At the time of writing, it is not yet apparent how the developments since the signature of Greece's first Memorandum of Understanding with the EU and IMF in June 2010 will play out in the next European Parliament election, scheduled for May 2014. What already seems clear, however, is that the forthcoming contest will be part of a new period, in which the dynamics of the Greek European debate and of the parties conducting it will be rather different from 1994–2009. The aim of this chapter is to investigate, through analysis of Euro-election manifestos, the question of 'what kind of Europe' the Greek political parties envisaged during the very distinct period from the Treaty of Maastricht to the outbreak of the eurozone crisis.

Case selection

European Parliament elections have been famously described as 'second order national elections' (Reif and Schmidt 1980). The experience to date has been one of contests in which national parties fight each other within the national arena, often over national issues and with the outcome determined by the shifting national balance of power rather than by developments at the European level. This is far removed from the federalist dream of 'truly' European elections, in which voters would choose between pan-European lists putting forward competing views of the European Union. Nevertheless, it means that Euro-elections offer a good opportunity to examine national party positions. Even though the issue of European integration is not usually the central axis of party contestation, it is likely to have higher salience in European than in national or sub-national polls. For this reason, Euro-elections have been chosen as the field of study here.

Election manifestos offer the most official expression of the views of the party in central office and a 'shorthand' way of comparing party positions through documents of similar type and scope. Although the study of manifestos has now become established in comparative politics research, mainly due to the work of the Manifesto Research Group/Comparative Manifestos Project (MRG/CMP), so far there has been limited manifesto research on the Greek case. Examples to date include Konstantinidis (2004), who analysed the manifestos of three parties (PASOK, ND and the communist KKE) in the ten national elections of 1974–2000, and Gemenis and Dinas (2010) who focused on the 2004 Euro-election. The present research examines manifestos from the four Euro-elections of 1994, 1999, 2004 and 2009.

The electoral system used for the Greek Euro-elections – simple proportional representation with the whole country treated as a single constituency – has encouraged the participation of multiple parties: 40 in 1994, 41 in 1999, 23 in 2004 and 27 in 2009 (Teperoglu 2008 pp. 511–512, 290, 533 and Greek Ministry of Interior electoral data 2009). This is a very high number, even when compared with national parliamentary elections in Greece.[2] As a matter of necessity, therefore, the case selection is limited to significant parties, defined as those which won at least one EP seat in the election studied. This means five parties in each of the Euro-elections of 1994, 1999 and 2004 and six in 2009. For the 1999 contest, it was decided to add POLAN (Political Spring), which held a seat in the previous European Parliament and was a serious contender in this election too, winning 2.3 per cent of the vote. Its positions were therefore part of the mainstream pre-electoral debate. Moreover, this party currently has an additional interest, given that it was founded and led by Andonis Samaras, since 2009 the leader of New Democracy and, from June 2012, Prime Minister of Greece. Our research therefore covers eight different political parties and a total set of 22 cases (treating each party in each election as a separate case).

A significant challenge of manifesto research in Greece concerns the collection of the appropriate material. In only ten of our 22 cases were actual manifestos available. Just two parties, the left-wing KKE and SYN (Coalition of the Left and Progress, renamed the Coalition of Left Movements and Ecology in 2003), consistently published extensive 'Declarations' voted by their party Central Committee before each election. Similar documents were also produced by ND in 2004 and the Ecogreens in 2009. The absence of manifestos in the other 12 cases is itself an interesting finding, attributable to the Euro-elections' perceived lack of salience, with some parties apparently considering it was not worth producing lengthy position statements for these second order elections.

In any case, it raises the question of what alternative material to use. The practice of MRG/CMP, to substitute manifestos with pre-election speeches by party leaders, has been trenchantly criticised by Gemenis (2012), who shows with examples from Greece how the different length, thematic range and especially language register of these proxy documents distorts results. In several of our cases, internal party documents were available, providing notes on party positions for party cadres who would be making election speeches. We rejected these on similar grounds to Gemenis' arguments about the speeches but, above all, because they were not official party publications designed for the general public. Given that a political party manifesto is a written public declaration through which a party communicates directly with the electorate, the obvious substitute would appear to be the official election literature prepared specially for the election and distributed during the campaign.[3] The documents we used were drawn partly from the MRG/CMP collection and partly from party websites, but mainly from personal archives[4] of material collected at the time of the various elections.[5] Before moving on to examine the material, let us first present the party actors.

The players

As already mentioned, the Greek party system during this period was dominated by the two pro-integrationist parties of government. The centre-left PASOK and centre-right ND each won a minimum of around one-third of the vote and eight EP seats in all four Euro-elections. In terms of European alliances, ND had joined the European People's Party (EPP) some months after accession in 1981. PASOK participated in the EP Socialist Group from the moment of accession but initially attempted to maintain some ideological distance from West European social democracy by remaining outside the Socialist International (SI). An important signal of PASOK's ideological rapprochement with its EC partner parties came with its SI entry in 1989 while in the early 1990s it became one of the founding participants in the Party of European Socialists. Thus, during the period under consideration, the two leading Greek players were fully incorporated into the two dominant Euro-parties and increasingly aligned with the latter's policies. In the period of rapid deepening and enlargement of integration between the Maastricht Treaty and the onset of the eurozone crisis, both parties consistently voted in favour of European Treaty amendments and the accession of new members and both were keen supporters of eurozone entry.

Also permanent elements of the party system during this period were the two parties of the left, which won seats in all four Euro-elections. KKE (the Communist Party of Greece) won two or three seats in each Euro-election. The country's longest-lived political party, dating back to 1918, the KKE has consistently advocated a national road to socialism and maintained a hard Eurosceptic stance, apart from the brief period in the late 1980s mentioned above.[6] After its brief experience of government participation in 1989–90, the KKE's vote against the ratification of the Treaty of European Union in July 1992 signalled the Greek CP's return to its traditional role as an anti-system protest party. Subsequently, it maintained a hard eurosceptic position, opposing both enlargement and deepening of the European Union, voting against the ratification of all accession agreements and European Treaty amendments, and openly advocating a national 'rupture' with the EU. In the European Parliament, the KKE initially joined the old communist group. From 1994, it sat with the newly founded European United Left/Nordic Green Left group (GUE/NGL) but did not join the Party of the European Left in the 2000s.

SYN won two seats in the two Euro-elections of the 1990s, reduced to one in the two twenty-first century contests.[7] SYN was essentially the continuation of the left-wing alliance of the late 1980s without the KKE. Following the latter's withdrawal in 1991, SYN was reconstituted the following year as a unified party. Initially situated in the tradition of the pro-integrationist 'renewal left' born from the historic split of the KKE in 1968, SYN's enthusiastic pro-European stance gradually mutated as the party became increasingly disillusioned with the neoliberal direction taken by the integration process. As a result, SYN was the Greek party whose EU stance showed the most change over this period. By the late 2000s, the party had clearly redefined itself as part of the new European 'radical left'. While still favouring European integration in principle, it became increasingly critical in practice, a stance fitting the picture of soft euroscepticism as defined by Szczerbiak and Taggart (2008). The culmination of the party's European shift was the 2009 Euro-election which SYN contested as the leading component of SYRIZA (Coalition of the Radical Left), in alliance with a range of leftist grupuscules, all more eurosceptic than the party itself. The shift in party policy was reflected at the 'history-making moments' of European Treaty ratification in the national parliament. SYN voted in favour of the Treaty of European Union, abstained on Amsterdam and Nice, and voted against the European Constitution and the Treaty of Lisbon. However, SYN consistently voted in favour of EU enlargement while a rejection of the national road to socialism espoused by the KKE remained at the heart of party strategy. In the EP, SYN was a founder member of the GUE/NGL group and played a leading role in the foundation of the Party of the European Left in 2004.

Besides these two permanent components of the party system, four more ephemeral forces also won EP representation during this period. All were minor parties, winning one or at most two EP seats, and in three cases appearing in the EP as one-term wonders. Two of these parties were situated on the left and two on the right. In the case of the latter, their positions marked a break with the uncritical pro-Europeanism which had characterised the Greek right (mainstream and far right) throughout the Cold War.

POLAN (Political Spring), with 8.7 per cent of the vote, won two EP seats in 1994. Founded the previous year as an ND breakaway, POLAN was a nationalist party originally built around the single issue of the Greek refusal to recognise its neighbouring state under a name including the word 'Macedonia'. This nationalist strategy was combined with centrist economic policies.[8] In the 1993 national election, POLAN won 4.9 per cent of the national vote, making it the third largest political force, just ahead of the traditional third party, the KKE. On this initial electoral appearance, POLAN positioned itself firmly in the europhile camp, reflecting both the traditional policy of ND, the party from which it had splintered, and the role of party leader, Andonis Samaras, as the ND Foreign Minister during the Maastricht Treaty negotiation. At that time, POLAN called for Greece to play a leadership role in the creation of a united Europe. Subsequently the balance between nationalism and Europeanism in the party's programmatic statements seems to have shifted in favour of the former. This may be because the party's 1993 success was based on an appeal to a nationalist constituency which cut across the left–right axis. The result was often an uneasy balancing act between appealing to nationalist and Europeanist constituencies. A characteristic example was POLAN's 1999 Euro-election manifesto, in which conflicting demands for the preservation of national sovereignty and for a federal Europe appear in consecutive sentences, just above a call for EU enlargement to embrace Russia. The party's policy did not bring electoral success: POLAN disappeared from the national parliament in 1996 and from the EP in 1999. Following this failure, POLAN did not contest the 2000 national election and in 2004, Samaras rejoined ND, becoming party leader five years later.

The other party on the right was LAOS (Greek Popular Orthodox Rally), which won one EP seat in 2004 and two in 2009, also entering the national parliament in 2007. Founded in 2000 by a former ND MP, LAOS was a rather different party from POLAN, in the new mould of the West European radical right.[9] Its chief focus was the defence of the national identity – an identity in which the Greek Orthodox religion was deemed a fundamental element – against the threats of globalisation and, particularly, immigration. Although LAOS did not advocate Greek withdrawal from the EU, its fundamental position in defence of the nation-state meant its preference was for a 'Europe of Nations' at odds with the current reality of European integration. Not surprisingly, therefore, when the Treaty of Lisbon came up for ratification during its first national parliamentary term, the party voted against it. It had previously declared its opposition to the Draft Treaty establishing a European Constitution. LAOS also opposed Greece's adoption of the euro, both before and after the event, and during the 2007 national election campaign called for a referendum on whether Greece should stay in the eurozone. In the EP, LAOS participated in two Eurosceptic groups: the Independence/Democracy Group (2004–09) and Europe of Freedom and Democracy (2009–).

On the left, DIKKI (Democratic Social Movement) won two EP seats in 1999. DIKKI was a socialist splinter group, founded in 1995 by nostalgics for the old radical PASOK at a time when the latter, like many of its West European counterparts, was clearly shifting towards centrist 'Third Way' positions. Unlike the early PASOK, the party did not oppose EU membership itself, but declared its obdurate opposition to the neoliberal turn of European integration associated with the Maastricht Treaty. The central focus of DIKKI's European policy was its opposition to Economic and Monetary Union and the national economic austerity associated with it. In an echo of PASOK's 1970s slogan, 'EC and NATO the same syndicate', DIKKI's 1999 Euro-election material included a cartoon of the Greek prime minister caught between NATO, represented as a cigar-chomping US general, and EMU, depicted as a hooded hangman. During its single national parliamentary term, the party voted against the ratification of the Treaty of Amsterdam. In the EP, the party joined GUE/NGL, alongside KKE and SYN. After one term in each, DIKKI failed to be re-elected to the national parliament in 2000 and to the EP in 2004.

Finally, the Ecogreens won one EP seat in 2009. Founded in 2002 as the Greek component of the then European Federation of Green Parties, the party was from the start strongly influenced by the latter and clearly focused on Europe. The Ecogreens are 'decidedly Europeanist, in favour of an enlarged and federal EU with a Common Foreign and Security policy, a social and environmental Constitutional Treaty, and an EU with increased powers' (Gemenis 2009). In 2004 the Ecogreens became founder members of the European Green Party, with whom they sit in the European Parliament. The party is clearly positioned on the left, its policy positions including the abolition of NATO.

The above parties' position statements for the Euro-elections were analysed using the coding scheme of the INTUNE project as discussed in the introduction to this volume. Our total sample of 22 cases was broken down into a number of sub-groups in order to test some theoretical predictions concerning the party characteristics influencing stands on European integration. The first prediction distinguishes between government incumbents and opposition parties, suggesting the former will be more integration-supportive than the latter (e.g. Sitter 2001). In the Greek case, we have four incumbents (PASOK 1994 and 1999 and ND 2004 and 2009) and 18 parties that were in opposition at the time of the elections (all the other cases). The second theory posits a core–periphery distinction, proposing that the parties on the margins of the political spectrum will be more eurosceptic than those at its central core (e.g. Szczerbiak and Taggart 2000). There are eight mainstream cases (four manifestos from each of the two parties of government, PASOK and ND) compared to 14 'marginals' (covering six parties: KKE, SYN/SYRIZA, POLAN, DIKKI, LAOS and the Ecogreens).

Our third hypothesis concerns left–right ideology. In its early decades, European integration was predominantly supported by parties of the right and centre and often opposed by the left. This had changed in the period under examination, with the emergence of social democracy as a leading integration supporter and of a new eurosceptic current on the radical right (Hooghe *et al.* 2004). However, in the Greek case, the recent nature of PASOK's conversion and the late emergence of the radical right (after 2000) make it more likely that support for integration will come predominantly from the right rather than the left. This hypothesis will be tested by comparing the 14 cases from the left of the political spectrum (encompassing five parties: PASOK, KKE, SYN/ SYRIZA, DIKKI and the Ecogreens) with the eight cases from the three parties of the right (ND, POLAN and LAOS). Having introduced the players, let us now turn to the play.

The salience of European integration in electoral competition

The first question addressed in our research concerns the overall salience of European integration in our Greek parties' election material. To state the obvious, when conducting election campaigns, parties will focus on issues which they expect will win them votes, while avoiding issues which might divide their voters or reduce their appeal. Of course, that a particular theme is not mentioned in an election manifesto does not necessarily mean it is absent from the party's campaign. It may, for instance, appear in speeches by party candidates or emerge as an issue in TV debates. However, its presence or absence in the written election material prepared by party central office is significant, as the latter provides an official encapsulation of the public picture which the party aims to present of itself and its programme.

Throughout 1994–2009, there was never a point – and certainly never a Euro-election – when the deepening of European integration was not under discussion. However, this by no means guaranteed its salience at the national level. This point was investigated using two questions concerning the preferred level of decision-making and the policy scope of EU governance, capturing the two fundamental dimensions of the deepening debate. Examining our 22 cases, we recorded a positive result for salience if the manifesto included a minimum of one reference to at least one of these indicators. Despite the well-known tendency for Euro-elections to play out as second order national elections, the majority of our cases (17 out of 22) did include references to these themes. Nevertheless, this left five cases where party Euro-election manifestos did not include a single reference to either of the key axes of the deepening debate. In each of these cases, this 'European absence' was hardly accidental, but a conscious choice of electoral strategy, as will be discussed below.

As shown in Figure 8.1, the deepening of integration was more salient for marginal (85.7 per cent) than for mainstream (62.5 per cent), for left-wing (85.7 per cent) than for right-wing (62.5 per cent) and particularly for opposition (83.3 per cent) as opposed to governing parties (50 per cent). It was non-salient in at least one Euro-election for all three parties on the right (ND, POLAN and LAOS) but on the left, only for PASOK. Particularly notable was the 100 per cent salience for the four marginal parties of the left (KKE, SYN, DIKKI and Ecogreens), which always addressed the deepening of integration at every election. It seems that for Greek left-wing protest parties, Europe, whether for or against, was a key ideological issue for signalling their differences both from the mainstream parties and from each other. The classic example concerns the permanent contest for predominance on the radical left between KKE and SYN, in

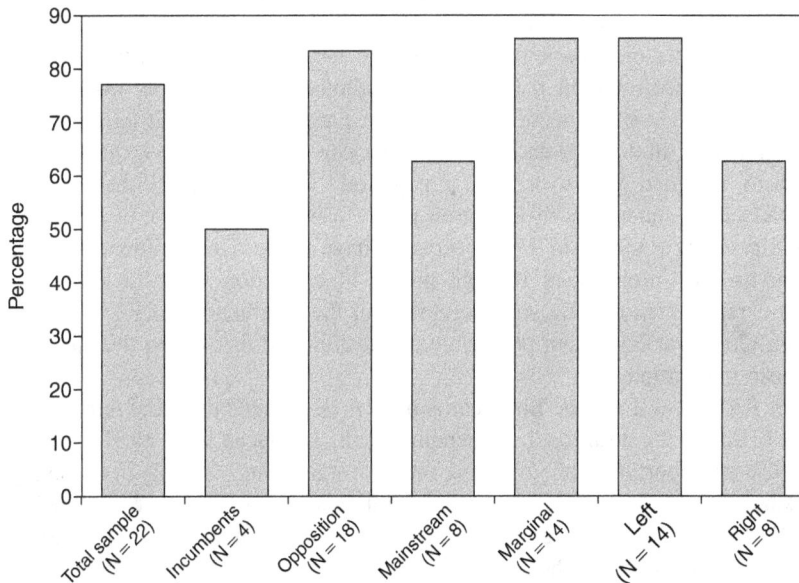

Figure 8.1 The salience of Europe in Greek electoral competition: percentage of Greek Euro-election manifestos referring to the deepening of integration, 1994–2009.

which diametrically opposed positions on integration served as a flagship of competing political worldviews. In contrast, the right-wing protest parties, with only 50 per cent salience of Europe, clearly preferred to compete on other issues. Meanwhile, the comparatively low salience of EU deepening for the pro-integrationist incumbent parties (50 per cent) requires further investigation, especially when compared to the higher salience (75 per cent) for the same parties when in opposition.

In fact, both cases of a governing party which did not mention its preferences regarding the deepening of integration concerned PASOK. In 1994, this partly reflected the generally low significance the party attributed to a contest sandwiched between its sweeping national election victory of October 1993 and the forthcoming local government elections of October 1994. Both the latter polls, concerning the allocation of domestic power, were of considerably greater strategic significance than the share-out of seats in the European Parliament. A second consequence of this string of elections was to leave the party low on resources. Partly for practical reasons, therefore, the governing socialists produced no election material of their own, circulating only a Greek translation of the Party of European Socialists manifesto (see Verney and Featherstone 1996). As a result, the party's programmatic statement for the Euro-elections consisted of a two-page Greek preface to the PES manifesto, signed by party leader, Andreas Papandreou.

However, 1994 was not an aberration. Limitation of PASOK's official manifesto statements on the issue of European integration was rather characteristic. In the 1981 dual national and European election, the party's 112-page manifesto included just one page on 'The accession to the European Communities', tucked away in a chapter on economic policy. In the 1984 Euro-election, the 97-page manifesto did not mention the EC at all, although admittedly it was supplemented by an eight-page election leaflet on the party's 'Untiring Struggle' in the EC. Meanwhile, in the dual national and European election of 1989, the 42-page manifesto included just over half a page on 'Europe'. In all these cases, PASOK's short statements of European policy were low in substantive content. In similar vein, PASOK in 1994 seems to have made a conscious choice to convey its pro-Europeanism through public identification with the PES programme, rather than making any assessment of the significance of EU membership for Greece or laying out programmatic positions of its own on the future of European integration.

That PASOK did not see European policy as favourable electoral terrain was probably due to the traditional 'ownership' of the European issue by ND, which never lost an opportunity of reminding the electorate of its own role in achieving Greek accession. The socialists' own U-turn in this area was another weak point. PASOK had no reason to remind either its pro-European voters of the party's former euroscepticism or those faithful to its original worldview of the party's striking ideological shift. Instead, the 1994 election document took the easier road of defining the party's European policy as 'aiming at the safeguarding of our national interests'. This was consistent with the party line adopted in the early 1980s, when PASOK's initial hard euroscepticism had been replaced by a new discourse about defending national interests from within the EC. In 1994, the 'national interests' reference also served as a reminder of the government's tough stance in imposing a trade embargo on the Former Yugoslav Republic of Macedonia four months earlier. The resulting referral of Greece to the European Court of Justice was followed by a rise in the government's popularity and a sharp drop in pro-EU public opinion. In this climate, dwelling on the future of European integration seemed a less successful strategy than reminding the voters of PASOK's willingness to stand up to its EU partners.

However, the low salience of Europe in PASOK's Euro-election manifestos was not confined to the period when the party was led by Andreas Papandreou. In 1996 the election of his successor was widely hailed as inaugurating a new era in Greek–EU relations. Kostas Simitis immediately made eurozone entry the central plank of his government programme. Under his leadership, 'probably for the first time since its 1981 accession, official Greece was finally in full mental and political accord with the European Union, seeing eye-to-eye with its integrationist core' (Pagoulatos and Yataganas 2010 p. 198). Yet in 1999, the party's main Euro-election pamphlet, on the economy, did not mention the words 'Europe', 'European integration' or 'EU'. Its second pamphlet, on regional stability, referred only to integration into the European architecture as part of the solution to the Balkan problem. Its third pamphlet, aimed at women voters, stated that Greece's 'geo-economic position' was not unilaterally focused on the EU but also embraced the Balkans and the Mediterranean.[10] Thus, although PASOK by this time was clearly positioned in the pro-integrationist camp, it appears that in the 1990s the promotion of its European policy was not considered essential to selling the brand. This changed in the 2004 Euro-election, under the new leadership of Georgios Papandreou. By this time, Greece's eurozone entry under a PASOK government in 2002 gave the socialists strong European credentials of their own, allowing them to compete with ND in this area.

Equally striking was the low visibility of European issues in ND's 1999 campaign, its first under the leadership of Kostas Karamanlis, nephew and namesake of the party's founder. Throughout the two previous decades, ND's image as a pro-European party had been considered an essential part of its appeal. The party had always made considerable electoral use of the elder Karamanlis' role as the architect of Greece's EC entry. Yet in ND's first election campaign under the leadership of the younger Karamanlis, its 1999 'New Start' did not express preferences on the deepening of integration. Instead, it centred on 'Ten Priorities', with the only EU-related reference being the instrumental 'increasing absorption of Community funds'. While asking 'What Greece do we want in EMU?', ND did not express any vision of what kind of Europe Greece should prefer.

The 1999 Euro-election, occurring past the midpoint of a second PASOK government term, was seen by both major parties as a dress rehearsal for the forthcoming national contest. In their election material, both parties focused on each other, painting a bleak picture of their opponent's record in office. That neither party saw European issues as a useful tool may have been partly because by 1999, PASOK and ND were pursuing rather similar European policies. In particular, they shared a central commitment to EMU entry, entailing the implementation of unpopular economic austerity to meet the criteria. Six months before the election, the third stage of EMU had started – without Greece, the only EU member-state which had wanted but failed to join. Thus, at this point, the EMU entry drive seemed a case of all pain and no gain. Moreover, this Euro-election, like its predecessor, played out against the backdrop of the violent breakup of Yugoslavia. The NATO bombing of Kosovo, which ended just three days before the election, was extremely unpopular in Greece where 'it reignited old positions of anti-Westernism' (Kazamias and Featherstone 2001 p. 91), in turn conducive to euroscepticism. Therefore, for both PASOK and ND, in the 1999 Euro-election European integration did not seem a vote winner.

Our two other cases concern marginal parties of the right. In 1994, POLAN's central mobilising strategy – the claim to be the only political force capable of defending Greek national interests – had suffered a dynamic challenge from the PASOK trade embargo against FYROM. In this context, the party sharpened its nationalist discourse to the point of adopting a confrontational stance towards the EU. Directly competing with PASOK in terms of national interest discourse, POLAN adopted the election slogan 'Strong Greeks–Equal Europeans', while its campaign keynote was the statement that 'We are pro-European but at the same time we give battle to safeguard our country's rights'. POLAN's chief line of attack against PASOK and ND was to claim their membership of European parties had compromised their independence and resulted in them accepting policies damaging to Greece, notably on employment and the Macedonian question. This claim was enlivened with inflammatory rhetoric about a Greece 'continually kowtowing in apology' to its European partners. (POLAN itself was non-aligned within the EP.) Beyond this, the manifesto did not engage with European integration, but sent a signal to pro-European voters through a symbolic European cover, juxtaposing the Greek and EU flags.

Finally, for LAOS, spelling out its position on Europe was never central to this party's competition strategy. LAOS preferred to focus on an anti-immigrant discourse with growing appeal in a decade when undocumented immigration was becoming an increasingly explosive issue. In 2009 the party, already established in the national parliament and now fighting its second Euro-election, already had its sights set on government participation. Its aim was to present itself as an effective and responsible defender of national interests. Its 24-page election pamphlet focused exclusively on comparing the party's record in a series of European Parliament votes on Macedonia, Turkey and Cyprus with those of the other Greek parties, whose stance was attributed to 'obligations of enslavement' to their pro-integrationist EP groups.

The 'deepening deficit' in each of these four cases influenced the dynamics of the thematic debate on Europe, to which we will now turn.

The thematic content of European integration in electoral competition

Identity

It has been suggested that the Treaty of European Union, with its deep penetration of national sovereignty and the innovation of European citizenship, significantly increased the salience of identity as an issue in the integration debate. As noted by Liesbet Hooghe (2007 p. 7), 'In the early decades of European integration, Euroscepticism was rooted in opposition to market integration. Since the Maastricht Treaty, it has taken on an additional dimension: defence of the national community.' The rise of national identity politics is not only linked to the deepening of integration, but also reflects the emergence of globalisation and its consequences as a predominant political issue during the same period. One result has been the rise of right-wing populist parties, for whom 'the basis of their success lies in their appeal to identity and their exploitation of anxieties about losing one's identity in a denationalising world' (Kriesi 2009 p. 224). Meanwhile, the difficult process of Treaty ratification, signalling an apparent end to the 'passive consensus' under which the majority of the population had allegedly accorded European integration their tacit toleration, was followed by considerable debate about the construction of a European demos.

In Greece, identity issues had constituted a key axis of disagreement in the pre-accession debate on European integration. In a Europe divided by the Cold War, the question of where Greece belonged had constituted a basic dividing line. The political forces had vehemently contested the nature of both 'Europe' and Greece as well as the compatibility of EC membership with national identity. Proponents of accession, often stressing the Greek roots of European civilization, had presented 'Europe' as Greece's natural habitat and participation in European integration as something like a 'return to the roots'. In contrast, their opponents had argued the EC was a creation of monopoly capitalism which threatened national cultural identity and had championed a view of the country as belonging simultaneously to different geographical regions, of which Western Europe was only one (Verney 1994). Meanwhile, during the post-Cold War era, Greece was rapidly developing a new kind of identity crisis, centred on the survival of the Greek nation under the dual challenges of globalisation and mass immigration. This was to result in heated national debates on issues such as identity cards ceasing to signify religious affiliation or non-nationals carrying the flag in school parades (Verney 2002).

Despite this European and national context, identity as an explicit theme was of rather low salience in our Greek parties' post-Maastricht Euro-election material, mentioned in only half our cases (11 out of 22). As shown in Figure 8.2, identity was of lower than average salience for mainstream parties (mentioned in three of eight cases) and particularly for government incumbents (with only one reference out of four cases). This is partly attributable to the 'absence of Europe' in three of our mainstream manifestos (PASOK 1994 and 1999, ND

1999) mentioned above. Contrary to what might be expected, identity was of equal salience (50 per cent) to left and right. Not only the mainstream ND but also the new right-wing parties, POLAN and LAOS, each mentioned identity in only half their manifestos. The radical right LAOS, for whom identity was normally a key mobilising issue, was silent on this issue in its 2009 election leaflet as on European integration in general. On the left, six out of the seven cases to reference identity concerned KKE and SYN (three cases each), compared to one case for PASOK.

For all the Greek parties, reference to identity in their election material appears almost random and incidental rather than a central element of their European strategies. Moreover, identity was not the object of an interparty dialogue in which parties answered each other's arguments in their manifestos. By 1994, 15 years after accession and in a Europe gradually reuniting after the end of the Cold War, the question of 'where Greece belonged' appeared to have been resolved. Only one Euro-election manifesto (ND 1994) mentioned this theme.

Meanwhile, no new central theme had emerged to replace this old question and provide a common core to the identity debate. Instead, the identity references were rather disparate and all the parties seemed to be talking about different things. Five cases (four parties) talked about elements making up the national identity. This included all three right-wing parties, which mentioned national identity in one manifesto each. LAOS (2004) referred to the role of the Orthodox Church, POLAN (1999) to religion, language, traditions, morals and the importance of the family, and ND (1994) to the ecumenical nature of Hellenism

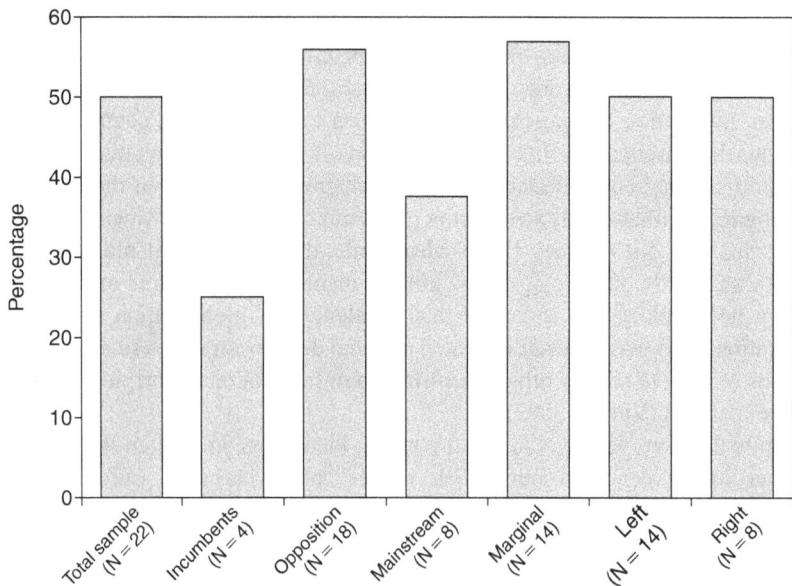

Figure 8.2 The salience of identity in Greek Euro-election manifestos, 1994–2009.

which had allowed it to become the basis for contemporary global civilisation. On the left, the KKE (2004 and 2009) described cultural tradition, popular culture and language as 'part of the History and consciousness of the people' and a tool of resistance to corrosive imperialist ideology. The other four left-wing parties did not refer to national identity.

In contrast, European identity was mentioned by only one right-wing compared to three left-wing parties. Five cases (three parties) referred to elements making up the current European identity. In two cases (ND 1994, SYN 1999), these concerned the role of Greek civilisation in European culture. The most significant European identity theme, however, was the European social model, mentioned in three cases. For SYN (1994 and 1999), the rights won through the long history of European political and labour struggle were elements of the European identity which required defence against neoliberal attack. Meanwhile, PASOK (2004) referred to 'the achievements of the social state' as part of Europe's 'major comparative advantage', along with its 'intellectual capital, knowledge, education, research, civilisation ... and the quality of its political and legal culture'. Two cases mentioned a vision for the future European identity. For ND (2004), the future Europe should be based on 'justice, freedom, democracy, the rule of law, solidarity and Christian humanism' while SYN (1994) preferred a multicultural, anti-racist model. Only one manifesto talked about the current European identity-building process. This was the KKE (1994), which denounced the EU goal as 'the undermining of national policies and traditions' in order to shape a 'quiet', subservient 'European' consciousnessness and homogeneous 'European citizens'.

Representation

The democratic deficit, an issue from the early years of integration, became particularly visible in the post-Maastricht era. The continuing transfer of ever more significant competences to the European level without a corresponding democratisation of EU institutions meant decision-making was increasingly removed from citizens' control. The series of public rejections of European Treaties, from the Danish 'no' to Maastricht to the Irish rebuff of Lisbon, suggested increasing popular disaffection with this model, undermining the legitimacy of integration and making the democratic deficit into a high profile issue. From a positive viewpoint, this period also saw a continual expansion of the powers of the European Parliament and therefore of democratic control, beginning with the introduction of the co-decision procedure in the Maastricht Treaty. The current democratic functioning of the EU was of higher salience than identity in our Greek manifestos, appearing in 77.3 per cent of cases (17 out of 22). There seemed to be little difference in salience between incumbents (75 per cent) and the opposition (77.8 per cent) or between mainstream (75 per cent) and marginal parties (78.6 per cent). However, ideology played a significant role, with this issue mentioned by 92.9 per cent of left-wing cases compared to only 50 per cent on the right.

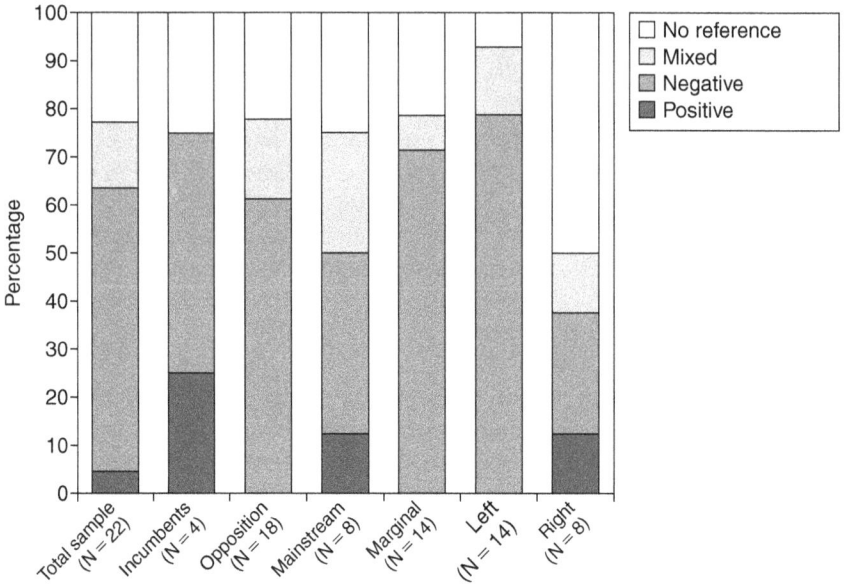

Figure 8.3 Attitudes towards the current functioning of EU democracy in Greek Euro-election manifestos, 1994–2009.

The evaluation of EU democracy by our Greek parties was overwhelmingly negative (13 cases, or 59 per cent of the total). Apart from LAOS, which did not mention this issue at all, the other seven parties, whether eurosceptic or pro-integrationist, offered a purely negative assessment on at least one occasion. Opposition parties were critical more often (61.1 per cent) than government incumbents (50 per cent) and marginal (71.4 per cent) more often than mainstream parties (37.5 per cent), while there was a particularly significant difference between left (78.6 per cent) and right (25 per cent). Of the parties which mentioned this issue on more than one occasion, however, only the KKE was systematically negative every time while PASOK and SYN each also made one mixed assessment and ND one mixed and one positive. The latter, focused on the role of the European Parliament, was the sole positive case in our sample. There was also quite a difference in tone between the communist party's denunciations of an unredeemed anti-democratic integration, designed to serve the interests of the ruling class and the multinationals, and the criticism voiced by PASOK, SYN and the Ecogreens, often linked to references to their joint proposals with other progressive forces for the democratisation of the EU.

The process of institutional deepening, including the repeated extension of the use of qualified majority voting and the growing strength of the European Parliament, meant the mode of cooperation among nation-states at the European level was under continual renegotiation during this period. For our Greek parties,

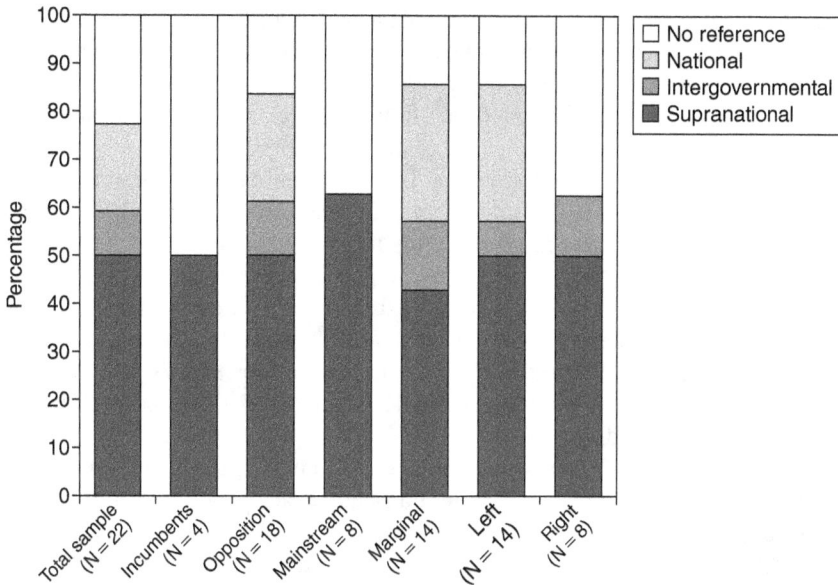

Figure 8.4 Preferences on EU decision-making as expressed in Greek Euro-election manifestos, 1994–2009.

the nature of EU-level decision-making was an issue of equal salience (again mentioned in 77.3 per cent of cases) with the functioning of democracy. All parties expressed a preference on this topic on at least one occasion and all were consistent: none changed preferences between elections and the only issue was whether they would mention the issue or not. The majority preference, supported by five parties and expressed in 50 per cent of total cases, was for supranationalism. Rather surprisingly, there was no difference in support for supranationalism between government and opposition or between left and right (all at 50 per cent). The only differentiation was between mainstream (62.5 per cent) and marginal parties (42.9 per cent).

As might be expected, the hard eurosceptic communist party was a fervent advocate of national decision-making, while the left-wing DIKKI and the radical right LAOS both indicated an intergovernmental preference. The other five parties – PASOK, ND, POLAN, SYN and the Ecogreens – not only supported supranationalism but also all explicitly declared their support for a federal EU on at least one occasion (POLAN in the rather *sui generis* fashion mentioned above). Indeed, as early as 1994, two Greek parties, ND and SYN, were already calling for a European Constitution. This reflected the emergence of federalism as a buzzword in the Greek European debate in the early 1990s, following the Greek government's enlistment in the pro-federal camp during the Maastricht negotiation. Greek support for federalism was based on a belief that it would offer smaller states greater decision-making influence than intergovernmental-ism, while also serving two important national interests: a common security policy entailing mutual territorial defence and a redistributive budget promoting economic and social cohesion.

Of all our cases, SYN's manifestos from 1994 and 1999 contain the most detail on the future institutional shape of the EU, calling *inter alia* for the elec-tion of European Commissioners by the European and national parliaments, the direct election of the Commission President, transparency in all EU decision-making procedures, greater involvement by national parliaments and NGOs, the strengthening of the Committee of the Regions, and especially for political control of monetary policy. This contrasted with PASOK's relative silence on European issues in both these elections. By 2009, however, there had been a clear qualitative shift. While the SYRIZA manifesto referred only to a decisive role for the European Parliament, PASOK mentioned the European Citizens' Initiative, an upgraded role for the European and national parliaments, and the direct election of the Commission President. Meanwhile, the Ecogreens called for a clear separation of powers, greater transparency and new ways of involving national parliaments, citizens and NGOs in EU decision-making. In 2009, SYRIZA had clearly downgraded the pro-European dimension in its election strategy while both PASOK and the Ecogreens were now competing strongly on the pro-European left.

Scope of governance

The Maastricht Treaty intensified the debate on the limits of integration by inau-gurating a major expansion of EU competences into policy fields central to national sovereignty, such as external and internal security. Meanwhile, the Treaty's definition of subsidiarity and institutionalisation of an EU decision-making role for sub-national government fuelled discussion on the appropriate level of decision-making competence. To investigate this theme, Greek prefer-ences on this topic were examined in five high-profile policy areas: foreign and defence, justice and crime, immigration, social (including employment) and environmental policies. Scope of governance, mentioned in 14 cases (63.6 per cent), attracted more attention than identity but less than representation. Parties often seemed more interested in talking about the content of policies than indi-cating at which level they should be decided. For example, both KKE and SYN were very critical of the Schengen Treaty but neither explicitly addressed the question of decision-making in the field of free movement. Overall, scope of governance was more salient for the opposition (66.7 per cent) than for govern-ment parties (50 per cent) and particularly for the left (71.4 per cent) than the right (50 per cent), while there was no difference between mainstream (62.5 per cent) and marginal cases (64.3 per cent).

In terms of policy areas, foreign and defence was the most significant, men-tioned by seven parties in 13 cases (59 per cent). The level of interest in this subject was partly due to the rapid and major developments in this field, from the launching of the Common Foreign and Security Policy to the inauguration of the European Security and Defence Policy in just a few years. Meanwhile, with the end of the Cold War and the transformation of Greece's Balkan neighbourhood into a warzone, EU membership was seen by successive Greek governments as a vital source of security. Indeed, in the Maastricht negotiation, the Greek government prioritised the Common Foreign and Security Policy over all other issues (see Ioakimidis 1993 ch. 7). Contrary to what might be expected, foreign and defence policy was more salient for opposition (61.1 per cent) than for government (50 per cent), for marginal (64.3 per cent) than for mainstream (50 per cent) and, overwhelmingly, for the left (71.4 per cent) rather than the right (37.5 per cent). This can be partly attributed to the KKE's consistent emphasis on this area as a key theme of its opposition to integration. While the communists clearly opposed EU policy competences in any area, this was the only one in which EU scope of governance was singled out for explicit mention.

Foreign and defence policy was followed in terms of salience by social (five parties, ten cases), environmental (five parties, seven cases), immigration (three parties, five cases) and justice and crime policies (one party, two cases). As might be expected, environmental policy was predominantly an issue of the left (mentioned in 42.9 per cent of cases) with little interest on the right (12.5 per cent). It was also more of an opposition (27.8 per cent) than a government issue (12.5 per cent) while there was no appreciable difference between mainstream (25 per cent) and marginal parties (28.6 per cent). Immigration had the opposite profile: a concern of the right (37.5 per cent) rather than the left (14.3 per cent), the government (50 per cent) rather than the opposition (16.7 per cent) and the mainstream (50 per cent) rather than the margins (7.1 per cent). Social policy ran somewhat counter to expectations, more likely to be mentioned by the right (50 per cent) than the left (42.9 per cent), by government (50 per cent) than by opposition (44.4 per cent) and especially by mainstream (62.5 per cent) rather than marginal parties (35.7 per cent). The latter can be explained not only by the lack of explicit reference from the KKE but also to three mentions from ND. This reflects the finding by Konstantinidis (2004) that after the fall of its 1991–93 government, associated with neoliberal policies, ND was trying to promote a more socially sensitive image. Finally, justice and crime was an ND monopoly, mentioned by the party on both occasions in which it was in government.

In terms of decision-making level, it was striking that in an era of multilevel governance, not a single Greek party referred to a role for sub-national government, whether alone or in collaboration with another level of governance. In fact, only one party (SYN in 1994) mentioned the potential role of sub-national government as the 'third partner' in Europe, alongside the EU institutions and the national governments. This was despite the fact that five months after the 1994 Euro-election, Greece held its first elections for a new second tier of local government at the prefecture level. Even in 2009, after 15 years of functioning, the prefectures had not impinged on the Greek parties' conceptions of European policy-making. It remains to be seen whether a new territorial restructuring in 2010 replacing the prefectures with 13 regional governments, will influence this picture in the future.

As can be seen from Figure 8.5, across all policy areas, the leading preference, in cases where one was expressed, was for the EU to play a substantive
policy role. This suggests support for supranational governance, consistent with
our findings under the theme of EU decision-making procedures. Care should be
taken, however, in suggesting this necessarily implied an exclusive supranational
competence. Parties were not always very explicit about the decision-making
procedures they envisaged. It would be hard to imagine, for example, that the
nine cases in which parties declared support for an EU foreign and defence
policy meant they imagined this completely replacing national policy. In three
cases, parties explicitly referred to mixed competences, with parallel national
input in the specific policy area. Two of these concerned parties which on other
occasions, referred only to an EU role in the specific policy area.[11] This suggests
that at least in the Greek case, the 'supranational' and 'mixed' categories should
probably both be counted as indicating support for expanding the limits of integration. That an exclusive national preference appeared so seldom was due to
the fact that the KKE, whose national policy-making preference is implicit
throughout its manifestos, only explicitly referred to this in relation to foreign
and security policy. In terms of breakdown among our sub-groups, the supranational preference, mentioned in 50 per cent of total cases for at least one policy
area, remained constant at this level both for incumbents and opposition parties
and for left- and right-wing cases. Only in the marginal–mainstream pairing

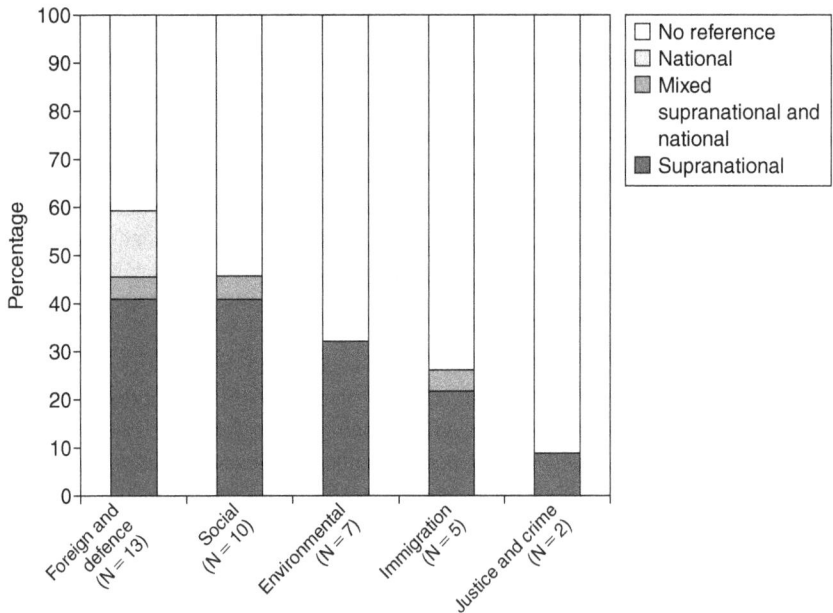

Figure 8.5 Decision-making preferences by policy area in Greek Euro-election manifestos, 1994–2009.

were the former more likely (62.5 per cent) than the latter (42.9 per cent) to support EU policy competence.

Party positions on scope of governance remained consistent diachronically. The only exceptions were the two examples of support for mixed competences which seem unlikely to indicate an actual change of preference. Party preferences also remained stable across different policy areas, suggesting the influential factor was the basic stance towards European integration rather than the specific dynamics of policy-making in a particular field. PASOK, ND, POLAN, SYN and the Ecogreens all supported supranational policy competences in the policy fields they mentioned. The KKE was alone in stating a preference for exclusive national competences in any of our policy areas. Scope of governance was not addressed at all by LAOS, in line with its general downplaying of European issues. Nor does the issue appear in the 2009 SYRIZA manifesto, marking a significant break with the consistent references to three specific policy areas (foreign and defence, social and environmental policies) in the SYN manifestos of 1994–2004. Finally, DIKKI offers a rather interesting case. Despite its opposition to 'Maastricht', DIKKI supported supranational policy competences in some policy areas. It called for an EU defence policy, including protection of its members' external borders, while simultaneously insisting on the national right to autonomous foreign policy action. The party also wanted the EU to be active on the environment. On social policy, DIKKI not only called for European policies on employment creation and social cohesion but also made a surprising – and revolutionary – call for EU action in the areas of health, welfare and pensions.

Patterns and conclusions

Summing up patterns of competition, governing parties were less likely than the opposition to compete on issues of European integration. This was reflected in the thematic content of their statements on Europe: incumbents hardly referred to identity (no references to national identity, one to European identity), made fewer references than the opposition to scope of governance but were equally likely to discuss representation. With regard to policy areas, government participants were more likely to talk about social policy and immigration and less likely to refer to foreign and defence or environmental policy. In terms of support for integration, they were somewhat less critical than the opposition of the current functioning of EU democracy. Confounding theoretical predictions, however, governing parties were no more likely than the opposition to make statements supporting supranational decision-making or scope of governance.

For mainstream parties, European integration was also less salient than for their marginal opponents. They made far fewer references to identity, whether national or European, but were equally likely to discuss representation or scope of governance. Mainstream parties showed far greater interest in social policy than the marginals while making more references to immigration and less to foreign and defence policy, with no difference between them on the environment.

In terms of support for integration, they were considerably less negative about current EU democracy than the marginal parties. They were also significantly more supportive of supranationalism in both decision-making and scope of governance. In this case, therefore, theoretical expectations were fulfilled with the two parties at the core of the system more integration-supportive than those on the margins.

Given that the group of governing parties is a subset of the mainstream cases, our results indicate that the same parties took a more favourable stance towards European integration when out of power than when in government. As explained above, this outcome was essentially due to the shift in PASOK's competition strategy, entailing a new emphasis on the party's pro-European credentials from the 2004 Euro-election onwards. This finding underlines the solid nature of the pro-integrationist consensus between Greece's two main parties during this period. Neither party when in opposition made the tactical eurosceptic shift suggested by Sitter's theory. Instead, for both PASOK and ND, their support for integration was a strategic choice. They preferred to mobilise support by criticising their rival's handling of European issues rather than by challenging the basic direction of European policy.

Examining our third prediction, concerning ideological orientation, right-wing parties were significantly less likely to compete on European issues than the left. They made more references to national and fewer references to European identity. While equally interested in scope of governance, they showed considerably less interest in issues of representation. Thematically, right-wing parties showed more interest in immigration and social policies and less interest in foreign and defence policy and the environment than the left. With regard to support for integration, parties of the right were considerably less likely to make negative statements about the current democratic functioning of the EU. However, contrary to our expectations, right and left were equally likely to support supranational decision-making and policy-making competences.

In fact, our research showed that during the period under examination, there was considerable support for deeper integration among Greek political parties, including some opposition and marginal parties and those on both sides of the ideological spectrum. Parties supporting integration included some normally regarded as at least soft eurosceptic. As mentioned above, the most detailed strategy for the EU's institutional deepening could be found in some SYN manifestos while DIKKI was apparently prepared to envisage a significant expansion of EU social policy competences into areas currently reserved for the nation-state. This suggests that, contrary to the way in which it is normally envisaged, the basic distinction in the Greek debate was not that between parties supporting or opposing the current direction of integration. Indeed, in the one question measuring attitudes towards the latter, all the Greek parties (except LAOS, which did not mention it) expressed a negative opinion at least once about the functioning of EU democracy.

Rather, what emerges is a fundamental distinction between the parties which were prepared to envisage further European integration and those which were against. In this regard, only the communists insisted on a return to the nation-state. In its 1994 Euro-election manifesto, the party explained that each state should move ahead on its own, carrying out its own revolution while waiting for the rest of the European countries to follow suit. The two small parties of the right also emphasised the nation-state, which for LAOS should function in the context of a European confederation with relations based on cooperation rather than integration. In contrast, POLAN rather confusingly situated the nation-state in a European federation without providing clear indications of what it had in mind. However, POLAN's ambiguous stance suggested that, in contrast to KKE and LAOS, this party, like the others examined here, was open to the deepening of integration. Thus, in the period after Maastricht and before the crisis, the Greek party consensus in favour of integration extended beyond the system's mainstream core, also embracing all the marginal parties with the exception of the two at the furthest ends of the political spectrum. While the parties had varying views on the direction they wanted Europe to take, all saw Greece's future within a framework of European integration. This confirms the picture of pre-crisis Greece as an overwhelmingly pro-European country before the impact of economic turmoil after 2009.

Notes

1 On the change in PASOK's policy, see Featherstone 1988 ch. 7; Kazakos 1992; Verney 1996; Moschonas 2001. Compared to the interest in PASOK, there is rather a dearth of literature on New Democracy's European policy, especially in English.
2 For example, 17 and 19 parties contested the 2004 and 2009 national elections.
3 One objection to such literature – that, unlike manifestos, it has not been approved by party congress – is not so relevant in the Greek case, where with the exception of the left-wing KKE and SYN, manifestos are usually not voted by party organs but produced by central office.
4 The personal archives were those of Susannah Verney and Eftichia Teperoglu. The authors would particularly like to thank the latter for sharing her material with us.
5 A complete list of the documents selected, not included here for reasons of space, is available from the lead author (deplan@otenet.gr).
6 On the KKE's European policy, see Dunphy 2004 pp. 103–112.
7 On SYN's European policy, see Tsakatika 2009 and Dunphy 2004 pp. 103–112.
8 On POLAN and its political strategy, see Ellinas 2010 ch. 5. To date, there has been no study of the party's European policy.
9 On LAOS and its strategy, see Ellinas 2010, Psarras 2010; on its European policy: Vasilopoulou 2010 ch. 6.
10 A position reminiscent of the description of Greece as simultaneously European, Balkan and Mediterranean used by PASOK in the 1970s to counter ND's slogan of 'Greece belongs to the West'.
11 ND on immigration and SYN on social policy.

References

Dunphy, R. (2004) *Contesting Capitalism? Left Parties and European Integration*, Manchester: Manchester University Press.

Ellinas, A. (2010) *The Media and the Far Right in Western Europe: Playing the Nationalist Card*, Cambridge: Cambridge University Press.

Featherstone, K. (1988) *Socialist Parties and European Integration: A Comparative History*, Manchester: Manchester University Press.

Featherstone, K. and Verney, S. (1990) 'Greece' in J. Lodge (ed.) *The 1989 Election of the European Parliament*, Basingstoke: Macmillan: 90–106.

Gemenis, K. (2009) 'A Green comeback in Greece? The Ecologist Greens in the 2007 parliamentary election', *Environmental Politics*, 18(1): 128–134.

Gemenis, K. (2012) 'Proxy documents as a source of measurement error in the Comparative Manifestos Project', *Electoral Studies*, 31(3): 594–604.

Gemenis, K. and Dinas, E. (2010) 'Confrontation still? Examining parties' policy positions in Greece', *Comparative European Politics*, 8(2): 179–201.

Hooghe, L. (2007) 'What drives Euroskepticism?' *European Union Politics*, 8(1): 5–12.

Hooghe, L., Marks, G. and Wilson, C. (2004) 'Does left/right structure party positions on European integration' in G. Marks and M. Steenbergen (eds) *European Integration and Political Conflict*, Cambridge and New York: Cambridge University Press: 120–140.

Ioakimidis, P.C. (1993) *European Political Union*, Athens: Themelio [in Greek].

Kazakos, P. (1992) 'Socialist attitudes towards European integration in the eighties' in T.C. Kariotis (ed.) *The Greek Socialist Experiment: Papandreou's Greece, 1981–85*, New York: Pella Press: 257–278.

Kazamias, G. and Featherstone, K. (2001) 'Greece' in J. Lodge (ed.) *The 1999 Elections to the European Parliament*, Basingstoke: Palgrave Macmillan: 89–99.

Konstantinidis, G. (2004) 'The changing content of Greek parties' electoral manifestos: the value of flexibility', *Hellenic Political Science Review*, 24: 105–142 [in Greek].

Kriesi, H. (2009) 'Rejoinder to Liesbet Hooghe and Gary Marks', *British Journal of Political Science*, 39(1): 221–224.

Moschonas, G. (2001) 'The path of modernization: PASOK and European integration', *Journal of Southern Europe and the Balkans*, 3(1): 11–24.

Pagoulatos, G. and Yataganas, X. (2010) 'Europe othered, Europe enlisted, Europe possessed: Greek public intellectuals and the European Union' in J. Lacroix and K. Nikolaidis (eds) *European Stories: Intellectual Debates on Europe in National Contexts*, Oxford: Oxford University Press: 183–202.

Psarras (2010) *Το Κρυφό Χέρι του Κατατζαφέρη: Η Τηλεοπτική Αναγέννηση της Ελληνικής Ακροδεξιάς* [*The Hidden Hand of Karatzaferis: The Televisual Rebirth of the Greek Far Right*], Athens: Ekdoseis Alexandreia.

Reif, K. and Schmitt, H. (1980) 'Nine second-order national elections: a conceptual framework for the analysis of European election results', *European Journal of Political Research*, 8(1): 3–44.

Szczerbiak, A. and Taggart, P. (2000) 'Opposing Europe: party systems and opposition to the Union, the Euro and Europeanisation', SEI Working Paper No. 36, Brighton: Sussex European Institute.

Szczerbiak, A. and Taggart, P. (2008) 'Theorising party-based Euroscepticism: problems of definition, measurement, and causality' in A. Szczerbiak and P. Taggart (eds) *Opposing Europe? The Comparative Party Politics of Euroscepticism*, Oxford: Oxford University Press, Vol. II: 238–263.

Sitter, N. (2001) 'The politics of opposition and European integration in Scandinavia: is Euro-scepticism a government–opposition dynamic?' *West European Politics*, 24(4): 22–39.

Taggart, P. (1998) 'A touchstone of dissent: Euroscepticism in contemporary Western European party systems', *European Journal of Political Research*, 33(3): 363–388.

Teperoglu, E. (2008) 'Οι Ευρωεκλογές στην Ελλάδα' ['Euro-elections in Greece'], PhD thesis, University of Athens.

Tsakatika, M. (2009) 'The Greek coalition of the left: turning eurosceptic?' *International and European Politics* 14: 143–161 [in Greek].

Vasilopoulou, S. (2010) 'Euroscepticism and the radical right: domestic strategies and party system dynamics', PhD thesis, London School of Economics.

Verney, S. (1990) 'To be or not to be within the European Community: the party debate and democratic consolidation in Greece' in G. Pridham (ed.) *Securing Democracy: Political Parties and Democratic Consolidation in Southern Europe*, London: Frances Pinter: 203–223.

Verney, S. (1994) 'Panacea or plague: Greek political parties and accession to the European Community, 1974–1979', PhD thesis for King's College London.

Verney, S. (1996) 'The Greek socialists' in J. Gaffney (ed.) *Political Parties and the European Union*, London: Routledge: 170–188.

Verney, S. (2002) 'Challenges to Greek identity', *European Political Science*, 1(2): 12–16.

Verney, S. and Featherstone, K. (1996) 'Greece' in J. Lodge (ed.) *The 1994 Elections to the European Parliament*, London: Frances Pinter: 107–121.

9 Czech Republic

Vít Hloušek and Petr Kaniok[1]

Introduction

The Czech Republic is not usually ranked among countries supporting European integration enthusiastically and unreservedly. The fall of the Czech government midway through the Czech presidency of the EU Council, and especially the complications the Czech president Václav Klaus created around the ratification of the Lisbon Treaty, remain in living memory (Rybář 2010, 51–52). Klaus's Eurosceptic attitude is sometimes identified with the Czech political mainstream, but as we shall see the spectrum of opinions expressed by Czech political parties is substantially wider.

Almost immediately after the fall of the communist regime, the slogan 'Return to Europe' appeared in the country, to which Czech politicians promptly added that the return was to be symbolic, as Czech lands had formed an integral part of European history until the onset of the Communist rule. Only in the mid-1990s had these general ideas been transformed into actual efforts to approach the EU with full membership as the ultimate aim.[2] Apparent in election campaigns, the dynamics of growing interest on the part of Czech parties in European issues has corresponded to this: it has been observable in national parliamentary elections since 1998 and peaked in the last parliamentary election preceding EU accession in 2002. The attitudes of the relevant Czech parties towards European integration had become stable by then. While the Christian and the Social Democrats (as well as the then relevant liberal Freedom Union) can be described as having been pro-European parties, the Communists can be classified as having stood somewhere between soft and hard Euroscepticism. The Civic Democrats were soft Eurosceptics, believing that there is no alternative to Czech membership in the EU, but that the EU's political system does not work well and ought to be reformed in a number of areas, generally weakening the supranational and strengthening the intergovernmental character of the Union (Kopeček and Šedo 2003).

It is important for our research that attitudes of the Czech parties have remained essentially unchanged since the 2002 election (Havlík 2011a). The Social (ČSSD) and Christian Democrats (KDU-ČSL) have remained pro-European and the Civic Democrats (ODS) have kept their ambivalent soft

Eurosceptic position.[3] Only the Communist Party (KSČM) has taken something of a pragmatic turn. Since May 2004 its appeals against Czech membership in the EU have ceased, although a very critical attitude towards the present character of the EU remains in its programme. Generally speaking, KSČM no longer uses its Euroscepticism to mobilise voters and, except where European Parliament elections are concerned, it is virtually silent on the matter of European integration.

The just-outlined approach of the Communists who do not employ their Euroscepticism to mobilise voters points to an important trait in Czech party politics, namely the low salience of European integration issues in party programmes and especially in their mobilisation strategies. Generalising the matter somewhat we can say that the dynamics of development of Czech party programmes from the mid-1990s had been marked by a fairly steadily increasing importance of integration issues. To simplify, this trend had been in direct proportion to the real prospects of Czech membership in the EU, reaching its peak in the campaign preceding the 2002 election of the Czech Parliament's Chamber of Deputies. Since then, interest in European integration among both parties and voters has consistently decreased, however. Although the problems of the EU and of Czech membership in it remain a constant in the party programmes, the real importance of these issues in campaigns is minimal. Some exceptions aside,[4] Czech political parties remain relatively unaffected as far as direct effects of Europeanisation are concerned (Hloušek and Pšeja 2011).[5]

Otto Eibl's large-scale study, which maps the Czech political space from the perspective of both parties and electorate (2011, chapters 7 to 9), produces results which support our thesis. It is becoming apparent that parties devote much more space to issues of national politics, both in their programmes and in inter-party discussion, and that European integration is at the periphery of their interest. But this is hardly surprising as Czech voters are not interested in European integration either and when they choose a party they focus on domestic issues. In terms of how European integration is discussed, we could say that the political mainstream is fairly pragmatic. This is probably connected with another factor suggested by Tim Haughton (2009) in his attempt to explain the prevailing Czech attitude to the EU. In addition to reasons that were ideological and economic in character, as well as those of a more *realpolitik* nature, one of the key factors favouring Czech accession was the feeling that the country would be weak and vulnerable if it was to remain outside. This is in line with the fact that – with the exception of a few cases that were seized upon by the media as newsworthy and could be used politically, such as the ratification of the Lisbon treaty – the Europeanisation of the individual Czech policies has been progressing fairly smoothly, and that the Czech politicians have been pragmatically adjusting their strategies in consideration of the country's EU membership. With an equal pragmatism, they do not turn integration issues into bones of political contention.

In other words, in practical politics there is not much space either for radical rejection of, or excessive enthusiasm for, the EU, although there have been some rhetorical exceptions to this, as we shall see below from programmes for the

2004 and 2009 elections of the European Parliament (EP). In the following sections of the chapter we will subject these programmes to a qualitative content analysis. Focusing mainly on parties which gained seats in the EP, we will then compare both elections in terms of the structure and themes of the election programmes and draw some general conclusions.

Party positions in 2004

The 2004 election of the European Parliament had a specific quality in that it took place shortly after Czech accession to the EU. This is one of the reasons why the election programmes were fairly brief. The programme of the victorious Civic Democratic Party only contained 1960 words, whereas its election programme for the 2002 election of the Czech Parliament's Chamber of Deputies contained 7716 words and in 2006 the party needed as many as 26,456 words to express its position. The programmes of other parties relevant at the time exhibit similar imbalance.[6] However, during the period between the parliamentary election in summer 2002 and accession of the Czech Republic to the European Union in May 2004 in particular, European issues had been abundantly present in other programmes and campaigns of the Czech parties[7] and the programmes for the EP election were thus mostly summarising and repeating positions already adopted.

A certain lack of experience on the part of Czech parties had become apparent in the form of the election campaign: the Social Democrats came up with a modified version of the campaign used for the election of the national parliament, whereas most of the other parties hedged their bets on a strategy 'cribbed' from local elections (Šaradín 2007, 47). In particular, the oppositional Civic Democrats declared openly that they intended to use the election campaign to unleash a robust critique of the governing coalition consisting of the Social Democrats, Christian Democrats and the liberal Freedom Union–Democratic Union.[8] In this sense, the issues and rhetoric in the campaign – notably the focus on domestic political issues and mutual attacks between the contestants – did correspond to the theory of second-order elections (Bradová and Šaradín 2004, 191–195 and 203–205; Linek 2005, 984–991; Rulíková 2004; Šaradín 2007, 48–52). Our aim in this chapter is not to analyse the campaign but the contents of the election programmes.

Thirty-two Czech parties, movements and coalitions stood for the 2004 election of the European Parliament. Our analysis will only focus on the programmes of those entities which gained seats in the EP, namely ČSSD, KDU-ČSL, KSČM, Independents, ODS and SNK-ED. The character and number of documents analysed preclude the possibility that a statistical analysis would produce relevant data. We will therefore employ qualitative content analysis on the election programmes, aiming to describe and compare their contents in three dimensions: identity, representation and policies.

In specifying the important themes of the 2004 election programmes of the Czech parties we can rely on Petr Buchal's (2004) summary analysis. Specifically, the campaign at the time was about evaluating the conditions negotiated for Czech accession. Although the governing parties did not comment on the issue, all opposition parties criticised the negotiated conditions as being insufficiently favourable to the Czech Republic. Even the governing parties promised to negotiate with the EU over interim periods involving unequal conditions concerning the free movement of people, and also over subsidies to Czech farmers. Essentially all of the programmes mentioned the issue of maximising the flow of money from EU structural funds, mostly without any detailed elaboration. The theme of Czech national interests appeared in the parties' programmes in a very vague fashion. None of the parties specified what this concept encompassed and the Christian Democrats did not talk about national interests at all.

In terms of the programme structures for the 2004 election of the European Parliament, it is surprising that practically all of the parties observed lacked any clear statements about identity. The parties did not deal with issues of either national or European identity.[9] Likewise lacking were mentions of the cultural determinants of these identities.[10] A partial explanation can be sought in the fact that the Czech Republic is a highly homogeneous state both ethnically[11] and territorially.[12] Another reason that was probably more important at the time was that the parties had already given vent to their opinions on these issues in the campaign ahead of the EU accession referendum, and in the discussion about the relationship between the Czech Republic and the EU which took place in the 1990s. The generally accepted slogan of 'Return to Europe' had an implicit subtext: the Czech Republic is part of Europe and Czech national identity does not clash with European integration.

Explicit emphasis on co-operation with ideologically and politically similar parties from other EU member countries in the European Parliament was a specific element in some of the 2004 programmes (ČSSD, KSČM, ODS). Given the fact that this was the very first election of the EP in the Czech Republic, some parties (ČSSD and ODS) briefly introduced the institution and its competences in their programmes.

Let us look first at the presentation of general attitudes towards the EU and the role of the Czech Republic in the Union. Interestingly, in 2004 the Czech parties which strongly supported the EU project and Czech accession were cautious on their general vision of European integration and their own attitudes towards the Union. In the introduction to its programme, KDU-ČSL simply summarised the EU as 'a community of peace and stability ... prosperity ... solidarity ... values'. ČSSD valued more positively the impact of the EU on national politics and the economy (MEMBERSHIP) and implicitly supported further deepening of the EU in terms of supranational decision making (EUDEC). But the programme which described its party's general position on Europe most comprehensively was that of SNK-ED. It emphasised that the EU provides new opportunities, and that the Czech Republic should accede to the EU as a self-confident and active partner: 'We want to be a country that co-operates, one which is a respected co-creator of European integration.' But in terms of national activities within Europe (NATACT) the SNK-ED also contained elements of accommodation, explicitly pointing out the necessity of Europeanising Czech political culture. The Civic Democrats also described EU accession as an opportunity, but warned emphatically about the EU's continuing 'federalisation' and its tendency to put smaller member countries on an unequal footing. Generally speaking the ODS programme advocated flexible and essentially multi-speed integration. This attitude reflects well the position of ODS as a soft Eurosceptic party which does not question integration as a whole but is critical of many trends in contemporary EU development.

Parties with clear Eurosceptic orientation obviously used their election programmes to criticise the EU. The Communists in particular emphasised the disadvantages of the conditions of Czech accession. They also criticised the circumstances in Europe at the beginning of the twenty-first century more generally, circumstances caused in their view by the dominance of neo-liberal policies and undue influence of organisations such as NATO, WTO and IMF on European politics. The KSČM programme outlined a very negative image of contemporary European development and talked about economic stagnation, militarism, anti-social policies and turning away from democracy. In its programme the KSČM also outlined its intention to co-operate intensively in the European Parliament with other parties of the European left to achieve 'a radical change of the present EU orientation'. The Communist programme was silent on overall Czech strategy in the EU (NATACT), however. The programme of the Independents appraised Czech accession as a mixture of opportunities and threats, pointing out that the EU is not only 'a friends club' but also a place where countries have to seriously fight for their interests.

In the programmes of ODS, KSČM and SNK-ED, general statements on the European Union overlapped with issues of representation, the question of democratic deficit and how the latter ought to be resolved (EUDEM). Although the term democratic deficit was not explicitly mentioned in any of the programmes, the issue of how democratic and effective decision making is in the EU was addressed by the parties.

SNK-ED took a rather cautious approach to the problem of democratic deficit. The programme supported the adoption of the so-called Constitution for Europe, but it also featured a sweeping critique of excessive regulation and weak performance of the EU's administrative environment. In general the European Democrats' vision of the EU's future was characterised by an emphasis on the development of the free market and a liberal conception of integration. Interestingly, ODS did not use its election programme to explicitly criticise the democratic deficit either. This can be explained with reference to the discussion at the time which focused on the specific Draft Constitution as proposed by the European Convention. ODS believed this Constitution to be useless and, in the points where it strengthened supranational decision making, disadvantageous for the Czech Republic. The Independents also focused on criticising the Draft Constitution proposed by the Convention. The Communists, by contrast, addressed the problematic state of democracy in the EU explicitly. In its programme the KSČM pleaded for 'the democratisation of European institutions (including the

European Parliament), which would reduce the gap that presently exists in terms of decision making between citizens, national parliaments, and the centre from which the EU is directed'. The Euro-optimistic parties, namely the Christian and Social Democrats, did not address the question of democratic deficit at all, but did explicitly support the project of the so-called Euro-constitution. Like SNK-ED, ČSSD was in favour of the Draft Constitution and the Christian Democrats even named EU institutions whose influence should be strengthened. Yet in line with the generally reserved stance in the Czech political debate on the federalist vision of the EU, Euro-federalism was not explicitly espoused, not even by parties relatively closest to this vision, i.e. the Christian and Social Democrats, who preferred the more equivocal language of deepening and strengthening of integration.

The issues of governance and policies featured prominently in the 2004 programmes of the Czech political parties, both in terms of space devoted to them and substance. Let us look first at how the programmes accentuated (or not) selected policies that featured in the programmes with varying frequencies. At one end of an imaginary axis stand ČSSD,[13] SNK-ED and the Independents, parties which opined on none of the selected policies. Whereas with ČSSD and the Independents the main problem was the extraordinary brevity and generality of their election programmes, SNK-ED dedicated most of its programme to a presentation of its domestic policy. This can be explained by the relative novelty of the party at the time and its need to use every channel possible to communicate its 'first-order' programme.[14]

At the other end of our imaginary axis stand ODS, KSČM and above all KDU-ČSL, parties which showed interest in at least some of the policies observed. Out of those, ODS only dealt with social and migration policies.[15] Whereas in social policy (SGSOC) the party clearly preferred the national level of governance and refused its Europeanisation (as it did with tax policy), in asylum and migration policy (SGIMMI) it demanded EU-wide co-ordination.

The programme of KSČM was exceptionally interesting in selected areas. The party addressed almost all of the policies observed except matters falling under the Ministries of Justice and Interior (SGJHA) and those concerning migration (SGIMMI). Despite its general Eurosceptic attitude, KSČM demanded either dominance of supranational governance (SGDEF) or a blend of supranational and national governance (SGFORE, SGSOC, SGENV). It must be added, however, that in their programme the Communists linked those hopes with the transformation of the EU as a whole, so that there would be greater redistribution and state or supranational regulation. Their position in foreign and defence policies was in turn linked with their long-term opposition to the US presence in Europe, and their demand for NATO dissolution. In a strict sense this was not an acceptance of common foreign and security policy or European security and defence policy. Among the Czech parties relevant in the last decade, KDU-ČSL had the most federalist programme, and this was apparent in the policies observed. KDU-ČSL addressed all but social and environmental policies (SGSOC, SGENV), believing that they ought to be executed by combined supranational and national governance. The party specifically enumerated the tools that would strengthen EU governance in foreign and security policies. A certain exception to the general federalist drift of the Christian Democrats' election programme was family policy, to which this party – oriented chiefly towards the Catholic electorate – dedicated substantial attention, writing in its programme explicitly: 'We do not agree with the initiatives of certain European institutions, enticing member states to become involved in law-making incompatible with traditional family values.'

Party positions in 2009

As was the case with programmes for the 2004 election of the EP, the 2009 election and its results do not offer sufficient data to make a reliable statistical analysis. In this second EP election in the Czech Republic, seats were obtained by only four of the 33 parties who put up their candidates. Moreover, the party manifestos either entirely or substantially omitted the dimensions in which this publication analyses the European programmes of the parties. We will therefore submit the 2009 election programmes to the same kind of qualitative content analysis we used previously, using a coding scheme employed to create the dataset for this publication. We will nevertheless add dimensions and themes which the Czech parties accentuated over and above the indicators provided, themes which are specific to Czech circumstances. One such theme is the Czech presidency of the EU Council in the first half of 2009, which had the added interest of the fall of the Czech government in March (Kaniok and Smekal 2009).

In terms of analysing election manifestos, the Czech presidency and the fall of the cabinet are also important for another reason. The fall of Mirek Topolánek's government and the subsequent period in which the political elites found themselves unable to come up with an alternative coalition led to these elites' plan to call an early election for autumn 2009.[16] As such, many political parties started a long election campaign in spring 2009 to cover both European and national elections. The consequence of this was that parties published programmes ahead of the European election which, in addition to European issues, also had to take into account the domestic agenda as much as possible, precisely because the parties had to woo voters for the early election of the national parliament. Due to this structural circumstance, the 'European' programmes were diluted by domestic issues much more than is usually the case. This remains true despite the fact that ČSSD for instance attached to its national programme for the EP election the generic programme of the Party of European Socialists (PES) written for the same purpose.[17] Among the parties analysed, ČSSD was the only one that incorporated a document of its parent Euro-party into its programme.

During the 2004–2009 term the position of certain Czech parties which gained seats in the first EP election changed. The Independents had disintegrated by 2004. Their two MPs Jana Bobošíková and Vladimír Železný then created their own entities under whose banners they sought to defend their seats in 2009.

Jana Bobošíková created the association Sovereignty-Party of Common Sense, whereas Vladimír Železný's project was entitled Libertas.cz. The Euro-optimist formation SNK-ED went through a similarly turbulent development which resulted in part of the leadership leaving in 2008 for the newly established European Democratic Party. Needless to say, none of the new or reconstructed parties won seats in the EP and this chapter therefore does not analyse their programmes.[18]

In terms of the structure and conceptualisation of their programmes, the parties analysed can be divided into two categories. The first encompasses entities which have published extensive and compact programmes containing coherent and often very detailed visions (ODS, ČSSD, KDU-ČSL). These three parties were very concrete in a number of policies and went into great detail. KSČM, by contrast, only issued a two page manifesto for the election which presented a generic programme in bullet points. Characteristically, this second type of programme usually employs negative rhetoric; KSČM focused more on what it does not want in the EU, whereas the first type of programme allowed the parties to present their positive visions as well.

Let us turn now to an analysis of concrete dimensions, to which parties dedicate varying degrees of attention. In evaluating the importance of these dimensions one must carefully consider their contents. Respecting strictly the indicators defining the dimensions, one arrives at a different picture than when one considers the additional policies and topics that Czech parties have brought into their manifestos. In the former approach, the programmes are dominated by the dimension of representation, simply because the Czech parties have expressed their views on policies other than those preferred by the coding scheme. Contrariwise, when all common policies are taken into account, the main determinant becomes the dimension of governance and policies, with greater importance placed on common policies.

The dimension of representation was clearly present in the programmes, although it did not manifest itself solely in the indicators observed. An example of this can be already seen in the first indicator: the evaluation of Czech membership in the EU (MEMBERSHIP). Half of the parties analysed (ODS, KSČM) did not do any evaluation whatsoever. It is interesting that KDU-ČSL and ČSSD, that is parties which are generally considered Euro-optimist, had mixed views about the membership which was not therefore evaluated in clearly positive terms.

The parties devoted somewhat more attention to the decision making process in the EU (EUDEC). ODS in particular treated this theme at length, expressing its preference for the intergovernmental character of European integration. The party explicitly defined two possible directions for the EU's future development: it will either take the direction towards 'a closed regional power bloc with the greatest degree of legal, political and economic unity – something of a European state' or it will choose the 'path of a flexible, economically open and constantly enlarging whole, which will lead towards the concept of flexible or variable integration'. ODS clearly preferred to support the latter option and to criticise federalist tendencies. KDU-ČSL and ČSSD did not deal with EU decision making in their programmes, whereas KSČM was explicitly in favour of increasing the European Parliament's competence while also criticising unjustified transfers of political power from nation states to supranational institutions.

Czech parties viewed the role of their country in the EU (NATACT) soberly. Manifestos generally advocated an active Czech role in co-operation with other countries, but differed in how they understood this active role and the premises on which their conceptions were based. For instance, ČSSD and ODS shared a vision in which an active role for the Czech Republic might secure its national interests, whereas ČSSD (and KDU-ČSL) explicitly understood European politics as domestic politics, ODS, on the contrary, took defence of, and lobbying for, national interests as its starting point. ODS also differed from other parties in that its contextualisation of the role of the country in the EU was substantially inflected by Czech presidency of the EU Council and its evaluation of the presidency.[19] The party devoted significant space to introducing a new political group in the European Parliament, the European Conservatives and Reformists (ECR), into which its MEPs would enter after the election, as they eventually did. ČSSD also mentioned ECR in its manifesto, but in negative terms.

In terms of understanding the EU's democratic deficit the parties were divided evenly. Whereas ČSSD and KDU-ČSL did not devote much space to this problem in their programmes, KSČM spoke out explicitly in favour of 'stronger competences for the European Parliament and national parliaments instead of uncontrollable bureaucracy' and against 'increasing bureaucracy, nonsensical norms and opaque systems for deciding common matters by the EU's executive bodies'. ODS was also explicitly critical of European bureaucracy. None of the parties has grappled with the problem of democratic deficit in a complex fashion, however.

As we already said above, for the Czech case the dimension of governance and policies must be divided into two sections which construct two different pictures. The first picture is constructed by the indicators covering selected policies; the second by those of the first plus other policies that were actually present in the programmes, policies that often exceeded the selected ones in breadth, depth and attention devoted to them.

In terms of dividing competencies, some of the selected policies contained certain interesting elements. KDU-ČSL was the greatest advocator of the supranational model of decision making, preferring its exclusive use in most of the indicators observed. The only exception to this was the social policy where KDU-ČSL favoured a mixture of supranational and national levels. KDU-ČSL was also the Czech party which granted the most attention to the policies observed, dealing with all of them except environmental policy (SGENV).

Other parties were not as consistent, either in the breadth of their interest or in preferring one model for dividing competencies between the EU, nation states and, potentially, the sub-national level. In terms of dividing competencies, the Social Democrats were the second biggest advocate of the supranational model, proposing its sole use in immigration (SGIMMI) and defence (SGDEF) policies.

For social policy (SGSOC) the party opted for a split of competencies between national and supranational levels. ODS and KSČM, meanwhile, were explicit only on two policies observed: social and defence. Whereas ODS preferred to grant competencies in both areas to nation states only, KSČM preferred a division of competencies between national and supranational level.

The Czech parties showed no interest whatsoever in environmental policy (SGENV), as none of the programmes dealt with it explicitly. Foreign policy (SGFORE) was similarly neglected, as among the parties studied here only KDU-ČSL dealt with it.

All of the parties dedicated the same amount of attention, or even more, to alternative EU policies, particularly energy and economic policies, framed by the context of the economic crisis. The first policy in particular was dealt with extensively, with ODS proposing 'the most European solution possible', emphasising the need to deepen integration. The importance of this policy for ODS is obvious from the fact that the party dedicated five pages to it. KDU-ČSL also devoted significant space in its programme to this policy and advocated a supranational approach; ČSSD opted for the same model of decision making in energy policy.

The second policy not taken into account by the indicators but featuring prominently in the programmes of the Czech parties was economic policy. Here the parties generally adhered to their previous positions on the division of competences. ODS opted for an ad hoc division of competences between the EU and nation states, believing that the role of the EU was to observe strictly the four freedoms, whereas member states would adopt concrete measures in their capacity of sovereigns. Contrariwise and in line with their general focus, ČSSD and KDU-ČSL tended to prefer a Europe-wide solution to the economic crisis.

KSČM's programme was rather problematic in terms of policies. Rather laconic and mixing together attitudes on exclusively national issues with proclamations pertaining to the European level, it was indicative of the party's general stance rather than expressing its opinions on specific European policies.

We have left the dimension of identity for the very end of our analysis of the 2009 election, as this dimension did not play a relevant role in Czech parties' programmes. It was only briefly mentioned in ČSSD's programme in connection with national identity (IDNAT), and completely ignored by other parties. The theme of national culture and its protection (NACULT) was not explicitly treated by the manifestos. As far as European identity is concerned (EUCULT), ČSSD and KDU-ČSL made positive mentions of it; the other two parties were silent. KDU-ČSL was most specific here, listing explicitly the values that in the party's opinion define European identity: 'freedom qualified by responsibility, respect for every human being and for human work, solidarity with those who need it and a peaceful settlement of disputes'. The Christian Democrats were also the only party which referred to the EU's lack of identity as a problem threatening its ability to act. The programmes did not deal with issues of sub-national culture (SUBCULT) and identity (IDSUB) to any identifiable degree, which is not surprising given the character of the Czech Republic and of its party system: these issues do not play any role in the country's politics on the national level either.

Conclusion

This chapter has analysed the manifestos of European Parliament elections in the Czech Republic. A spatio-temporal comparison of the three dimensions analysed reveals that the parties dedicated most attention to the issues of representation and common EU policies. The agenda of identity, both national and European, played a marginal role. In terms of which levels of governance were preferred by the Czech parties for implementing individual policies, the crucial divider is between the national and supranational levels, because the sub-national level is not important in Czech politics.

Looking inside the individual dimensions, we see that in the dimension of representation the decisive indicator is the issue of defining the Czech Repub-lic's role within the EU. In this the Czech parties are consistently pragmatic and view their country as a co-operating partner. But stressing the advantages and disadvantages of Czech membership is not something that either Euro-optimistic or Eurosceptic parties do. This can be explained with reference to the fact that no relevant Czech party questions the country's EU membership. Parties like-wise do not emphasise the problem of democratic deficit; if it appears in their programmes at all, it takes the form of brief mentions of the need to decrease EU bureaucracy. Rather than suggesting that Czech parties think seriously about the EU's democratic deficit, this is more of a fragmentary reflection of the generally shared perception that the EU is too bureaucratic.

ODS, which has been applying the concept of 'flexible integration' to the EU for a considerable time now, has presented the most developed arguments in the dimension of representation. The remaining three parties do not have such a detailed conception of EU organisation, not even the Euro-optimistic parties. Interestingly, none of them (and this includes the Euro-optimistic SNK-ED which was successful in the first election) advocates, explicitly or implicitly, a vision of a federalist Europe.

It is in the dimension of policy and governance that the parties observed are most active and communicative, but it nevertheless remains true that this dimen-sion cannot be explained solely in terms of the selected indicators. In 2009 in particular, parties were dealing extensively with other policies, such as those concerning energy and the economy. These two areas were the main priorities of the Czech presidency of the EU Council which was coming to a close at the time; in 2004, the same parties left these issues unaddressed. Czech parties also devote a great deal of attention to agricultural and cohesion policies, two areas of specific importance for new member countries which are not taken into account by the indicators selected. It is possible to say that in 2009 these pol-icies, together with the priorities of the Czech presidency, namely energy and economic policies, had completely pushed out environmental policy and common foreign and security policy. But given that the effect of the presidency is transitory, this situation is not expected to last.

The parties were fairly consistent in their preferred governance choices throughout the two periods and across the policies observed. KDU-ČSL is the greatest advocate of supranationalism. This attitude of the Christian Democrats is consistent in the long term and is one that they uphold in all policy indicators analysed. Social Democrats are behind KDU-ČSL in this sense, yet they have explicitly mentioned fewer common policies in both of their programmes than the Christian Democrats. ODS is likewise consistent, both in combining supranational and national models of governance and in the harmony between its general and concrete attitudes. The analysis of ODS's programme nevertheless leads us to the following question: to what extent does the persistent labelling of ODS as Eurosceptic reflect actual reality, and how much of it is rather a consequence of reproduced stereotypes? In other words, the question is whether it is methodologically tenable to describe the party's preference for a combination of national and supranational levels of governance as a manifestation of Euroscepticism, albeit tempered by the adjective 'soft'. In contrast, KSČM (which is the fourth stable component of the Czech party system) shows significant inconsistency in its programme. Whereas its first manifesto that we analysed treated the European agenda in a fairly comprehensive manner, in 2009 the party's attitudes on common policies were sketchy, expressed in terse bullet points. The Czech Communists' approach to European issues is decidedly contradictory: as far as their general attitudes to the EU and Czech membership are concerned, they are usually Eurosceptic, but when it comes to specific activities and policies, the party often prefers supranationalism or a combination of national and supranational decision making.

The identity dimension and the sub-national level of politics stand essentially outside the interest of Czech parties. This is especially true of the sub-national level of governance, to an outside observer the Czech Republic appears indeed culturally, ethnically and territorially homogeneous. In the 1990s parties existed in Czech politics that developed the theme of Moravian identity. In the 1996 election, the Moravians lost their position of relevant actor and despite attempts to unify and transform their parties never managed to recover it. Czech membership in the EU, an organisation which grants regional entities institutionalised attention, did not amount to a transformation in this respect and it seems unlikely that this will change in the future. We could likewise ask whether the current neglect of the issues of identity will continue. It seems that the relevant parties do not see a conflict between national and European identities and, some rare exceptions aside, do not feel the need to emphasise either of these identities.

The above findings and observations must be put in the following context. First, like in other EU countries, the positions of Czech parties on European integration are not determined solely by European elections or articulated only in documents published at those occasions. The European and domestic levels are increasingly permeating each other and it is often impossible to determine the cause and effect in their relationship. Second, only two EP elections have taken place in the Czech Republic thus far, both under specific circumstances: the first immediately after Czech accession, the second during the turbulent Czech presidency of the EU Council. Third, Czech experience with European integration remains fairly short and during the period observed has been fairly harmonic, to put it simply. During that time, the Czech Republic has been (and continues to be) a net receiver from the European budget. Throughout these two electoral terms substantial amounts of money flowed into the country without many hiccups via EU structural funds that has allowed a large-scale modernisation of the infrastructure. The individual operation programmes distributing the European money were viewed as a priori positive and uncomplicated. Indeed, the financial benefits of membership have been more important for the parties than discussions about the character of the EU and its future development. In the last couple of years (2011–2013) this view has been changing, however. The media is uncovering large-scale corruption networks connected with the distribution of EU grants, which sheds problematic light on the structural aid provided by the EU, as co-author and accomplice in the corrupt environment. Moreover, the money supply is no longer unproblematic, as from time to time the European Commission stops the payments of certain grants due to corruption scandals. Some political actors then interpret this as 'Brussels' revenge' for Czech Euroscepticism. Needless to say, since 2009 the overall atmosphere in the EU and the perception of European integration has been changing due to the economic crisis, with more criticisms of the EU appearing not only among politicians but also among voters. Only after the third Czech election of the European Parliament, which will take place in 2014 in an atmosphere of economic stagnation at best, will it be possible to assess the programmes of the Czech parties with at least medium-term validity.

Notes

1 This chapter has been written as part of the research project 'Europe 2020: A Horizon of Change of Relevant Actors of the Czech Republic's Political System' (Czech Science Foundation project GA13-24657S).
2 The developing relationship between the Czech Republic and the European Union is analysed in detail by Dan Marek and Michael Baun (2011), for example.
3 For ODS attitudes see Krutílek and Kuchyňková (2006). There are politicians in ODS, however, who do not share the otherwise mainstream soft Eurosceptic attitude, typical of the 2001 Manifesto of Czech Eurorealism, for instance. Moreover, opinion polls show that ODS's electorate shares a much more 'Euro-optimistic' vision in the long term than the party itself. This otherwise paradoxical fact could be interpreted as proof of the claim that the salience of EU issues for Czech voters' decision making is low.
4 In terms of programme, one such an exception is the Green Party (currently without parliamentary representation) which more than other parties integrated European issues into its programme and intertwined its vision of Czech politics with the realities of European integration (Hloušek and Pšeja 2011, 114–115).
5 This is also apparent from the fact that parties' stances towards European integration hardly matter in the process of putting together Czech governments, which are almost always coalitions (Hloušek and Kopeček 2012: 27–33). It was only after the 2002 election that the argument appeared claiming the new government, composed of left-wing ČSSD and right-wing or centre-right parties KDU-ČSL and Freedom Union, is made up from a coalition of pro-European parties and as such will ensure that the Czech accession to the EU will be completed smoothly (Havlík 2011b: 62–63).

6 The Czech Social Democratic Party described its vision of future EU development in 1448 words, the Association of Independent Candidates-European Democrats (SNK-ED) in 2380 words. The most extensive programme was created by the Christian Democrats with 3291 words. The Communists' programme contained 2240 words.

7 One must mention in particular the June 2003 referendum on Czech accession, for which Czech parties, both parliamentary and non-parliamentary, prepared campaigns which communicated to the voters their general positions on the EU and Czech membership in it (Vilímek 2005, 160–166).

8 The results of the European Parliament election have also confirmed the thesis that voters would punish the governing parties. Freedom Union failed to obtain any seats in the EP, whereas the Social Democrats lagged dramatically behind the result they obtained in the election of the national parliament, and only the Christian Democrats, who polled about 10 per cent of the vote, have achieved a standard and predictable result. The opposition parties and particularly the Communists have done well. The Social Democrats' result, who polled under 9 per cent of the vote, led to the resignation of the Social Democratic Prime Minister Vladimír Špidla, but the government coalition survived.

9 Only in the SNK-ED programme do we find an isolated mention of the compatibility between national and European identities.

10 The KSČM programme does contain, however, a vague mention of 'the advantages of national particularities' and of the need to construct 'a multicultural European reality'. SNK-ED declared in a similarly vague manner that Czech cultural traditions can serve as a basis for the country's success in the EU.

11 The most populous minority, the Romani, is not politically organised and its presence in Czech political discourse is therefore usually limited to the rhetoric of marginal extreme right parties (Mareš and Strmiska 2006).

12 There was only one relevant regional movement, that in Moravia and Silesia at the beginning of the 1990s, which was especially strong when the new form of the Czecho-Slovak federation was being decided. After Czechoslovakia's disintegration, the electoral support for and political relevance of Moravian parties decreased sharply, however (Strmiska 2000).

13 The programme of the Social Democrats was exceedingly laconic. In terms of policies and governance, it contained fragmentary and vague statements about developing the following: the European social model, a prospering and competitive economy which is at the same time socially responsible, European security and foreign policies, and general co-operation between member countries. Overall we can describe ČSSD's programme as strongly federalist. The problem lies in its declarative character which does not allow one to determine the level of governance on which the Social Democrats would prefer to implement individual policies.

14 The party European Democrats appeared in 2002, and in 2004 it formed a coalition with the political movement Association of Independent Candidates (SNK). In 2006 SNK and ED merged.

15 The programmes of ODS emphasised the necessity of reforming the CAP so that it would not discriminate against new member states. The party preferred transatlantic links in foreign and security policies. Generally speaking the Civic Democrats were in favour of equalising the circumstances under which new and old countries function in the EU.

16 The election eventually took place in the regular term in 2010, because following the complaint of one of ČSSD's former MPs Miloš Melčák the Constitutional Court annulled the early term of September 2009.

17 Analysis of ČSSD's programme is based on the national programme only and contents of the PES programme are not taken into account.

172 V. Hloušek and P. Kaniok

18 Another reason is that the programmes of many of these entities can no longer be found, as they either ceased to exist soon after the election (Libertas.cz), do not produce any noticeable activity (European Democratic Party) or are in constant flux of mergers and amalgamations with other parties (for instance, in 2011 Sovereignty became Sovereignty-Jana Bobošíková's Block).
19 ODS, the main governmental party at the time of the Czech presidency, dedicated one chapter (four pages) of its programme to this issue. The graphic design of the ODS programme was in fact heavily inspired by the logo of the presidency, employing its colour combination and referring to the visual design used for the presidency.

References

Bradová, E. and P. Šaradín (2004) 'Volební kampaň', in P. Šaradín (ed.), *Volby do Evropského parlamentu v České republice*, Olomouc: Periplum: 179–207.

Buchal, P. (2004) 'Analýza volebních programů', in P. Šaradín (ed.), *Volby do Evropského parlamentu v České republice*, Olomouc: Periplum: 209–235.

Eibl, O. (2011) *Politický prostor a témata v České republice v letech 2006–2008*, Brno: Centrum pro studium demokracie a kultury a Institut pro srovnávací politologický výzkum.

Haughton, Tim (2009) 'For business, for pleasure or for necessity? The Czech Republic's choices for Europe', *Europe-Asia Studies*, 61, 8: 1371–1392.

Havlík, V. (2011a) 'A-breaking-up of a pro-European consensus: attitudes of Czech political parties towards the European integration (1998–2010)', *Communist and Post-Communist Studies*, 44, 2: 129–147.

Havlík, V. (2011b) 'Česká republika', in S. Balík, Vlastimil Havlík, Vratislav Havlík, J. Kmeˆt and P. Svačinová (eds), *Koaliční vládnutí ve střední Evropě (1990–2010)*, Brno: Mezinárodní politologický ústav Masarykovy univerzity: 39–90.

Hloušek, V. and L. Kopeček (2012) *Záchrana státu? Úřednické a polopolitické vlády v České republice a Československu*, Brno: Barrister & Principal.

Hloušek, V. and P. Pšeja (2011) 'Europeanization of political parties and the party system in the Czech Republic', in T. Haughton (ed.), *Party Politics in Central and Eastern Europe: Does EU Membership Matter?* London and New York: Routledge: 101–127.

Kaniok, P. and H. Smekal (2009) 'The Czech presidency of the EU Council: no triumph, no tragedy', *Romanian Journal of European Affairs*, 9, 9: 59–79.

Kopeček, L. and J. Šedo (2003) 'Czech and Slovak political parties and their vision of European integration', *Central European Political Studies Review*, 5, 1 (www.cepsr.com).

Krutílek, O. and P. Kuchyňková (2006) 'ODS a evropská integrace', in P. Pšeja, L. Mrklas, P. Fiala, F. Mikš, M. Pink, J. Kyloušek, M. Mareš, S. Balík, M. Loužek, O. Krutílek, P. Kuchyňková, K. Zetocha, P. Žáček, P. Sokol, R. Chytilek, O. Eibl, A. Barták and J. Holzer, *Občanská demokratická strana a česká politika*, Brno: Centrum pro studium demokracie a kultury: 159–174.

Linek, L. (2005) 'Czech Republic', *European Journal of Political Research*, 44, 7–8: 983–993.

Marek, D. and M. Baun (2011) *The Czech Republic and the European Union*, London and New York: Routledge.

Mareš, M. and M. Strmiska (2006) 'Political participation by ethnic minorities in the Czech Republic', in T. Sirovátka (ed.), *The Challenge of Social Inclusion: Minorities and Marginalised Groups in Czech Society*, Brno: Barrister & Principal: 267–289.

Rulíková, M. (2004) 'The European Parliament Election in the Czech Republic June 11–12 2004', 2004 European Parliament Election Briefing No 9, Brighton, Sussex European Institute.

Rybář, M. (2010) 'Domestic politics and national preferences in the European Union', in D. Malová, M. Rybář, V. Bilčík, E. Láštic, Z. Lisoňová, M. Mišík and M. Pašiak, *From Listening to Action? New Member States in the European Union*, Bratislava: Devín: 33–56.

Šaradín, P. (2007) 'Česká republika', in P. Šaradín (ed.), *Evropské volby v postkomunistických zemích*, Olomouc: Periplum: 47–60.

Strmiska, M. (2000) 'Rise and fall of Moravian regional parties', *Central European Political Studies Review*, 2, 4 (www.cepsr.com).

Vilímek, P. (2005) 'Česká republika', in P. Fiala and M. Pitrová (eds), *Evropská referenda*, Brno: Centrum pro studium demokracie a kultury: 155–176.

10 Hungary

Réka Várnagy

Introduction

For a long time the Hungarian party system had not absorbed the question of European integration into its pattern of competition mainly because in spite of the conflicting nature of party politics the issue of integration was characterized by a high level of consensus both on the mass and the elite level. As in other countries of the CEE region EU accession was regarded as a necessity or an opportunity for the country to finally occupy the place it deserves in the European club. The lack of interest resulted in a low-profile campaign for the European Parliament dominated by domestic issues. However, in spite of its second-order nature, in 2009 the EP elections gained momentum as two new parties, the radical right-wing For the Right Hungary (*Jobbik*) and the green Politics Can Be Different (LMP), entered the political arena as relevant political actors with Jobbik winning three out of the 22 European parliamentary mandates. With the failure of the Alliance of Liberal Democrats (SZDSZ) to win any seat to the European Parliament, one of the most pro-European parties disappeared from the political arena, while hard Euroskepticism that used to be represented by extra-parliamentary parties became palpable with the strengthening of Jobbik. While the domestic political context was certainly the driving force of change, the stance and the interaction of parties regarding the European process cannot be neglected: the growing number of Euromanifestos presented and the appearance of high-profile politicians on party lists suggest that Hungarian parties started to use the European political arena and define themselves in the European dimension as well. The fact that the new pattern of party system emerging at the EP elections was further reinforced at the 2010 general elections also supports the assumption that European and national level politics strongly interact.

The aim of this study is to present on the one hand how Hungarian parties relate to the European question and on the other hand how party dynamics evolve in the European dimension. Both aspects are critical in order to understand if, how and where parties support or hinder the European process. Party-related variables drawn from mainstream literature on party attitudes such as party ideology, mainstream–radical stance and government–opposition role will

be analyzed along with impact of the old–new member state dichotomy suggested by Conti (2012) to evaluate how Hungarian party discourse on the EU fits
into the framework of the INTUNE project.

Theoretical and methodological considerations

The framework of this Euromanifesto project builds heavily on the hypothesis
established by mainstream literature on party attitudes namely that mainstream
parties tend to be supportive of the EU while Euroskepticism emerges among
radical parties; that center-left are the most pro-European while center-right
parties express more cautious views about the European process and that being
in government or in opposition might influence the attitudes of some parties with
opposition forces being more critical toward the EU (see Introduction to this
volume). Some of these assumptions have already been tested on the Hungarian
case and results mainly resonate with expected findings: relating to the 2004 EP
elections Bátory (2008) has shown that hard Euroskepticism only emerges at the
periphery of the political spectrum with mainstream parties representing pro-
Europeanism or soft Euroskepticism. Bátory also addresses the question of
ideology-based Euroskepticism suggesting that the relationship between radical
and mainstream parties, namely their coalition potential, also has a great influence on the stance they take since radicalism can inhibit coalition formation in
democracies where an overall consensus characterizes the question of integration
(2008, 275). Ideology-driven Euroskepticism is also tackled by Enyedi (2006)
who points out the problems arising when applying this model in the Hungarian
context. He argues that while in Western European countries the left–right divide
can mostly be translated into economic terms, in Hungary the left–right cleavage
encompasses strong cultural elements with the right rooted in a conservative/
anti-communist worldview and the left in a socialist-liberal tradition. He further
develops his argument by indicating that parties can send mixed messages about
their stances on the European integration with Fidesz, the most influential center-
right party being one of the best examples. While in line with Taggart and
Szczerbiak's findings (2002, 2004) Bátory classifies Fidesz as being soft
Euroskeptic, Enyedi contradicts this view and points out that in the 2004 EP
campaign, Fidesz led a two-faced campaign with populist rhetoric accompanied
by a less visible pro-European side reflected in its elaborated program and in its
elaborated and highly visible EP website (2006, 163). Finally, concerning the
government–opposition divide no clear pattern emerges due to the fact that in
2004 and 2009 there was no variation in the government–opposition divide since
a Socialist-Liberal coalition was in government in 2004 and the Socialist party
governed in minority in 2009.

Besides these general assumptions, new considerations on party attitudes
have also emerged that complement these hypotheses. Some of these originate
from the case-study approach authors take and thus they endorse specific
context-based explanatory variables. In this sense the radical–mainstream party
divide is further developed by Bátory (2008) who points out the importance of

coalition potential by arguing that in the Hungarian context hard Euroskepticism can hinder the coalition-making potential of parties and thus even radical parties with strong stances on Europe tend to be more open to compromise in case of potentially becoming partners in a coalition. This question also relates to government–opposition dynamics suggesting that parties are not only influenced by their actual role in the political arena but also by their expectations and future-oriented strategies. In this dimension the timing of the EP elections is crucial since opposition–government dynamics can be different when the elections are mid-term or when they are close to the parliamentary elections and thus can be considered as a run-up race.

A new explanation also emerges from a territorial divide pointing out the differences between old and new member states. A general expectation is that Euroskepticism is mounting (Taggart and Szczerbiak 2002) and more widespread in the Central-Eastern European region (Cotta and Russo 2012) and that further empowerment of EU institutions is less supported in new member states as they are more nation-centered and resist Europeanization of several policies (Real-Dato *et al.* 2012). Despite the overall consensus on the necessity of European integration documented in Hungary, the fact that the support for EU membership has been decreasing (Eurobarometer 71 2009) opens up the possibility of rising Euroskepticism in party attitudes especially in the case of new parties in which the traditional pro-European attitude characterizing parties born at the time of regime change is not rooted.

The overview of the theoretical considerations suggests that the Hungarian case is worthy of in-depth analysis as the assumed explanatory variables (mainly developed in the Western European or old member states context) may not apply directly in this country: the pattern in CEE countries is different from that in the Western European ones, the left–right divide has different implications and radical parties have become particularly prominent in the recent past. The analysis of the Euromanifestos issued for the 2004 and 2009 EP elections enables us to test these hypotheses on a dataset encompassing a wide range of variables that reflect the content of the party programs and thus the official party attitudes expressed toward the integration process. While the applied methodology allows us to gain insight into the party attitudes as expressed by the party in central office, certain methodological issues need to be addressed. The first concerns the validity of the opinions expressed in the Euromanifestos. Political discourse on the EU encompasses a wide range of communication channels such as public speeches, press materials, parliamentary debates, government and party programs. Different elements of the political discourse are born in different political contexts in which parties can follow various priorities such as complying with coalition requirements, painting a negative image of the competitors or answering the needs of a target. In this sense the institutional context for the Euromanifestos is identical: the campaign itself for the European Parliamentary elections, thus Euromanifestos or even the lack of them offers an important insight into the role of EU issues in the domestic party arena. While the narrow focus is certainly an advantage in this sense, it can also offer contradictory results compared to previous analyses that are more rooted in a case study approach. Investigating the 2009 EP campaign Mihályffy demonstrated that in the case of Fidesz the messages addressed in the broad campaign (including TV spots and billboard messages) are not identical to the messages expressed in the party program which is rather targeted to an elite group of party supporters (Mihályffy 2010). The same stands true for the Liberal SZDSZ which focused on policy issues in the program but built its campaign on becoming the "third political force" next to the left-wing government and right-wing opposition and on offering a viable alternative to the radical right-wing party Jobbik. In his analysis Enyedi (2006) also points out how different channels of communication are used to express different views on the Union which can sometimes be almost contradictory: the example of Fidesz can be cited again with its politicians often expressing more Euroskeptic views than the party's program would suggest. Despite the differences in messages the importance of Euromanifestos should not be underestimated as often they are the only comprehensive written documents that are issued in a European context. While even in a written form they often offer simplistic and linear arguments, following Conti's framework presented in the Introduction to this volume, Euromanifestos allow us to investigate parties' official stances, specific positions and preferences on the EU process, to assess whether they take pro-European or more Euroskeptical attitudes and to illustrate whether the EU question has been absorbed in the pattern of party competition.

The second methodological question concerns the dataset that includes Euromanifestos issued by Hungarian parties for the EP elections. Being a new member state EP elections have been held twice in Hungary, in 2004 and 2009 parties presented eight party lists at each election.[1] Out of the eight parties the four parliamentary parties – the Conservative Fidesz, the Conservative MDF, the Socialist MSZP and the Liberal SZDSZ – were able to establish a party list in both elections, while among the extra-parliamentary parties only the radical left-wing Workers' Party succeeded in presenting a party list twice (but only issued a Euromanifesto in 2009). However running at the EP elections does not necessarily imply issuing a Euromanifesto, a problem faced in other countries of the region as well (see Gagatek in this volume): some parties came up with documents that can hardly be labeled as manifestos (as for example a list of priorities for their EP groups), while others simply chose other forms of communication. As not all parties issued Euromanifestos for the elections, the Hungarian database includes the coding for nine Euromanifestos which is a rather limited number of cases especially if divided into subgroups based on ideology: two Euromanifestos issued by radical parties, one by the left-wing Workers' Party and one by the right-wing Jobbik both from 2009. On the center-left side we have three Euromanifestos: one issued by the governing Socialist party in 2004, one issued by the Liberal SZDSZ in 2009 and one by the green LMP also in 2009. On the center-right side, four Euromanifestos are present, two issued by the Conservative Fidesz and two by the Conservative MDF. Although the small number limits the possibilities of in-depth quantitative analysis, it still offers the opportunity for meaningful comparison: on the one hand the general characteristics of the two EP elections can be compared and on the other hand individual parties or parties belonging to the same subgroup (mainstream–radical, left–right) can be contrasted. In order to carry out this type of comparison it is useful to make a distinction between variables that are expected to remain stable and those that are supposed to follow a dynamic change. Following Conti's argument we can assume that ideology and the centrality along the political spectrum to be associated with continuity while the government–opposition divide is supposed to show discontinuity (2007, 201). As mentioned above in the Hungarian case the government–opposition role of the parties have not changed in between the two elections thus this should not have an impact on the outcome. An important change however occurred in the party system with two new parties, a radical right-wing one and a green one appearing on the scene and one radical right-wing party disappearing from the arena.[2] According to the hypothesis on the territorial cleavage, Euroskepticism is on the rise in new member states which suggest that new parties could express more anti-European attitudes than their antecedents. As Euromanifestos are not available for all parties though the analysis is complemented from other sources as well. The selection of parties that will be compared is further explained in the next section of the chapter.

The Hungarian political context: the party system and the European integration process

At the time of regime change three types of party emerged in the Hungarian political arena: the first labeled "successor party" was the Hungarian Socialist Party (MSZP) that after the collapse of the former state party reformed its image based on the West European Socialist tradition and became the dominant party on the left spectrum of the political scale. Despite its isolation at the time of transition, soon it broke the political quarantine and became a major actor in the party arena gaining 54 percent of mandates at the second democratic election and forming a government with the Liberal Party in 1994. Right after the modernization of the MSZP a radical left-wing group split from the main party and the Hungarian Workers' Party was founded with the aim of following the communist tradition. While the party is still present in the political arena, it has not succeeded in gaining parliamentary representation in the last 20 years. The second type of party, the agrarian Smallholders (FKGP) and the Christian Democrats (KDNP), was rooted in the pre-communist period and were reformed after the transition. These parties managed to build an image based on their historical legitimacy which was strong enough to be included in the right-wing governments of 1990 (FKGP and KDNP) and 1998 (only FKGP). Finally internal conflicts had eroded both parties by 2002 with the KDNP reemerging as an ally to the Conservative Fidesz in 2006. The third type of party was the so-called "new party" born at the time of regime change. On the right-wing spectrum the conservative Hungarian Democratic Forum (MDF) emerged as a conglomerate party incorporating several different political streams. Despite its early success of winning the first democratic elections and forming a coalition government, due to internal differences the party soon eroded into smaller organizations. Among others the radical right-wing Hungarian Justice and Life Party (MIÉP) was founded by former MDF members in 1993. After governing in coalition with Fidesz in 1998–2002 the MDF struggled to uphold its parliamentary presence until 2010 when it dropped out of the legislative arena, while the MIÉP succeeded in entering the parliament only in 1998. Along the MDF two liberal parties also emerged as "new parties": the Liberal Alliance of Free Democrats (SZDSZ) and the Fidesz-Hungarian Civic Union (Fidesz).[3] During the first government the biggest opposition party was the Liberal SZDSZ which quickly became one of the fiercest opposition to the right-wing coalition. With the MSZP searching for a partner among the democratic parties and the SZDSZ looking for an ally to turn down the right-wing government, the first Socialist–Liberal coalition was born in 1994 followed by similar coalitions in 2002 and 2006. The Fidesz, born as a liberal youth party, soon began its transformation toward the right incorporating conservative values into its image. By 1998 the Fidesz was able to win the elections as the major center-right party in the Hungarian political spectrum and became the major opposition party in the following parliamentary cycles.

While a few small parties disappeared from the political landscape no relevant new actors entered the political arena in the first 20 years of Hungarian democracy except for the foundation of MIÉP in 1993. By the middle of the 1990s the Hungarian party system was regarded as consolidated, stable and even frozen (Ágh 1995; Márkus 1997). The left–right dichotomy became the decisive political divide as early as 1993–94 with no parties crossing the line at the times of coalition-building. Thus growing polarization has characterized the Hungarian political arena with the government–opposition dynamic following the left–right divide coupled with a growing tendency of bipolarization both on the elite and the mass level (Enyedi and Casal Bértoa 2011) which reached its peak by the 2010 parliamentary elections.

The growing political hostility and the conflicting nature of politics could suggest that the issue of European integration has been absorbed in political discourse and that many of its dimensions have been explored and debated. However, research carried out in this respect shows otherwise. According to Enyedi (2006) until 2002 the question of integration has not been represented as a conflict in Hungarian political discourse. He argues that the importance and necessity of the accession itself has never been debated since all parties were pro-European in this respect. Hungary has a relatively long tradition of European politics since the opening toward the EU already started in the late 1980s before the change of regime. A trade and cooperation agreement between Hungary and the EEC was signed in September 1988. Due to the change of regime in 1989 the opportunity of taking this cooperation further was considered and Hungary was invited for association negotiations in 1990. At this time all parties agreed on the importance of further strengthening cooperation with Europe, the Liberal SZDSZ and the

Conservative MDF even defined accession as an objective to achieve while the Socialist MSZP and the Conservative Fidesz included the prospect of accession in their program. The Europe Agreement was signed in December 1991 by the first elected Hungarian government headed by the MDF. During the election campaign of 1994 and 1998 the question whether to become a member or not was not present in the mainstream political discourse and although the questions of the accession negotiations were present in the political agenda, the costs and benefits of membership were not evaluated publicly. Euroskepticism however did emerge on the periphery of the political sphere. Bátory (2008) notes that the radical right-wing Hungarian Justice and Life Party expressed views that fall into the category of hard Euroskepticism since its foundation in the early 1990s. But despite being anti-European the party had never opposed the accession itself directly and the party even signed the formal declaration of support to the accession project in 2000. Bátory explains this relatively moderate attitude by the party's parliamentary presence and its objective of developing its coalition potential toward Fidesz in case a right-wing government would be in need of its parliamentary support. However after the lost elections in 2002 the party has returned to its radical rhetoric campaigning for a "no" in the 2003 accession referendum (Bátory 2008, 272–273). A similar tendency can be observed in the case of the Hungarian Workers' Party which originally resisted the idea of European integration based on its rejection of foreign influence. The pressure of repeatedly not gaining parliamentary representation in 1998 motivated the party to take a more permissive stance on EU affairs and promoted voting "yes" at the accession referendum in order to present itself as a viable coalition partner on the left side of the political spectrum (Bátory 2008, 274). The first mainstream critics concerning the accession process emerged in 2002 when Brussels published its plan concerning the reduced agricultural funds available to new member states, a case of concern for all in the CEE region. At that time the MSZP accused the governing Fidesz of not defending national interests. The second period of political discourse on the EU started when the issues concerning Hungary's future within the EU came to the forefront. According to Lakner (2004) the fact that the Conservative party lost the elections in the same year gave further impetus to the development of a political debate concerning integration as since this date a right-wing party has been in the position of opposition. Thus by the 2004 EP elections it became politically possible to criticize the EU without questioning Hungary's membership or suggesting opting out of integration.

While the 2004 elections were fought by the "old parties" rooted in a pro-European tradition, the 2009 elections produced a new situation.

In order to understand fully the impact of the 2009 elections the results of the following parliamentary elections in 2010 should also be considered. After being present in the parliament for five parliamentary cycles the Liberal SZDSZ and the Conservative MDF did not gain parliamentary representation in 2010. These parties had already achieved poor results at the EP elections with the Liberals not gaining any mandates and the MDF barely reaching the required 5 percent threshold securing only one mandate in the EP. On the other hand two new parties entered the parliament in 2010: Jobbik gained 12 percent of votes and 47 seats out of the 356, which is a result quite similar to that of the 2009 EP elections. The LMP which did not succeed in winning an EP mandate with 2.6 percent of votes in 2009 increased significantly its support base and obtained 15 mandates (4 percent) at the parliamentary elections. These numbers indicate that despite the fact that the EP elections can be considered as second-order elections where voters feel more "free" to express their preferences and to vote for opposition and/or new and/or small parties (for latest confirmation of this hypothesis see Hix and Marsh 2011), the new pattern of party competition emerging at the 2009 EP elections proved to be long-lived enough to change the parliamentary composition and earn the title of critical elections in 2010 (Enyedi and Benoit 2011).

In order to present how parties addressed the question of European integration in the two elections and evaluate the similarities and the differences, the framework elaborated within the INTUNE Euromanifesto project will be applied. First, the general characteristics of the two elections will be compared followed by a thematic overview including the questions of identity, policy and representation. Within each topic a party-based comparison aimed at discovering the changes in party attitudes will be presented. For parties such as the Fidesz and the MDF, the base of comparison is evident since these parties issued Euromanifestos for both elections. For other parties the following scheme will be applied: in order to understand the dynamics of radical right-wing Euroskepticism the Euromanifesto of Jobbik issued in 2009 will be analyzed in detail and will be contrasted to the 2004 program of the radical right-wing MIÉP. As MIÉP did not issue a Euromanifesto at the time of running for EP elections, the comparison will be based on other available data sources in order to gain an insight to the dynamics of Euroskepticism. On the other side of the political spectrum we can find the Workers' Party of which only the 2009 Euromanifesto is available. As opposed to the strengthening of the radical right-wing rhetoric, left-wing Euroskepticism did not seem to gain general ground with the Workers' Party, reaching 1.83 and 0.96 percent in the two EP elections, respectively, and so detailed comparison is not carried out in this chapter. Concerning the center-left, one major actor, the MSZP, only issued an official Euromanifesto for the 2004 elections, in 2009 it just produced a leaflet which cannot be considered a program. While the content of the leaflet was not coded in the project, some of its relevant elements will be compared to the 2004 Socialist Euromanifesto. In the conclusion of the chapter the results of the analysis will be interpreted in the light of the hypotheses suggested by the comparative literature and reported in the Introduction to this volume: the growing Euroskepticism characterizing the region, the ideological divide, government–opposition dynamics along with radical–mainstream party type influence the party attitudes toward the EU.

European discourse in the Euromanifestos

Taking a first glance at the dataset including the Euromanifestos of the 2004 and 2009 elections we can observe a significant imbalance of available data for the events: for 2004 we have only three Euromanifestos coded while in 2009 there are six of them, in 2004 only mainstream parties (and not all of them) are included as opposed to 2009 when there is a wide range of parties from both sides of the political spectrum. This asymmetry already suggests that while European Parliamentary elections are often considered second-order (Bátory and Husz 2006), they did gain momentum in Hungary's political agenda. While in 2004 extra-parliamentary parties did not issue an official party program addressing European issues, in 2009 we can find three of them among the parties presenting Euromanifestos. One possible explanation can be the growing salience of European issues although this assumption is not backed up by other indicators as for example the percentage of voting was almost identically low in the two elections (38 and 36 percent respectively). An alternative explanation is that European elections can act as a testing ground for new messages, new tools of campaign or even new parties. The 2009 elections were suitably timed, one year before the general elections to be used as a large-scale opinion poll and a demonstration of strength. With the coalition government breaking down not long before the elections, the economic crisis worsening and the prime minister stepping down at the same party congress where the official Socialist EP list was accepted, the political climate offered a good chance for new parties to make an appearance on the political scene and for opposition parties, especially for Fidesz, to highlight the importance of EP elections and try to position itself as a critical match in the political game. Several factors underline this explanation: according to the rhetoric of Fidesz, the EP elections opened a chance to express dissatisfaction with the government and even to express the need for early elections. Jobbik also recognized the opportunity and instead of staying away from the campaign and discouraging voters as it did in 2004, the party came forward with a detailed program, extensive campaigning and a party list headed by the top party politicians. The LMP also used this opportunity to present itself and its politicians by introducing a list headed by the top politicians of the party along with popular figures of the cultural sphere in order to build a certain intellectual image of the party. Moreover, appearing on the political scene was not limited to the national level as parties also aimed at building an international profile during the campaign: the nomination process became more balanced, the application of gender and other quotas was more frequent and experience at the EU level was rewarded (Ilonszki and Jáger 2006; Várnagy 2010a). Parties also emphasized their embeddedness in the European political context by inviting representatives of their European party families to campaign events and also by referring directly to their European ties in Euromanifestos. Often the content of the Euromanifestos overlapped with the program of European parties to a great extent: in 2009 the Liberal Euromanifesto of SZDSZ bore similarities to the European Liberal Democrat and Reform Party's manifesto accepted in Stockholm in 2008. The Fidesz also included elements from the European People's Party's manifesto and also devoted a subsection to present its role and activities within the European Party. Radical parties also use European references: the Jobbik mentions the British National Party while the Workers' Party associates itself to the European Left.

The heterogeneity of the Euromanifestos resulted in a more complex overall evaluation of European integration. While in 2004 only Fidesz sent mixed messages about European impact on country matters, in 2009 the parties' opinions vary from very positive evaluations to a clearly negative view of the EU. Although negative evaluations were only present in radical programs, among the mainstream parties not only Fidesz but also the LMP sent mixed messages possibly endorsing the overall mixed sentiments of the population. The change in the political climate toward the EU was further emphasized by the fact that both new parties expressed concerns toward the EU while the two parties regarded as most pro-European either did not issue a Euromanifesto or did not evaluate on the impact of integration. While the overall attitude toward the EU is more negative, among mainstream parties the role of Hungary was still perceived as cooperative with only the Workers' Party expressing the need to defend or even reject the Union. The radical right-wing Jobbik torn between its radical image and the fact that membership in the EU is still seen as a value (a problem faced by MIÉP in 2004) offered a twofold solution with speaking about the need to either opt out of the EU or to initiate changes that defend more Hungarian national interests. This latter possibility is taken further in the program by declaring that decision-making competencies should be shifted back to member states instead of supranational empowerment, coupled with a strong critique of European intergovernmental decision-making that is regarded as a "club of political elites". Regarding the level of decision-making the radical right-wing program is clearly incoherent as it calls for more democracy on the EU level but rejects supranational decision-making processes. The Workers' Party is less radical in this sense as it calls for more intergovernmental decision-making which actually dilutes the party's strong anti-European rhetoric based on the need to reject the integration process fully. With reference to the level of decision-making missing from more than half of the Euromanifestos we can conclude that the topic is not a salient element in party discourse. In 2004 as well as in 2009 among the mainstream parties only the Fidesz program talks explicitly about the modes of decision-making with identifying policies where a "stronger Europe" is needed with more supranational power such as in the field of foreign policy and policies where intergovernmental decision-making is preferred. A common element in the Socialist Party's declaration and the Fidesz program is that both express support for the Lisbon Treaty which points toward a positive evaluation of further integration. The general picture emerging from the Euromanifestos thus reflects the overall social and political dynamics: in 2009 there is a wider palette of opinions expressed in the official party attitudes accommodating more critical voices. However, looking at the dynamics of change in individual parties this trend is not evident since the Fidesz and the MDF which presented Euromanifestos at both elections had the same characteristics: the Fidesz presented a very detailed program (the longest one on both occasions) focusing on the critics to the Hungarian government with a mixed message concerning the integration stating "within a stronger Europe, a stronger nation". The MDF presented a short program on both occasions emphasizing its anti-establishment image and the heavy criticism toward both political sides. On the other hand if we contrast the program of the radical right-wing Jobbik with the official statements of MIÉP in 2004 and the Euromanifesto of the Workers' Party with its campaign in 2004 we can observe a trend of radicalization: the left-wing critics are among the harshest in 2009 while the Jobbik swings its program between the rejection of the Union and the need for its radical change. Interestingly the emergence of a more nation-centered view can also be detected in the Socialist declaration which bases its messages on the better representation of national interests in the EU framing the question as an issue of competence or incompetence of Hungarian parties in dealing with the EU also observed in the Polish case (see Gagatek in this book). Although the differences observed in the general tone of the elections are more the product of the smaller and new parties coming out with written programs, it would be a mistake to regard this phenomenon as peripheral: the results of the 2009 elections show that parties showing more positive attitudes lost ground while the radical right-wing force, Jobbik, gained important support.

Based on the general evaluation we would expect a wide range of opinions emerging concerning the analyzed fields: identity, scope of governance and representation. However, only the governance dimension seems to meet this expectation since the most important characteristic of the other two fields is their lack of saliency.

Certainly short programs issued by most parties (with the exception of Fidesz and Jobbik) tend to be rather instrumental, focusing on policy issues without much reference to more ideological factors such as identity, culture or democracy. The pragmatic nature of Euromanifestos does not even result in a detailed policy program though, as most programs are rather similar to a "to-do list" enumerating programs or strategies that should be elaborated without talking about how this should be done. Still most programs include some kind of reference to policies: the most salient issue is social policy with almost 90 percent of programs mentioning this aspect followed by environmental policy (67 percent) and foreign, justice and crime policies (55 percent). The importance of social policy can be explained by the deepening economic crisis and growing unemployment which can easily be translated into popular messages. The dominance of economic-related policies observed also in the Czech case (see Hloušek and Kaniok in this volume) resonates with the pragmatic nature of European discourse and the fact that the economic crisis needed to be addressed in all countries affected. In this field programs tend to address different levels of decision-making by suggesting solutions not only on the European level, but also on the national level thus the preferred decision-making is in most cases supranational and national. On the other hand environmental policy is often regarded as a European affair with three programs calling for supranational and three calling for mixed national and supranational decision-making. The same is true for foreign policy which incorporates a special Hungarian phenomenon: the treatment of Hungarian minorities living outside the national border. One driving force behind EU membership was the idea that the EU would be beneficial for building closer ties with Hungarians living outside Hungary. The growing saliency of the field (only Fidesz mentioned it in 2004 while five programs contained references in 2009) suggests a certain disappointment and that expectations toward the EU are still high in this respect, something translated in the manifestos with a call for a common European framework securing minority rights. Crime and justice policies became less salient but much more nation oriented with Fidesz opting for mixed solutions in 2004, MDF calling for a stricter supranational framework in both years and radical parties promoting national-level decision-making in 2009. Finally defence and immigration policies were rather neglected in both years with Fidesz referring to them, MDF mentioning them in 2004 and the Workers' Party taking a strong stance on the need for national armed forces in 2009. In line with the experiences of the other CEE countries, among the policies not coded in the INTUNE project, agricultural programs deserve special attention: as mentioned before reduced agricultural funds were among the first European issues debated in the national sphere causing disappointment in the new member states and opening the opportunity to criticize the accession requirements and import a conflict into the domestic political game. Ever since, agriculture has remained a sensitive issue where almost all parties feel the need to stand up as defenders of national interests.

On the individual party level the only meaningful comparison appears taking a look at the stance of Fidesz which became more pro-European in 2009 as, except for social policies, the program only talks in favor of supranational decision-making. The sovereignist approach is most visible in the Workers' Party's program while the radical right-wing Jobbik maintains its dual approach and lists the need for stricter national policies along with the need for stricter European policies. The most European-centered policies are declared by the SZDSZ which only talks about European competencies in its program. A similar view is taken by LMP which also focuses on European competencies, but also includes the need for compatible national-level decision-making including thus a national element in its program. Interestingly the center-left Socialist Party is much less specific in this sense: in its 2004 Euromanifesto and 2009 declaration there is almost no reference to the preferred level of decision-making in spite of the fact that the party's messages are very functional and focus on policy issues.

Elements concerning identity and representation were only found in half of the Euromanifestos which can be either explained by the low level of importance associated or simply by the fact that most programs are rather short and not very well elaborated. Where representation is referred the tone is negative: while in 2004 Fidesz sent mixed messages in this field, by 2009 its evaluation of European democracy became negative citing it as one of the main problems of the EU that needs to be tackled. According to our expectations in 2009 the two radical parties also expressed critical views on European democracy, with Jobbik strongly expressing its discontent with the democratic deficit, the lack of control by the people on European affairs that is further worsened by the lack of information which disables citizens from exercising their civic rights.

In the domain of identity we can observe a clear shift of focus from the European level to the national one: while in 2004 all three Euromanifestos contained explicit references to a common European identity, in 2009 only two right-wing parties, the Fidesz and Jobbik, mention European identity and/or European culture.

National identity on the other hand is referred to in four out of the six Euromanifestos in 2009 which stands in line with findings in other CEE countries where the nation and the representation of the national interest at the European level became the main point in the debate on Europe. This trend indicates an important change in party attitudes: while the accession period was characterized by adaptation and political success and was understood in terms of meeting EU requirements, by the time of the second EP elections the need to fight for national interests and thus to become more of a partner than just a mere follower appeared in the political discourse in the CEE countries. Another common phenomenon observed in the region is the lack of reference to sub-national identity which can be explained by the homogeneous nature of societies and the low importance of territorial cleavages. Still, in the Hungarian case, it is worth mentioning that in 2009 a new party representing the interests of the Roma minority ran at the EP elections and, while it did not issue a proper Euromanifesto, its official documents clearly reflect that the party bases its image on the importance of the Roma subculture and on the representation of the special interests of this community. The party only received 0.46 percent of the votes casted which indicates that, similar to the Czech case (see Hloušek and Kaniok in this volume), the minority–majority cleavage has not yet been formed as deliberate collective action and institutionalized interest articulation and representation are missing (in spite of the existence of various organizations claiming to do so). However, with Jobbik building also heavily on the issue of the Roma minority in the negative sense,[4] and mainstream parties including Roma candidates in their EP lists, it seems that the issue is gaining salience in the framework of European elections.

Conclusions

Looking at Euromanifestos we can conclude that in line with our expectations, Euroskepticism is on the rise in Hungary with radical critics gaining momentum both at European and national elections. Explanatory variables such as ideological divide, government–opposition and mainstream–radical dynamics do not seem to offer a complete explanation though and complementary factors such as coalition potential and the new–old party dichotomy should be considered. Concerning the impact of ideological divide no clear pattern emerges as the right-side of the political spectrum is characterized on the one hand by the radicalization of the far right and a more pro-European attitude emerging on the center-right. On the left side of the political spectrum a pro-European attitude is reflected in the declaration of the MSZP and in the manifestos of the Liberal SZDSZ and the green LMP with only the radical left expressing Euroskepticism. Still due to the lack of elaborated Euromanifestos and the very instrumental nature of the programs the left cannot be regarded as a determined supporter of the European process. The opposition–government dichotomy is hard to analyze due to the fact that in both elections the Socialist MSZP was the major governing party and the Conservative Fidesz was the biggest opposition party. Still, it seems that the focus on domestic matters is more palpable among opposition parties: Fidesz offers hash criticisms of the government in its program while among smaller parties the negative evaluation of all major political actors is the main trend. The fact that Fidesz offered a more pro-European program with critical remarks mainly addressed to the government (and not to the EU itself) could be explained by the fact that the party was preparing for a governing role soon and thus did not act as an opposition party at the elections. With the Hungarian party system moving toward the two-party model (or even showing signs of a one dominant party model based on 2010 results), opposition parties tend to be the smaller parties with no hope for a governing position, their stance on the EU could be labeled as more Eurosceptic in general. The most relevant cleavage seems to be the mainstream–radical divide with radical parties presenting more critical Euromanifestos than mainstream ones.

Contrasting the elections of 2004 and 2009 suggests that a certain trend of radicalization is also present with the radical right expressing more elaborated and more critical views and the Workers' Party offering a radical program. This trend could be explained by the coalition potential suggested by Bátory (2008) as in 2009 Fidesz was expected to win the elections alone and thus Jobbik was not counting on the possibility of becoming a coalition partner. Along with coalition potential, a difference among new and old parties is also emerging: while the parties born in the first half of the 1990s were socialized in a more pro-European climate where Euroskepticism could not gain ground among voters, new parties are more free to offer criticism of the EU. The most telling example is LMP which is often contrasted with the Liberal SZDSZ due to the fact that it occupied the political vacancy created by the disappearing liberal party: while the SZDSZ Euromanifesto was clearly the most pro-European, the LMP also included references to the problems of the integration process. However, this old–new cleavage might not hold for long as mainstream parties also feel the need to react to voters' change of opinion which is reflected in the fact that the main message emerging from the old parties' Euromanifestos is: who can better represent Hungarian interests in the EU? The heavy focus on policy matters can be explained by this phenomenon since policies are the most tangible expressions of national interests. The lack of reference to preferred decision-making levels might also be rooted in this nation-centered view since while in certain cases supranational decision-making can be advantageous (as in the case of extended minority rights), in other instances it can be regarded as a threat to national interest. Mainstream parties that try to avoid appearing Euroskeptic find it easier to remain silent in this respect. This message is in line with expectations (see introduction) of new member states being overall more cautious toward the European process.

Ultimately, a twofold picture emerges: along with rising Euroskepticism, Hungarian parties along with other CEE parties seem to focus more on national interests and issues emphasizing the importance of national identity instead of European ones. Both EP campaigns reinforce this phenomenon by bringing domestic issues into the spotlight. The dynamics of party competition are thus defined not by European issues, but the characteristics of the domestic political arena which confirms

Conti's (2012) expectations of a more national introverted political contestation of the EU in these countries. Still a certain level of Europeanization is tangible in the Hungarian party system: in their content Euromanifestos build heavily on the programs presented by European parties, European networks are highlighted in the campaign and in a sense nomination processes are becoming more EU conforming. Despite the dominance of domestic issues, the emerging critical voices enable a political discussion about European issues (especially the competent representation of national interests) and introduce the integration process into the patterns of party competition as well as into public debate.

Notes

1 In order to present a party list the collection of 20,000 signatures is needed.
2 Among the extra-parliamentary parties running in 2004 and 2009 several changes had occured but parties gaining less than 1 percent of votes are not included in the analysis.
3 Fidesz has changed its name several times since 1990: it is referred to by its current name in this chapter.
4 Talking about "Roma crime" and even allegedly taking part in violent actions organized by paramilitary organizations in settlements inhabited by Roma people. See Várnagy (2010b) for more detail.

References

Ágh, Attila (1995) "The 'early freezing' of the East Central European parties: the case of the Hungarian Socialist Party", *Budapest Papers on Democratic Transition*, 129, Budapest: Hungarian Center for Democratic Studies Foundation.

Bátory, Ágnes (2008) "Euroscepticism in the Hungarian party system: voices from the wilderness?" in: Alex Szczerbiak and Paul Taggart (eds): *Opposing Europe? The comparative party politics of Euroscepticism*, Oxford: Oxford University Press: 263–276.

Bátory, Ágnes and Dóra Husz (2006) "Az első magyarországi európai parlamenti választások" [The first European Parliamentary elections in Hungary], in: Hegedűs István (ed.): *A magyarok bemenetele: Tagállamként a bővülő Európában* [*The accession of Hungarians: being a memberstate in the enlarging Europe*], Budapest: DKMKKA-Budapesti Corvinus Egyetem Politikatudományi Intézet: 155–180.

Conti, Nicoló (2007), "Domestic parties and European integration: the problem of party attitudes to the EU, and the Europeanisation of parties", *European Political Science*, 6, 2: 192–207.

Conti, Nicoló (2012) "The EU in the programmatic statements of domestic parties", in: Heinrich Best, György Lengyel and Luca Verzichelli (eds): *The Europe of elites: a study into the Europeanness of Europe's economic and political elites*, Oxford: Oxford University Press: 192–207.

Cotta, Maurizio and Frederico Russo (2012) "Europe á la carte? European citizenship and its dimensions from the perspective of national elites", in: Heinrich Best, György Lengyel and Luca Verzichelli (eds): *The Europe of elites: a study into the Europeanness of Europe's economic and political elites*, Oxford: Oxford University Press: 14–42.

Hix, Simon and Michael Marsh (2011) "Second-order effects plus pan-European political swings: an analysis of European Parliament elections across time", *Electoral Studies*, 30, 1: 4–15.

Enyedi, Zsolt (2006) "Az európai integráció hatása a kelet-európai és a magyar párt-stratégiákra" [The impact of European integration on Eastern-European and Hungarian party strategies], in: Hegedűs István (ed.): *A magyarok bemenetele: Tagállamként a bővülő Európában* [*The accession of Hungarians: being a memberstate in the enlarging Europe*], Budapest: DKMKKA-Budapesti Corvinus Egyetem Politikatudományi Intézet: 155–180.

Enyedi, Zsolt and Fernando Casal Bértoa (2011) "Patterns of party competition 1990–2009", in: Paul Lewis and Radoslaw Markowski (eds): *Europeanising party politics? Comparative perspectives on Central and Eastern Europe after enlargement*, Manchester: Manchester University Press: 147–168.

Enyedi, Zsolt and Ken Benoit, (2011) "Kritikus választás 2010: a magyar pártrendszer átrendeződése a bal-jobb dimenzióban" [Critical elections 2010: the restructuration of the Hungarian party system in the left–right dimension], in: Enyedi Zsolt and Szabó Andrea-Tardos Róbert (eds): *Új képlet: A 2010-es választások Magyarországon* [*New formula: the 2010 elections in Hungary*], Budapest: DKMKA: 17–42.

Eurobarometer 71 (2009) National Report on Hungary, spring.

Ilonszki, Gabriella and Krisztina Jáger (2006) "A magyarországi delegáció az Európai Parlamentben 2004–2006: hasonlóságok és eltérések" [The Hungarian delegation in the European Parliament 2004–2006: similarities and differences], in: Hegedűs István (ed.): *A magyarok bemenetele: Tagállamként a bővülő Európában* [*The accession of Hungarians: being a memberstate in the enlarging Europe*], Budapest: DKMKKA-Budapesti Corvinus Egyetem Politikatudományi Intézet: 215–238.

Lakner, Z. (2004) "A Magyar pártok és az Európai Unió: az EU mint belpolitikai kérdés 1990–2004 között" [Hungarian parties and the European Union: the EU as an issue in internal politics between 1990–2004], *Politikatudományi Szemle*, 2004/1–2: 141–157.

Márkus, György (1997) "Az anomáliák normalitása: befagyott pártrendszer-cseppfolyós partook" [The anomalous normality: a frozen party system and liquid parties], in: Kurtán Sándor, Péter Sándor and László Vass (eds): *Magyarország Politikai Évkönyve 1996-ról* [*Political yearbook of Hungary 1996*], Budapest: DKMKA: 109–118.

Mihályffy, Zsuzsanna (2010) "Biztosra menve: a Fidesz-Magyar Polgári Szövetség kampánya" [Playing for sure: the campaign of Fidesz-Hungarian Civic Union], in: Mihályffy Zsuzsanna and Szabó Gabriella (eds): *Árnyékban: az európai parlamenti választási kampányok elemzése* [*In the shadow: the analysis of European Parliamentary campaigns*], Budapest: Studies in Political Science, Institute for Political Science, HAS, 36–56.

Real-Dato, José, György Lengyel and Borbala Göncz (2012) "National elites' preferences on the Europeanization of policy-making", in: Heinrich Best, György Lengyel and Luca Verzichelli (eds): *The Europe of elites: a study into the Europeanness of Europe's economic and political elites*, Oxford: Oxford University Press: 67–93.

Taggart, Paul and Aleks Szczerbiak (2002) "Europeanisation, Euroscepticism and party systems: party-based Euroscepticism in the candidate states of Central and Eastern Europe", *Perspectives on European Politics and Society*, 3, 1: 23–40.

Taggart, Paul and Aleks Szczerbiak (2004) "Contemporary Euroscepticism in the party systems of the European Union candidate states of Central and Eastern Europe", *European Journal of Political Research*, 43, 1: 1–27.

Várnagy, Réka (2010a) "Jelöltállítás a 2009-es európai parlamenti választásokon" [The selection of candidates at the 2009 European Parliamentary elections], *Politikatudományi Szemle*, 2010, 4: 9–24.

Várnagy, Réka (2010b) "Hungary", *European Journal of Political Research*, 49, 7–8: 1001–1008.

11 Poland

Wojciech Gagatek

Introduction

The question of Poland's EU membership has been always perceived in the categories of *raison d'être*, as an undisputable chance to become finally a member
of the democratic and wealthy club of countries. As with most issues related to
foreign affairs, there was a shared understanding that they should not become an
issue for party competition. From that point of view, until the early 2000s, only
marginal parties expressed their opposition to EU membership. The mainstream
parties, regardless of their ideological profile, strongly supported Poland's EU
membership (Markowski 2007; Zuba 2009). However, the time of acceding
negotiations showed that this national unity over EU issues will not last indefin-
itely, and that some parties will try to capitalise on politicising the issues of EU
integration. In 2001, two parties rejecting EU membership won representation in
the national parliament. During the first election to the European Parliament in
2004, the voters could choose between openly federalist, moderately pro-EU,
moderately Eurocritical and overtly anti-EU membership parties. However, how
specific and accurate were party preferences on EU integration? How do they
structure domestic competition over EU affairs? These are the principal research
questions. The chapter starts off with a short introduction to Polish party politics.
Then it moves to the qualitative analysis of the party manifestos adopted for the
2004 and 2009 elections to the European Parliament. The manifesto coding was
carried out within the INTUNE project, thus focusing on four major areas:
general attitudes towards Europe, identity, policy scope and representation. The
pros and cons of basing analysis on manifesto content are discussed in the Introduction to this volume. This short time span is the main reason to use the qualitative, rather than quantitative, analysis, with the latter seemingly better suited to
document programmatic change, and the former better able to capture the com-
plexity and detail of the actual programmatic supply.

From the point of the aims of this volume, this chapter faces two principal
challenges. First, the majority of theoretical explanations available in the comparative literature have been developed in reference to Western Europe only.
The question then arises whether we can hypothesise possible explanations of
the Polish case in relation to general theoretical explanations. By studying the

Polish example we can contribute to verifying some of them in a different context. Second, and related, the INTUNE coding process was also operated on the same coding scheme, developed primarily in relation to Western European cases. For example, the question of regionalisation and regional identity is not an issue in Poland. For this reason, as in other Central and Eastern European countries (see Hloušek and Kaniok or Várnagy in this volume), with regard to many variables it was not possible to code some items at all. Nevertheless, it was possible to illustrate party positions on the EU and how they make the EU an issue of party competition.

The main political parties of the 2000s

Polish politics have been commonly described in the literature as totally unpredictable and fluid, with a fragmented and highly volatile party system, where even the mainstream parties disappear after one election (Casal Bértoa and Mair 2010). Nevertheless, politics in that time has been run by six parties whose participation in government and basic approach to the EU is described below.

The early 2000s started with a government of the Democratic Left Alliance (SLD) and the agrarian Polish People's Party (PSL) (for a general introduction to the Polish elections, see Millard 2009). From the very beginning, SLD tried to build its credibility as a responsible player, enthusiastically oriented towards EU membership. From this point of view, it contrasted itself with some right-wing parties, accusing them of backwardness and various Europhobia. This was particularly visible on the occasion of the 2004 EP campaign and the national parliamentary campaign held one year later. A similar approach was taken by the centrist Union of Freedom (UW), which later coalesced with SLD in national elections. A positive, although not always consistent approach, toward EU membership was expressed by the centre-right Civic Platform (PO). A slightly less enthusiastic although still positive attitude came from the conservative Law and Justice party (PiS), which favoured Polish EU membership, although rejected greater political integration, favouring instead the "Europe of the nations" approach.

Two parties that won parliamentary representation in 2001 rejected EU accession. In the first place we should mention the overtly anti-EU League of Polish Families (LPR), a nationalist party with a fundamentalist Catholic message, whose principal rejection of the EU was rooted in the defence of Polish national identity and the Catholic religion. This party was one of the two major forces calling for rejecting the EU accession treaty in the national referendum of 2003. Another one was the agrarian, populist Self-Defence of the Republic of Poland (*Samoobrona*) of charismatic leader Andrzej Lepper, whose Euroscepticism was based to a greater degree on economic, anti-liberal arguments and less on religious motivations, focusing on criticism of the outcome of accession negotiations, which in its opinion would make Poland a second-order EU member. The accession referendum of 2003 was then fought with the mainstream parties on the one side, which to a varying extent but nevertheless supported the accession agreement (SLD, UW, PO, PiS, PSL) and LPR and Samoobrona calling to vote no. In the end, the pro-European side prevailed, with 77 per cent of voters supporting EU membership (Markowski and Tucker 2010; Szczerbiak 2011).

Poland joined the EU on 1 May 2004, and a month later the first election to the European Parliament was held. While PO won (24.10 per cent of the vote), the polling gave surprisingly good standing for LPR (15.92 per cent) and Samoobrona (10.78 per cent), with PiS finishing third (12.67 per cent), and the governing SLD scoring a dismal defeat (9.35 per cent). Seats were also gained by UW (7.33 per cent), PSL (6.34 per cent) and a splinter group from SLD, namely Social Democracy of Poland (SDPL, 5.33 per cent of the vote). However, the biggest surprise came after the 2005 national election, when a government of PiS–LPR–Samoobrona was created. Since this time, Polish party politics has been characterised within the frame of dominant competition between two centre-right parties, PO and PiS, with other parties playing a secondary role. In the PiS–LPR–Self-Defence government, European integration remained in the hands of PiS, which also had its own president of Poland, Lech Kaczyński. Due to internal friction in the coalition, and corruption allegations against Samoobrona leader and Deputy Prime Minister Andrzej Lepper, the coalition broke up and after a short period of PiS minority government, an early election was held in 2007. PO managed to win quite overwhelmingly (41.51 per cent of the vote), and established a coalition government with PSL: the two Eurosceptic parties LPR and Samoobrona grossly failed to reach a 5 per cent electoral threshold, thus failing to win representation in Parliament. Similar patterns of political competition characterised the 2009 election to the European Parliament, with PO scoring an overwhelming victory (44.43 per cent of the vote), PiS finishing second (27.40 per cent) and the Eurosceptic LPR (running this time as *Libertas*) failing to win seats, and thus disappearing from the political scene (Gagatek *et al.* 2010).

Analysing party manifestos

Given that our main source of reference is party manifestos, a few words should be devoted to illustrating the extent to which political parties value their programmatic work and adopt various policy documents. In general, we can say that the only parties that consistently adopt separate manifestos for the elections to the EP are SLD and PSL. In 2004, SLD had its own manifesto, whereas in 2009 it adopted as its election document the manifesto of the Party of European Socialists (PES), of which it is a member. PSL in both cases had its own separate although quite vague policy document for EP elections. The case with other parties varies. For example, while PO had a separate manifesto for the 2004 elections, it failed to offer any programmatic document in 2009, instead presenting a one-page list of priorities of its group in the EP (EPP-ED). For this reason in 2009 its programme was not included in the analysis. PiS had a manifesto for the 2004 elections, but in 2009 it failed to produce a separate European manifesto, instead referring to the general party programme it adopted in 2009.

Nevertheless, out of all the Polish parties running for seats in 2004, PiS clearly produced the most detailed manifesto, and the high amount of space devoted to European issues in its general programme of 2009 is sufficient to code the main elements of the INTUNE codebook. Other parties tended to produce some electoral documents, although of different length and character. For example, neither LPR nor Samoobrona produced any manifestos for either the 2004 or 2009 EP elections, presenting instead letters to the voters from the chairmen, or some short list of priorities. Based on the analysis of the other chapters in this volume, we can point out that letters to the voters seems to be a Polish specificity. In some cases (as the example of PiS and LPR shows), they are the only programmatic document on offer. In 2004, the Samoobrona leader presented short, separate letters to the following social groups: the unemployed and homeless, farmers, forest officers, the handicapped, students, pensioners, veterans, doctors and to some other social groups. These letters were put on the website and cited in the elections. In each of these letters Lepper discussed the benefits and challenges of EU membership, focusing on the social group in question, followed by a number of electoral promises. The possible explanation of this phenomenon relates to the nature of leadership in Samoobrona and also in the LPR, where the leader had an indisputable position, weight and voice. Overall, these letters seem to be of equal importance as the election manifestos, and the added value of this analysis is to integrate them with Euromanifestos.

It can be said that manifestos are used in the electoral campaign only to a limited extent. Most parties hardly refer to them in the electoral literature, and the contents of the manifestos are hardly used in political battle. As shown above, given the lack of consistency, only the manifestos of SLD-UP, PSL and PiS could be compared between 2004 and 2009. The other parties either failed to produce manifestos in both or in one of the EP elections. Considering the limited time of Polish membership as well, this chapter resigns from documenting programmatic change and instead tries to build a general picture pertaining to the period from 2004 and 2009, where necessary clearly indicating where the source of data does not come from manifestos. Below we will focus on analysing the content of the 2004 and 2009 election manifestos and equivalent programmatic documents.

The party positions in 2004

The 2004 election took place virtually during the honeymoon of Polish membership in the EU. Quite expectedly, the patterns of political contestation typical for the accession referendum governed the 2004 campaign to the EP. We will structure the following analysis along four dimensions of the INTUNE codebook. First, we will discuss general attitudes towards the EU, the Polish role within the EU and the EU decision-making system. Second, we will move to discuss patterns of identity, particularly in the axis European–national–subnational identity. Third, we will discuss the domain of EU policies and scope of governance by focusing on parties' preference for levels of competence for certain policy areas.

Finally, we will conclude with the domain of representation and democracy, and in particular with regard to the opinions and solutions to EU democratic deficit. Exactly the same structure will be used in the case of the analysis of the 2009 programmes.[1]

General attitudes towards the EU

The only party that explicitly rejected EU membership and called for an exit was LPR. Unfortunately, the party did not issue a manifesto, so an approximation of its views on the matter can be indicated on the basis of the letter to the voters written by LPR chairman, Roman Giertych, as follows. After the positive result of the 2003 EU accession referendum, "Poland is at the edge of the abyss". In order to revert this "tragedy", LPR will strongly support an initiative for an exit referendum. According to Giertych, during the referendum campaign the majority of political parties lied with regard to the benefits of EU membership and now the Poles begin to see through it. Due to EU membership, Poland is losing its sovereignty, and in the case that the Constitutional Treaty is ratified, it will lose its independent statehood. However, when this exit will prove not to be possible, it will become necessary to do all possible in order to dilute the scope of integration and minimise the impact of the EU on Poland. Particular importance is placed on the need to defend Christian values within the EU.

A slightly less principled opposition to EU membership was expressed by populist, agrarian Samoobrona. Here, similar to the case above, there was no manifesto, so we need to revert to the letter to voters by the Self-Defence chairman and the letter signed by the candidates of Samoobrona, as follows. Accordingly, Samoobrona is not against Poland's EU membership, but strongly rejects the outcome of the accession negotiations, which were carried out "on the knees" and led to discriminatory results for Poland. In particular, it is argued that as a result of EU accession the price of agricultural products on average will increase by 10 per cent, and the income of farmers will drop down by 50 per cent. In other words, Samoobrona does not reject EU membership, but calls for the renegotiation of the accession treaty, and, specifically, to change provisions on the production quotas in agriculture, transition periods in the employment sector and the amount of direct subventions to Polish farmers. At the same time, Samoobrona supports a Union of independent, sovereign states, based on the concept of the Europe of fatherlands.

Yet another rather Eurosceptic approach was presented by the ultra-liberal Union for Real Politics (UPR). While not calling for an EU exit, UPR strongly rejects the current direction of EU integration. Most importantly, it rejects the development of the EU into supranational and federal direction, and, in particular, it is against the EU constitution. It calls to limit the powers of EU institutions, such as the European Parliament (the national parliament can do the same job as the EP much more effectively and cheaply) and the European Commission (undemocratic and unaccountable). In short, the EU should remain an international organisation, favouring a loose cooperation of independent states. The economic independence of Poland would enable it to carry out a market-oriented liberal economic policy, which seems to be hindered by the EU. The difference with LPR is that the Euroscepticism of UPR is based on economic grounds, whereas LPR reverts more to the rhetoric of the defence of the nation and its values, which are in danger with EU membership.

All the other serious parties running for seats expressed support for EU membership, to greater or lesser extent. PO perceived the membership of Poland in the EU as both

> a hope and a challenge. A hope for peace, stability and development of civil society. A challenge is to care about constant and harmonious development of European integration to the benefit of all its participants, our own contribution and a mark of our identity in the united Europe.

Overall, in the language of the PO there is a lot of care about the future of European integration, and an emphasis on the symbolic end of the period of detachment of Poland from the democratic world. EU membership does not limit, but strengthens, Poland's sovereignty and the freedom of the Polish people. It is an opportunity to "regain our due place in Europe". While approving the provisions of the Constitutional Treaty, PO strongly supports an increase of powers of the European Commission and the European Parliament, as well as greater use of majority voting. For example, the EP should receive the right to elect the president of the European Commission, which will be then approved by the European Council. The manifesto of PO sees a role of Poland in establishing the Eastern dimension of EU external policy, with a view to preparing a ground for future EU membership of countries such as Ukraine. The EU should be able to speak with one voice to a greater extent than today, and Poland should actively participate in the development of the Common Foreign and Security Policy. Finally, PO emphasise that in order to achieve its ambitions, Poland should build stable relationships and a good level of agreement with all European partners.

In its manifesto, SLD-UP uses similar rhetoric to PO when it argues that the EU enlargement of 2004 is a chance to finally close the post-cold war division of Europe. Similarly, it approves the greater prerogatives of EU institutions, explicitly mentioning the EP. The Constitutional Treaty is also perceived in positive terms, as a chance to provide a basis for a "strong and democratic Europe". However, rather than focusing on the benefits of EU membership for Poland, SLD-UP presents a general vision of the EU and states that European integration is an opportunity "to achieve social democratic values: solidarity, equality, freedom, justice and democracy". This ideological perspective is emphasised many times. SLD-UP favours a social Europe, able to maintain and create new jobs, guarantee gender equality and help less developed regions of the world.

The programme of the PSL is rather vague, limited to some very general goals. These are mainly related to ensuring that both new and old member states are treated in the same way, and that transition periods both in the labour and agricultural fields are removed. The manifesto refrains from taking a clear-cut position about the benefits of Poland's membership. However, it is quite clear that PSL favours an intergovernmental mode of EU decision-making system, calling for the maintenance of unanimity in the matters related to Poland's vested interests and observance of sovereign rights of all EU member states (MS). Altogether, the PSL will be guided by the need to "strengthen the role of national states within the framework of the Europe of fatherlands". This is stated even more strongly in the letter to voters from the PSL chairman, Janusz Wojciechowski,

> let us elect MEPs that will look after Poland and our national interests. Let us elect MEPs whom the EU flag will not shout the white-red colours [i.e. Polish national colours], who will not forget our anthem. Who will not supplant our religion, culture and language.

Finally, a mixed approach is presented by PiS. On the one hand, their manifesto notes that economic terms of Poland's entry to the EU are "unfavourable". This statement must be read within the complex dynamics of Polish party politics of the time. Although it is not elaborated in the manifesto, we can point that PiS was highly critical of the way the SLD-PSL coalition government led accession negotiations. So the critique of these "unfavourable" economic conditions was mainly targeted against SLD, rather than a sign of their rejection of the EU membership. On the other hand, in their view, the EU is dominated by "shallow" economic interests and does not want to increase budgets for structural and cohesion policies. The strong voting power of Poland as stipulated in the Treaty of Nice gives a chance to secure a good outcome in EU budget negotiations and an opportunity to make up for the unfavourable economic terms of accession. The EU should remain based on an intergovernmental mode of work, with the European Council and the Council of Ministers remaining the key players. The other institutions such as the Commission and the EP are important, but their role and competencies should not be increased.

Identity

In this domain, our research questions concerned whether parties refer to the European, national and subnational identity, such as common culture, values, customs, history or traditions, and whether by doing this, they try to differentiate the in-group from the out-group. The first conclusion is that none of the Polish parties referred in any way to the subnational identity, either in positive or negative terms. The reason for this is that the issue of regional or local identities in Poland is not an issue for political competition. At the time of the election, there was not a single regionalist party in Poland (defined as one that calls for a greater autonomy for the region in which it operates), and regionalisation, as understood within West European terms, has not yet reached Poland. The real question was then about the extent to which the national and European layers of identity will be revoked by the parties. While it seems to be almost certain that the Eurosceptic parties will mostly refer to the national identity, the question is about the extent to which the pro-EU parties will refer to European identity.

The result is that none of the parties build any arguments based on common European identity, but this does not mean that even the pro-European parties emphasised national identity. For example, the nature of the short electoral manifesto of SLD did not allow coding it either as focusing on European or national identity. Similarly, the only sentence in the programmatic documents of Self-Defence which could suggest an emphasis on the national identity label is

> while taking a decision about who to support in the elections to the EP, let us not forget that we are a proud nation of almost 40 million people, faithful to its common Christian traditions developed over the period of one thousand years.

However, if these issues were raised in more than a few words, then at minimum it was stated that the EU should respect the variety of national identities, traditions and customs. PO used such a phrase to indicate that it is against the EU adopting laws that would undermine these basic European values and customs. Furthermore, PO rejected the tendencies to Europeanise and unify cultural policies, because in this area "we particularly value cultural autonomy and diversity of nations and regions of Europe". A similar approach is shared by PSL and PiS. The latter added that "culture has been and will be one of the most important vehicles of national traditions", and that the proposals for unification of cultural policy are proof of a lack of faith in the vitality of Polish culture and a lack of understanding of EU policy to help national cultures which altogether make up a European heritage. Poland should bring its cultural heritage to the EU, in particular concerning its Christian and Solidarity movement ideals. Quite expectedly, a strong reference to the Polish nation is visible in the programme of LPR. Any European identity labels or symbols (such as the EU anthem *Ode to Joy*) are treated there pejoratively. Instead, LPR aims to organise the nation in the circumstances of EU membership, primarily in reference to its Christian roots.

Policies and scope of governance

This domain is most difficult to characterise, similar to other Central and Eastern European countries (see Hloušek and Kaniok, or Várnagy in this volume): the vast majority of parties did not devote any attention to the preferred level of competence for the various policies. Only UPR presented a straightforward proposal for the division of competences, in which the EU should be exclusively responsible for monetary issues (for those countries who have the common currency) as well as customs and immigration policy (due to the lack of internal borders and the functioning of the common market). All the other fields should remain the sole responsibility of MS. With regard to other parties, PiS expressed its criticism that "the so called EU constitution places many new competences to the EU institutions". As an example, it mentioned foreign policy as well as attempts to enter the cultural policy and coordination of economic and employment policies, which stands in contradiction with the aim to extend the degree of economic freedom in Poland. On the other hand, PO supported "the strict coordination of activities with regard to external and internal security". All the other parties remain silent on this dimension.

Representation and democracy

In this domain our attention was particularly placed on the question of democratic deficit, and, in particular, on positive and negative references to democracy in the EU. Here only three parties expressed any opinion on the topic and these were SLD and PO (with mainly positive references) and PiS (with mainly negative references). SLD is in favour of a "federal Europe", in which the adoption of the Constitutional Treaty will build a basis for a strong and democratic EU. Such a Europe should refer to the democratic mode of work as much as possible and engage citizens in the decision-making process. Overall, SLD was the only party that openly expressed its support for a federal conception of the EU. PO devoted a special section in its manifesto entitled "a Union that is close to citizens". The citizens will only start to support and identify with the EU when it becomes transparent and understandable. For this reason the citizens should have a real influence on the decisions taken in the EU. In particular, PO expressed its approval for the European citizens' initiative and provisions strengthening the role of national parliaments as stipulated in the Constitutional Treaty.

A totally opposite view is presented by PiS. In the first place, among the dangerous phenomena it identifies there is the democratic deficit, a growing alienation of EU institutions in relation to national democratic communities and an impression of a lost democratic legitimisation due to integration processes. However, the recipe for these illnesses is not an increase of powers and competences of EU institutions, or, more generally, a greater level of political integration, but rather the strengthening of national parliaments by including them in the process of creating common rules of European integration. Only through national parliaments can the distance between citizens and the integration processes be reduced. Finally, UPR devotes only a few lines to the question of democratic deficit by calling for full transparency of all EU decisions, documents and meetings, such as those of the European Council and "in those places where there is no transparency, fraud, corruption, nepotism and one-sidedness rule".

The party positions in 2009

The political situation in 2009 was much different from in 2004. Not only because five years had passed since 2004, but mainly because the 2005, and particularly, the 2007 national election campaign significantly altered the patterns of political competition. Since this time, the two main competitors are two right-wing parties, PO and PiS, whereas once almighty SLD does rather badly in the opinion polls. As far as political actors are concerned, the only changes worth mentioning are the fact that former politicians of LPR with some prominent figures from the national-Catholic circles of other right-wing parties decided to run for seats as the Polish section of Libertas; a small group of very religiously oriented politicians led by Marek Jurek split up from PiS and established the Right of the Republic of Poland (*Prawica RP*), and that Union for Freedom (now renamed the Democratic Party) established a coalition with the Social Democracy of Poland named the Alliance for the Future – Centre Left (*PdP-Centrolewica*) (see Gagatek *et al*. 2010).

General attitudes towards the EU

The programme of Libertas Poland was a mix of old arguments of LPR derived from the nationalist and Christian influence and a few ideas that Libertas and its leader Declan Ganley wanted to promote all over Europe, in particular the rejection of the Lisbon Treaty (see Gagatek 2009). Accordingly, on its website it stated:

> today Libertas is the most serious political force that proved to be able to unite numerous political clouts in order to fight for the most important cause – the defence of Polish interest and the restoration of Christian civilization in Europe.

Among the key slogans was the maintenance of the Polish national currency (because the adoption of the euro would increase prices and deprive Poland of "currency sovereignty"). On the other hand, the impact of Libertas Europe was clearly visible in the proposals regarding EU decision-making. The majority rule should become a default decision-making procedure, but MS should maintain the right to veto EU laws in some sensitive areas. However, every new piece of legislation in the EU should be voted in the EP. Overall, Libertas Poland combined the previous negative attitude towards the EU and the nationalistic reasoning of LPR with some rather federally oriented proposals derived from the general programme of Libertas.

The Samoobrona did not propose any programmatic document for the 2009 election. The only official document was a selection of previously published proposals compiled by the spokesman of Samoobrona. For this reason, the programme of Samoobrona was very similar to the one proposed in 2004, with some parts of the 2009 programme copied and pasted from the 2004 one. In short, while Samoobrona is not against Poland's EU membership, it will try to do everything possible to renegotiate the accession treaty, which, using the same arguments as previously, it believes is unfavourable to Poland. Likewise, it repeated its belief in the Europe of fatherlands, the rejection of dominance of the biggest states and the two-speed Europe. Additionally, in the letter to the voters, the chairman of Samoobrona advertised his own achievements as the Minister of Agriculture in the coalition government of 2006–2007, including an increase of the milk production quotas and the introduction of an embargo on strawberries from China (which was a threat to Polish farmers).

UPR updated its principal opposition to the greater level of political and economic European integration. This time it stated its objection to the Lisbon Treaty, because it undermines Poland's sovereignty, limits economic freedom and ignores Polish traditional values and identity. Furthermore, it means "a total submission to the law adopted in Brussels, resignation from national foreign policy, national currency, a factual surrender of national sovereignty". Referring to the positive outcome of the 2003 referendum, for UPR the year 2009 sees that "instead of a Europe of free nations a bureaucratic empire is being built. We do not want to be its province!"

On the pro-European side, PO did not adopt any manifesto for the 2009 elections, submitting only a short list of EPP-ED priorities, and a report of the achievements of its MEPs in the 2004–2009 EP legislature. On the other hand, SLD adopted as its own main election document the PES Manifesto "People First: A New Direction for Europe". As in other cases when national parties adopt such a Euromanifesto, we only have an approximation of views of a national party, due to the lowest common agreement method that leads to the adoption of such Euromanifestos (see Conti and Memoli in this volume, Gagatek 2009). Nevertheless, the PES manifesto presents a number of benefits of EU integration, such as, a large EU economy leads to more jobs, less poverty and greater trade exchange with third countries. It also emphasises various EU freedoms, such as freedom of movement of labour. The operation of the euro currency to a large extent is considered to defend the EU against the effects of the global economic crisis. Overall, as it can be expected from the Euromanifesto of a European party federation, rather than focusing on the benefits of EU integration to Poland and on the country-specific problems, the PES manifesto builds a general programme for the whole EU, and is particularly competitive against the EPP family.

A much more country-specific manifesto was offered by PdP-Centrolewica. The manifesto starts from confirming that the choice to join the EU was right, for a number of political and economic reasons, which altogether allowed Poland to achieve "a historic success". Among the benefits enumerated by PdP-Centrolewica is the flow of EU structural and agricultural subsidies, the freedom of movement of labour, and access of Polish companies to the common market. Poland has all the capabilities to play a more active role within the EU, particularly by proposing "constructive initiatives" for the entire EU and close and strategic cooperation with the most important partners. PdP-Centrolewica situates itself clearly in favour of greater political integration in Europe, in particular by granting the EU more competences according to the subsidiarity principle and by strengthening the community method.

A few months before the 2009 EP election, PiS adopted its new, very comprehensive general programme, with large parts devoted to the EU. Compared to the 2004 document, this time PiS unequivocally states that EU membership is beneficial to Poland's security and economic development, in particular through the common market and the subsidies from structural and agricultural funds. EU membership offers a number of action instruments, which can be used to the benefit of Poland and the EU as a whole. Additionally, it stated that "the status of a large Member State requires from us to actively participate in all areas of EU functioning". These aims can be achieved by entering into various coalitions with MS (in areas subject to the majority rules) or, if necessary, by acting alone (in areas subject to unanimity). Overall, we see a big change of rhetoric compared with the 2004 document. On the other hand, PiS confirmed its principal vision of the EU as a Europe of nations, governed according to the intergovernmental mode, in which the Council of Ministers stands over other EU institutions. On the other hand, unlike in 2004, it unequivocally approved a number of benefits of EU membership. Like PiS, PSL in 2009 declared it "acknowledges the usefulness of Poland's EU membership", particularly for farmers but also for other social and professional groups. The PSL manifesto is silent on the preferred mode of decision-making within the EU, or the competences of various EU institutions, except for the fact that PSL approves the Europe of fatherlands approach. Finally, a splinter group from PiS, Prawica RP, presented a similar general attitude towards Europe as PiS, although emphasising Christian principles to a much greater degree. Accordingly, Poland, due to its geopolitical position and history, must play an active role in Europe, and avoid "drifting in the stream set up by the dominating EU member states". Like for PiS, the European Council and the Council of Minister should remain the decisive EU institutions.

Identity

Like LPR in 2004, Libertas in 2009 clearly refers to national identity and a number of elements differentiating Polish culture and identity. "Freedom means independence of state, sovereignty of the nation as well as freedom in family life: the right to live, to bring up children according to own beliefs, in the faith of fathers, based on own national culture." The EU should not try to promote a unified cultural policy, but respect the variety of national cultures. Samoobrona repeated verbatim its 2004 statement that Poland is a proud nation, faithful to its own, Christian traditions. UPR did not devote any attention to either European or national identity.

On the pro-European side, the PES manifesto adopted by SLD does not raise any issues of identity. The same goes for PdP-Centrolewica. But the PSL manifesto contains references to both European and national identity and values. The latter is exemplified in the aim of PSL to

the widest application and solid establishment of European values in Poland and in all EU Member States – a respect for a peaceful development and human and civil rights, freedom, democracy, solidarity, justice and dignity of people, rooted in the Christian tradition and ethics of Europe.

At the same time, the PSL emphasises the defence of Polish state interests, cherishes national culture and identity, and fights for better protection of Poles in the world.

The PiS manifesto strongly emphasises national identity and its differentiating elements in relation to Polish EU membership. One of the parts of the manifesto seems to be worth quoting in full:

> While accepting the national community as a natural and positive phenomenon, one has to accept the obvious fact of the existence of competition between nations, which if carried out in a civilized manner, is a driving force of the material and spiritual development of nations and of the entire world. Some political elites in Europe attempt to exclude competition mechanisms between the nations and replace them with bureaucratic forms of supranational uniformization. In the short run, by weakening the patriotic motivations, this risks slowing down the development dynamics; in the long run, this is dangerous because it ignores national pride as a strong element of identity ... and puts the idea of international cooperation at risk of discredit and rejection.

PiS adds that one can be a wholesome citizen (that means having civil rights and an ability to influence public authority) only within the nation state. Accordingly, for obvious reasons the EU and other international organisations are unable to become democratic organisations replacing MS. PiS notes and rejects some tendencies leading to the weakening of cohesion of the Polish nation, and here even refers (pejoratively) to the term known as "transfer of loyalties". For this reason, special care must be placed on both traditional and new institutions uniting the nation that are able to wake up national motivations, such as Polish media and Polish schools. This adjective "Polish" is emphasised particularly, and the "foreign capital" in the public education system in Poland is perceived negatively. Overall, we have here an acclamation of national identity and culture that must be protected against various perils, to which the manifesto attaches particular weight. Likewise, Prawica RP echoes similar concerns, but is much more oriented towards the Christian character of the Polish nation, identity and customs.

Policies and scope of governance

Similar to 2004, Polish political parties remain silent on the preferred level of competencies of certain EU policies. The only exception is SLD, but this is quite expected due to the nature of the PES manifesto, which proposed a number of areas for EU action, such as a European Pact for the Future of Employment, common rules on migration to the EU (with full respect to the competencies of MS in this area), common controlling of external borders, a European Pact on wages, which will guarantee equal pay for equal work and set up a minimum wage in all MS. PiS strongly states that on no account should the EU regulate matters related to morality and family law. Otherwise there is nothing to report about.

Representation and democracy

Libertas perceives democracy at the EU level in a negative light. First, non-elected, non-accountable and overpaid EU bureaucrats decide on many key issues impacting Poland and the Polish people. The solution is to drastically reduce EU bureaucracy and introduce a system in which officials will be accountable for their decisions. Furthermore, EU Commissioners should be accountable before their national parliaments, whereas the President of the Commission before the European Parliament. These slogans were derived from the general programme of Libertas. As mentioned above, the fight against "EU bureaucratic empire" is also quite important in the programme of UPR. Prawica RP ridicules some of the key terms that are typical of the discourse on EU democracy such as "European society" and "EU democracy", calling them utopian. The EU does not need any such democratisation (as examples they quote the election of the President of the Commission by popular ballot, pan-European referenda or the strengthening of the EP), but "a greater respect and solidarity of countries and nations of Europe" and the intergovernmental mode of decision-making. The PiS manifesto states that the problem of transparency and democratic legitimisation of decisions taken by the EU is an important issue. Given that a European nation does not exist and will not develop, it is not possible to determine its will by calling a referendum or election. Hence it is necessary to think of other means which will guarantee a greater influence of citizens of all MS on EU affairs via national mechanisms of political representation. Out of those parties that expressed any opinion on the matter, the only positive approach was presented by PdP-Centrolewica. It pointed out that the EP is the only democratically elected EU institution and has an important influence on many issues regulating daily life of EU citizens. However, the manifesto notes that the EU is in some areas too bureaucratic and detached from the daily lives of EU citizens. That is why a more direct link between EU activities and the daily life of EU citizens must be established.

Discussion and conclusions

One of the greatest challenges of studying manifesto content is that in order to explain programmatic change we need to turn to a much greater number of sources, including internal party dynamics, party system change, electoral developments, etc. However, despite the limitations of the Euromanifesto analysis, they are the official party stance on EU affairs and seem to be a good approximation of party attitudes towards Europe. In some cases, however, they are not sufficient. Other analyses pointed a low salience of EU issues in party programmes not only in Poland, but generally in Central and Eastern Europe and elsewhere (Haughton 2009). The Polish case is interesting because the level of salience varies between the parties and over time, with – quite expectedly – the most Eurosceptic LPR giving most prominence to EU affairs in the electoral campaigns of 2000s (Szczerbiak 2011). However, in order to understand how parties use EU integration as an issue in political competition, the programmatic offer is clearly not enough. Both in the 2007 national parliamentary elections and in the 2009 EP election (and indeed since the early 2000s) the main electoral theme revoked in relation to the EU was the manifesto party's competence and/or other party's lack of competence in dealing with the EU and other MS that was used as a political weapon against the competitors. For example, in 2007 and 2009 the questions of competences concerned the negotiating tactics with the EU (regarding for example the Lisbon Treaty negotiations), the quality of representation and the choice of political group in the EP (whether it is better to be a member of a large or small political group), friendly acquaintance with heads and prime ministers of other MS (whether friendly relationship of Donald Tusk with Angela Merkel is a sign of Tusk's strength or weakness), etc. For this reason, Szczerbiak (2011) believes that EU affairs in Poland have been treated as an issue over which parties compete in order to set who represents Polish interests in the EU most effectively.

To summarise, how divided are Polish parties over EU integration issues as far as the Euromanifestos are concerned? It seems that out of four dimensions analysed here, the best suited indicators are the preference for either supra-national or intergovernmental decision-making system, and, relatedly, opinions on the issue of representation and democracy, which are highly correlated. Here political parties in Poland clearly differ and their preferences have the highest level of salience. The least explanatory powers have the identity and policy dimensions, for different reasons though. In the first case, all Polish political parties did not revoke either European or subnational identity patterns. The key reference point is the nation, national culture and custom. Certainly, the more Eurosceptic a party, the greater the emphasis on the role of the nation, but even the pro-European parties tend to refer to national values and stand against any attempts of the EU to regulate sensitive issues, such as those related to morality. The policy dimension, on the other hand, is the least discussed point in Poland. In 2009, particular emphasis was placed on the question of when Poland should join the Eurozone. But the issues of the preferred level of competence for migration, employment or social policies are left intact, or are subsumed to a more general pattern suggesting a rather reserved approach towards granting the EU more competencies. Even the PO, which in 2004 expressed its support to the increase of powers of EU institutions, referred more to the aim of bringing citizens closer to the EU (by for example electing the President of the Commission by direct ballot), rather than to give the institutions more policy competences. Here Poland is not an exception to the wider trends in new MS, where parties are silent on many issues that are quite important in the old MS (Conti 2012). The explanation of this trend can be threefold. First, as pointed out above, some problems pertinent to Western Europe are not existent in Poland, with migration and anti-immigrant parties being the case in point. Second, as far as policy scope is concerned, for Polish parties the most important points of reference are foreign policy (by which they primarily refer to the Eastern dimension) and agricultural policy, but it is more problematic to explain why justice, employment and social policies are not discussed at all. Even the party that has justice in its name and which seems to "own" issues related to law and order, namely PiS, is silent on the preferred level of competences in this area. On the other hand, the left parties that traditionally claim issue ownership in employment and social policies refer to these areas only as broad values, but not devote any attention to what EU competencies in this field should be. Finally, one would need to move above the content analysis of the manifestos and do research on how these documents are adopted, and, in particular, who decides on priorities and what the role of experts on EU affairs and MEPs tends to be (see Szczerbiak 2011 for some ideas).

In general, it seems safe to conclude that party attitudes seem to be linear across almost all the dimensions of the INTUNE codebook. This is particularly visible as far as the less enthusiastically oriented parties are concerned, namely LPR, PiS, Prawica RP, Samoobrona and UPR. Certainly, the degree of their scepticism varies (with only LPR classified as "hard Eurosceptics"), but overall a preference for the intergovernmental mode of EU work (with much quoted slogan of the Europe of nations) perfectly correlates with negative references to EU democracy and emphasis on national identity, and, if discussed, with a preference for national policy competence in most areas. Conversely, the more pro-European parties such as PO and SLD combine positive general attitudes towards Europe with a preference for the empowerment of EU institutions and a greater involvement of citizens in EU affairs. However, even in this case reference to European culture or identity is rather absent. The clear exception in this linearity of attitudes is Libertas Poland, which as mentioned, combined nationalistic, religiously oriented Eurosceptic ideas of LPR (based on the defence of the Polish nation) with some federally oriented proposals of Libertas and its leader Declan Ganley (such as that the EP should have the right to vote on all EU legislation, which overall should be decided mostly by majority). Overall, Polish political parties are quite predictable as far as their EU attitudes are concerned, and from the score in one dimension one can reasonably predict their opinion in other dimensions. But even here one could quote some surprising features, such as the case of PiS, which despite many Eurosceptic views, supports the creation of a European army.

The literature commonly discusses the impact of various factors on party European attitudes, such as the left–right location, the status as a mainstream–radical party or government incumbency. The above analysis allows us to say that regarding the question of the impact of the left–right dimension on party attitudes, this factor does not play much role with regard to explaining the attitudes of the pro-European parties as we have left-wing (SLD, SdPL), centre (UW) and centre-right parties (PO) who belong to this category. On the other hand, it is almost certain that less enthusiastically oriented parties will be located on the right of the political spectrum, with the exception of Samoobrona (see below). So here Poland will not be an exception to the more general trends in Europe, with left or centre parties being more pro-European than the right. However, the difference between PiS and LPR on European matters is quite fundamental, not only in the degree of EU critique, but also in the quality of the arguments used. As far as government incumbency is concerned, the key problem here is causality, i.e. how to establish that a policy change in party attitudes resulted from the government experience and not from some other factors, be it political realism or simply a new electoral strategy. For example, in 2006, already after the 2005 elections but before signing a coalition agreement, LPR adopted a resolution quietening its principal rejection of EU membership voiced for the accession referendum of 2003 and EP elections of 2004, and during the period of the coalition it rarely spoke about the EU affairs (Zuba 2009). Former government experience did not lead Samoobrona and LPR (Libertas) to adopt an official Euromanifesto in 2009 (so nothing changed from 2004), and the governing PO did not adopt any Euromanifesto for 2009. Finally, the mainstream–radical divide is commonly believed to form the main pattern of contestation on EU affairs (Taggart 1998; Conti 2012). This question obviously depends how we define the two. Conti (2012) uses here an ideological criterion, grouping socialist, social democratic, Christian democratic and conservative parties and some other moderate parties as the mainstream (and pro-European), and communist, nationalist, far-right, far-left as the radicals (and anti-European). He finds this relation to be the best predictor of party attitudes towards the EU. Taggart and Szczerbiak (2004) developed a similar argument focusing specifically on Central and Eastern Europe, arguing that Eurosceptics are less likely to be found among the "core" of the political spectrum, defined as "parties of the government or potential parties of government". The logic behind this classification is that parties of the core are more responsible and less populist in their policy proposals because they face real or potential government responsibility, whereas parties out of the core put Euroscepticism at the centre of the fight against political establishment. The Polish case poses difficulties with both schemes. The Taggart and Szczerbiak scheme seems to be better suited to the study of the Polish case, given the difficulties in attaching traditional party labels to Polish political parties, and, in particular, because only LPR would be classified as radical within the Conti classification, and one would face difficulties in classifying Samoobrona (due to its populist nature, and a mix of left-wing, interventionist economic proposals with right-wing references to national identity, culture and religion). The approach adopted by Taggart and Szczerbiak worked perfectly as applied to the period of the accession referendum of 2003 and the first EP elections of 2004, but would need to be refined with regard to the 2009 elections, where LPR and Samoobrona had already had government experience in 2006–2007. Only the case of UPR (both in 2004 and 2009) can be clearly an indication of the functioning of the mainstream–radical divide. Otherwise, it seems that for each period of time one would need to come up with a list of mainstream and radical parties based on a subjective assessment. From this point of view, Poland can be categorised as a partial exception to the rule and, after LPR and Samoobrona joined the coalition government, one would come up with better predictions of general party attitudes towards Europe basing the assessment on the party's location on the left–right political spectrum.

Note

1 In all instances, I have used the texts of party programmes as compiled by Słodkowska and Dołbakowska (2005, 2010), my translations.

References

Casal Bértoa, Fernando and Peter Mair (2010) *Two Decades on: How Institutionalized are the Post-communist Party Systems?* EUI Working Papers 2010/03. Florence: European University Institute.

Conti, Nicolò (2012) "Party Elites and the Domestic Discourse on the EU", in *The Europe of Elites: A Study into the Europeanness of Europe's Political and Economic Elites*, ed. Heinrich Best, György Lengyel and Luca Verzichelli, Oxford: Oxford University Press.

Gagatek, Wojciech (2009) *European Political Parties as Campaign Organisations: Toward a Greater Politicisation of the European Parliament Elections*, Brussels: Centre for European Studies.

Gagatek, Wojciech, Katarzyna Grzybowska-Walecka and Patrycja Rozbicka (2010) "Poland", in *The 2009 Elections to the European Parliament: Country Reports*, ed. Wojciech Gagatek. RSCAS Books, Florence: European University Institute.

Haughton, T. (2009) "Driver, Conductor or Fellow Passenger? EU Membership and Party Politics in Central and Eastern Europe", *Journal of Communist Studies and Transition Politics* 25, 4: 413–426.

Markowski, Radosław (2007) "EU Membership and the Polish Party System", in *European Union and Party Politics in Central and Eastern Europe*, ed. Paul G. Lewis and Zdenka Mansfeldová, Basingstoke: Palgrave Macmillan.

Markowski, Radosław and Joshua A. Tucker (2010) "Euroscepticism and the Emergence of Political Parties in Poland", *Party Politics* 16, 4: 523–548.

Millard, Frances (2009) *Democratic Elections in Poland, 1991–2007*, London: Routledge.

Słodkowska, Inka and Magdalena Dołbakowska (eds) (2005) *Eurowybory 2004: Kandydaci i Programy*, Warszawa: Instytut Studiów Politycznych Polskiej Akademii Nauk.

Słodkowska, Inka and Magdalena Dołbakowska (eds) (2010) *Eurowybory 2009: Kandydaci i Programy*, Warszawa: Instytut Studiów Politycznych Polskiej Akademii Nauk.

Szczerbiak, Aleks (2011) *Poland Within the European Union: New Awkward Partner or New Heart of Europe?* London: Routledge.

Taggart, Paul (1998) "A Touchstone of Dissent: Euroscepticism in Contemporary Western European Party Systems", *European Journal of Political Research*, 33, 3: 363–388.

Taggart, Paul and Aleks Szczerbiak (2004) "Contemporary Euroscepticism in the Party Systems of the European Union Candidate States of Central and Eastern Europe", *European Journal of Political Research*, 43, 1: 1–27.

Zuba, Krzysztof (2009) "Through the Looking Glass: The Attitudes of Polish Political Parties towards the EU Before and After Accession", *Perspectives on European Politics and Society*, 10, 3: 326–349.

Appendix

Excerpts from the codebook for the analysis of texts.[1]

INTUNE project

The coding unit

The coding unit is *the entire document*.

To conduct the coding, you should proceed as follows. Read a whole unit, and assign codes applying the following scheme.

For example, if a text contains sentences such as the following...

Give national parliaments a say for the first time over proposed European legislation; enhance the role of the European Council, the body which represents the EU's members states; ensure that individual sovereign member states maintain control over core issues like tax, defence, foreign policy and future treaty change

...then, in the Coding sheet, you should assign value 2 (labelled "intergovernmental") to this unit under DOMAIN II → EUDEC.

Additionally, you should also copy and paste the above text in the Excerpt sheet, because saving relevant quotations will allow a qualitative analysis of texts. You should not inflate the Excerpt sheet with too many quotations, for each document you are allowed a maximum of three quotations per domain. When in doubt about how to save excerpts, always think that the reader will need such excerpts to find evidence of the codes you have assigned to texts. Therefore, saved excerpts should always be parsimonious in size but meaningful in content.

General rules

Rule 1. We are only interested in the manifest content of texts and not in any hidden content. You should not make any guessing, when references to a particular issue are missing, only use the no reference/not applicable codes. Any coding you do relying on previous knowledge and not on the manifest content of texts will result in misleading information.

Rule 2. Before using the no reference/not applicable codes you should make sure that reference to the issue you are analysing is really missing. Check the whole text one more time before assigning these codes that express lack of salience. This information is crucial, please be cautious when assigning such codes.

The coding scheme *(only the variables analysed in the volume are shown)*

MEMBERSHIP European impact on country matters

Favourable opportunities

Europe has mainly brought benefits and improvements to the country. Agreement and consensus are expressed for European integration processes.

Negative constraints

Europe has mainly limited and constrained the country without bringing positive results. Discontent is expressed for European integration processes.

Mixed

No reference

NATACT   National action in Europe

Leadership

A desire to influence, guide and direct European processes and major decisions dominates. Willingness to be at the forefront of bargaining and decision-making and not to stand on the sidelines.

Cooperation

Predominantly pledges in favour of working together to achieve a common aim, even taking an active part in Europe decision-making.

Defence/rejection

Preference for opting-out/withdrawing from the EU or some of its building-block policies (e.g. Monetary Union, Common Market). Strong protection of national interest(s) seen as threatened by the EU.

Mixed (any two or more categories)

No reference

EUDEC   EU decision-making

Supranational

Preference for decisions made by majority voting.

Positive mentions of this method of decision-making.

Positive mentions of the empowerment of the supra-national level.

Intergovernmental

Decision-making should be kept central to the member states and decisions in the EU made by unanimity. Negative mentions of the empowerment of the supranational level.

Mixed supranational and intergovernmental

National preference

European institutions are severely criticised, powers should be shifted back to member states. European institutions should have solely advisory or implementation functions.

No reference

SGFORE   Foreign policy
SGDEF   Defence policy
SGJHA   Justice and Crime policy
SGIMMI   Immigration policy
SGSOC   Social policy (includes employment)
SGENV   Environmental policy

The favourite level of competence is registered for each policy area. Combinations of different levels are registered only when mentioned explicitly.

Preference for:

Supranational only

National only

Sub-national only

Supranational + National

Supranational + Sub-national

Supranational + National + Sub-national

National + Sub-national

No reference

EUCULT   European cultural belonging

Reference

Reference to ascribed or acquired elements that define belonging to Europe, such as a common culture, values, customs, history or traditions

Reference to elements differentiating the in-group (the Europeans) from the out-group (the others).

No reference

IDNAT   National identity

Reference

Reference to national identity or to commonalities/similarities among the country citizens.

No reference

NACULT   National cultural belonging
          Reference
          Reference to ascribed or acquired elements defining
          membership or belonging to the nation, such as refer-
          ence to common culture, values, customs, history or tra-
          ditions. Reference to elements differentiating the
          in-group (nationals) from the out-group (foreigners).
          No reference

IDSUB   Sub-national identity
          Reference
          Mentions are made of sub-national identity or more
          generally of commonalities/similarities among local
          community fellows.
          No reference

SUBCULT   Sub-national cultural belonging
          Reference
          Reference to ascribed or acquired elements defining mem-
          bership or belonging to the sub-national identity(ies), such
          as reference to common culture, values, customs, history
          or traditions. Reference to elements differentiating the in-
          group (community fellows) from the out-group (outsiders).
          No reference

Note

1 Before coding the Euromanifestos, the coding system was tested on a standard text in English by all country experts. For the variables that are reported in the Appendix, the average of test's inter-coder convergence was 71.3 per cent, a rate considered adequate by Krippendorff (2004: 241) for reliable content analysis. Moreover, after the coding exercise, the variables with lower convergence rates were further simplified and made dichotomous in order to reduce the probability of coding errors and to approximate the rate of 80 per cent that was considered by Krippendorff as optimal.

Reference

Krippendorff, K. (2004) *Content Analysis: An Introduction to Its Methodology*, Thousand Oaks, CA: Sage.

Index

Page numbers in *italics* denote tables, those in **bold** denote figures.

For Product Safety Concerns and Information please contact our EU
representative GPSR@taylorandfrancis.com
Taylor & Francis Verlag GmbH, Kaufingerstraße 24, 80331 München, Germany

www.ingramcontent.com/pod-product-compliance
Lightning Source LLC
Chambersburg PA
CBHW062021270326
41929CB00014B/2277